Family Breakdown
A Legal Guide

Family Breakdown
A Legal Guide

By
Kieron Wood

Published by
Clarus Press Ltd,
Griffith Campus,
South Circular Road,
Dublin 8.

Typeset by
Deanta Global Publishing Services

Printed by
Sprint Print,
Dublin

ISBN
978-1-905536-65-8

To Rían, Grace, Molly, Billy and Teddy, who stayed
(relatively) quiet while I (allegedly) worked.

PREFACE

Introduction of Divorce in Ireland

The first referendum on divorce in June 1986 was defeated by a majority of almost two to one: 935,843 votes to 538,279. Much of the opposition came from the Catholic Church and the farmers' lobby, which was deeply concerned about the future of family farms.

But by the time of the second vote in November 1995, society had become markedly more liberal. Voters supported the proposed introduction of divorce by the narrowest of margins—818,842 votes to 809,728.

Former Fine Gael TD Alice Glenn argued that "a woman voting for divorce is like a turkey voting for Christmas"[1] but, following the referendum result, the government published the Family Law (Divorce) Act 1996. This marked a sea-change in Irish family law.

The judge in *Zappone and Gilligan v Revenue Commissioners*[2] described the introduction of divorce as "the most fundamental change of all" to the institution of marriage as it was understood at the time the Irish Constitution was written.

According to McKechnie J in *Foy v An tArdChláraitheoir*: "As a result of the 15th Amendment of the Constitution Act 1995, and the Family Law (Divorce) Act 1996, the permanency aspect of marriage no longer applies."[3]

Liberalisation of Irish Society

Since the introduction of legislation permitting divorce, the continuing changes in Irish society have been reflected by increasingly liberal and secular legislation at national and European level.

---

[1] The Alice Glenn Report May 1986, "A Woman Voting for Divorce is like a Turkey Voting for Christmas", *Irish Election Literature*, available from http://irishelectionliterature.wordpress.com/2009/09/10/the-alice-glenn-report-may-1986/, accessed 11 February 2014.
[2] Unreported, High Court, 14 December 2006.
[3] [2002] IEHC 116.

A 2010 report by the Family Support Agency and the ESRI showed:

- a fourfold increase in cohabitation in a decade;
- a substantial increase in numbers of people aged over 25 living with a partner;
- an increased rate of marital breakdown among those in their late 30s; and
- a 30 percent increase in relationship breakdown after the birth of the first child.[4]

Part of this may be due to a collapse in religious belief and practice. For example, in the 2011 census, the number of people who described themselves as having no religion rose to almost 270,000—an increase of 44 percent on the 2006 figure, and more than double the number of members of the Church of Ireland.

After judicial separation and divorce came same-sex partnership. The Civil Partnership and Certain Rights and Obligations of Cohabitants Act 2010 marked another fundamental development in Irish society, allowing the registration of same-sex partnerships, as well as imposing responsibilities on the growing number of opposite-sex couples who were cohabiting.

The Act also introduced allowed another radical change: cohabitants and civil partners were permitted to regulate their joint financial and property affairs, subject to certain formalities. Agreements could be set aside only in exceptional circumstances.

Pre-Nuptial Agreements

Yet, despite the fact that civil partners and cohabitants are now permitted by law to regulate their finances, prenuptial (the word means 'before marriage') agreements—which relate only to married, opposite-sex couples—remain contrary to public policy.

One of the effects of this can be to prevent couples marrying—particularly where one partner may have had a previous relationship breakdown and does not wish to risk losing a second home later in life. As a result, children

---

[4] Family Figures, February 2010.

(and partners) may be deprived of the constitutional protection guaranteed only to married couples.

The state should realise that marriages do break down, and should allow couples, following independent legal advice, to decide for themselves how they wish to organise their families and their finances for the future.

Other Concerns

Guardianship for unmarried fathers is another area of concern. There is still no national register of guardianship agreements in Ireland, despite the fact that Alan Shatter, Minister for Justice at the time of writing, as opposition justice spokesman told this author that he believed "the establishment of a guardianship register to be very much in the public interest".[5]

Another continuing problem is "limping marriages", which are recognised in one jurisdiction but not another. For example, under the 1995 Family Law Act, if an 17-year-old girl who is resident in the Republic marries an 18-year-old Northern Ireland resident in the North without court permission (as might well happen in a cross-border parish), the marriage would be legal in the North, but void in the Republic.

The government should also be doing what it can to preserve faltering marriages. Section 6 of the Divorce Act specified that "the minister may make regulations to allow for the establishment of a register of professional organisations whose members are qualified to assist the parties involved in effecting a reconciliation". Yet there is still no such register and, in practice, most separating and divorcing couples seem to take the traditional court route.

In a 2013 speech to a Law Society seminar,[6] Shatter recognised that "family breakdown and parenting disputes are particularly sensitive and painful areas". The minister said that Ireland should have "a dedicated and integrated family court structure that is properly resourced to meet the particular needs of people at a vulnerable time in their lives".

---

[5] Letter to author.
[6] 6 July 2013.

At present, if a case is adjourned, there is no guarantee that it will even come back before the same judge. The North's senior family law judge, Mr Justice John Gillen, told a Law Society conference in Dublin that he was the 12th judge to handle one family law case.[7] He recommended that a single judge should deal with one family—or at least that there should be comprehensive sharing of information and a collaborative, multi-disciplinary approach to family disputes.

Provision of Family Court Facilities

It might have been expected that such momentous changes in family law as the introduction of divorce and civil partnership would coincide with a new system of family courts with specialised judges, a comprehensive state-funded system to save faltering relationships and alternatives to the adversarial court system in the case of partnerships that could not be saved.

As long ago as 1996, the Law Reform Commission, in its report on family courts, said:

> The courts are buckling under the pressure of business. Long family law lists, delays, brief hearings, inadequate facilities and over-hasty settlements are too often the order of the day. At the same time, too many cases are coming before the courts which are unripe for hearing, or in which earlier non-legal intervention might have led to agreement and the avoidance of courtroom conflict.
>
> Judges dealing with family disputes do not always have the necessary experience or aptitude. There is no proper system of case management. Cases are heard behind closed doors, protecting the privacy of family members but offering little opportunity for external appreciation, criticism, or even realisation, of what is happening within the system. The courts lack adequate support services, in particular the independent diagnostic services so important in resolving child-related issues.[8]

The Courts Service said in 2007 that more than 40 court buildings had been built or refurbished under its capital investment programme. All of

---

[7] *Law Society Gazette*, November 2006, p 17.
[8] LRC 52-1996.

them were said to have the "consultation rooms and waiting facilities expected and needed for family law cases", including "specialised and separate facilities" to provide for "the dignity and privacy of family law litigants".[9]

But Shatter told the 2013 Law Society seminar that the current structure was still "far from ideal".[10] Family law had become "ever more extensive and complex", he said, and the introduction of the Civil Partnership Act and the Adoption Act in 2010 had brought "more challenges to an already complex and hard-pressed area".

The statistics bear out the minister's concerns. In 1997, the first year in which divorce was permitted in Ireland, 95 divorces were granted. The number rocketed to 1,421 in 1998 and peaked at 3,684 in 2007. Since then, the number of divorce decrees has remained fairly steady: there were 3,630 in 2008, 3,341 in 2009, and 3,113 in 2010. The number of remarriages more than doubled in less than a decade: from 21,400 in the 2002 census to 42,960 in the 2011 census.

The 2011 census also showed that the number of divorced people in Ireland had more than doubled in the previous ten years—and the figure is rising. In all, there were 87,770 divorced individuals living in Ireland in 2011: 49,685 women and 38,085 men. That's two-and-a-half times the number in the 2002 census.

The marital breakdown rate rose from 8.7 percent in 2006 to 9.7 percent in 2011, though the rates of marital breakdown are as high as 13.5 percent in Limerick city and 12.4 percent in Dublin city.

The Programme for Government promised a constitutional amendment in 2014 for a separate family court system staffed with specialist judges. Such a system is particularly needed because some of the family law courts—and even some of the judges—are not suited to family law hearings.

---

[9] Courts Service Annual Report 2007.
[10] 6 July 2013, 'A New Structure for Family Courts' Consultative Seminar in Law Society, addressed by the Minister for Justice, Equality and Defence Alan Shatter, TD.

"Just because a person has been a solicitor or a member of the Bar in practice for the minimum ten years required to be appointed as a judge, it does not mean that he or she has necessarily amassed the insight, qualities and expertise necessary to deal with all cases," said Shatter.[11]

The proposed specialised family law courts are to have their own structure, with "separate venues, adequate private consultation rooms and a co-located welfare and assessment service", together with in-court mediation facilities.[12]

Call me a cynic, but I'll believe it when I see it!

Kieron Wood
Barrister-at-Law
The feast of Candlemas

---

[11] 6 July 2013 Law Society seminar.
[12] *ibid*.

ACKNOWLEDGMENTS

Thanks to Paul O'Shea BL, Tabitha Wood BL, Andrew Nevin of PFP Financial Services, Fr William Richardson, Moling Ryan, Arran Dowling-Hussey BL, Gerry Curran, Geoffrey Shannon, Ken Murphy, Brenda Drumm and, of course, David McCartney of Clarus Press.

CONTENTS

TABLE OF CASES

Note: because of the in camera rule and the consequent anonymity of parties, cases with the same initials may be confused with one another when they are not necessarily connected.

TABLE OF LEGISLATION

Statutory Instruments

EU Materials

GLOSSARY OF LEGAL TERMS

A mensa et thoro: from table and bed (an earlier form of judicial separation)

Abatement: reduction of a legacy in a will

Access: the right of a non-custodial parent to see the children

Action: a civil court proceeding

Adjournment: postponement of a hearing by a judge on whatever terms he may impose

Ad litem: (for the suit), the appointment of a person to represent a child in an action

ADR: alternative dispute resolution (such as mediation, collaborative law or conciliation)

Adultery: sexual intercourse by a married person with someone other than his or her spouse

Affidavit: sworn written statement signed by a deponent, who swears that its contents are true to the best of his knowledge and belief. It must be witnessed by a practising solicitor or commissioner for oaths (who will charge for this service). In family law, an affidavit of welfare must be sworn in all divorce or judicial separation applications where there are dependants. An affidavit of means is required where any financial claim is being made

Ancillary relief: additional related orders available from a court

Annulment: declaration by a court that a valid marriage never existed

Appeal: challenge to a court decision in a higher court. Unless a stay is granted, the decision or ruling remains in force until it is varied or overturned by the higher court

Appearance: the act of replying to a summons or turning up in court and accepting its jurisdiction to try proceedings. A barrister or solicitor may make an appearance on a client's behalf

Appellant: person who brings an appeal

Applicant: person who brings a case to court; also called the petitioner. The person being sued is generally called the respondent

Arrears: accumulated debt which has not been paid by the due date

Assign: to give or transfer responsibility to another person. The person who receives the right or property is the assignee; the assignor is the person giving

Attachment and committal: bringing a person before a court, with a threat of imprisonment for failure to obey a court order

Attachment of earnings: court order for deduction of salary at source in order to pay, for example, maintenance or a debt

Audi alteram partem: (Latin: hear the other side) a principle of natural justice which requires that, where a decision may affect an individual's rights, that person has a right to be heard. It includes the right to receive notice of a hearing and to be legally represented

Barring order: an order preventing a person from entering the family home or joint property, or using or threatening violence against the other person or family members

Barrister: specialist in litigation and advocacy who receives instructions from a solicitor. Barristers may not normally deal directly with members of the public

Beneficiary: person who receives a gift under a will, or for whose benefit property is held by an executor or trustee

Bigamy: criminal offence of marrying another person while still in a valid marriage

Call-over: a hearing to fix the date on which a case will be heard

Canon law: the law of the Catholic Church, promulgated in 1983, which governs ecclesiastical nullity applications

Care order: an order placing a child in the care of the Health Service Executive until he or she reaches the age of 18, or for a shorter period, as decided by the judge

Case-law: published court decisions which establish legal precedents, binding lower courts

Case progression hearing: a pre-trial hearing before the county registrar to decide whether a case is ready for trial

Chambers: judge's personal rooms, where he may hear matters in private

Charge: form of security for payment of a debt

Chattels: household goods

Child: person under 18 (or under 23 and in full-time education for many family law purposes)

Child abduction: wrongful removal of a child from its parent, guardian or country of residence

Circuit Court: court above the District Court and below the High Court, with power to grant divorces and judicial separations and to award damages up to €75,000; or €60,000 in personal injury cases

Circuit Judge: judge of the Circuit Court, addressed as "Judge"

Civil partners: people of the same sex who have registered a civil partnership

Civil partnership civil bill: the document filed in the Circuit Court office to start proceedings under the Civil Partnership and Certain Rights and Obligations of Cohabitants Act 2010

Codicil: written amendment or addition to an existing will

Cohabitants: adults, whether the same or opposite sex, who live together as a couple in an "intimate and committed relationship"

Collusion: unlawful, and usually secret, agreement

Commissioner for oaths: a person who can administer oaths and take affidavits

Common law: judge-made law which has developed over centuries, also referred to as "unwritten" law. Common law as practised in Ireland may be contrasted with civil law systems (such as in France or Germany) where laws are set out in a written code

Common law spouses: colloquial term for unmarried partners

Conciliation: bringing spouses together with a third party to try to resolve differences

Conjugal rights: the right of one spouse to cohabit with the other

Consent order: court order agreed between both sides

Construction: legal process of interpreting a phrase or document. If a term is unclear or ambiguous, lawyers and judges must try and interpret (or construct) its probable intention and purpose

Consummation: completion (as a marriage is completed by sexual intercourse)

Contempt: deliberate disregard of a court order[1]

Costs: the legal expenses of an action, such as lawyers' fees, witness expenses and other fees incurred in bringing the matter to court. The rule is generally that "costs follows the event", which means that the loser normally pays the legal costs of both sides. The judge has the final decision and may decide not to make an order on costs

Counsel: barrister(s)

Counselling: giving advice with a view to resolving differences

Counterclaim: respondent's claim against applicant

---

[1] See *CF v JDF* [2005] IESC 45 in which a wife unilaterally changed the children's school, despite having joint custody with the husband.

Court fees: fees for bringing proceedings (but no court fees are payable in family law proceedings)

Court rules: procedural rules for the District Court, Circuit Court, High Court and Supreme Court

Cross-examination: at a hearing, each side calls its own witnesses and may also question the other side's witnesses under oath. Examination-in-chief is the questioning of a party's own witnesses; cross-examination involves questioning the other side's witnesses

Cross-petition: a claim by a respondent against a petitioner

Custody: care and charge of a child

De facto: (Latin: in fact) something which exists in fact, though not necessarily approved by law (*de jure*)

De minimis non curat lex: (Latin: the law does not concern itself with trifles) a common law principle whereby very minor transgressions of the law are disregarded

De novo: (Latin: anew) used to refer to a trial which begins all over again, as if any previous hearing had not occurred. A District Court appeal is heard by the Circuit Court *de novo*, with the court considering afresh all the law and facts

Decree, order or judgment: written order setting out a judge's decision

Deed of separation: voluntary agreement by a couple not to cohabit

Defence: formal response by the respondent to a claim, which may include a claim against the applicant

Defined benefit pension scheme: where retirement benefits are based on an individual's final pay and service with the employer

Defined contribution pension scheme: where employee and employer contribute to a fluctuating investment fund

Dependant: any natural or adopted child of either spouse who is under 18 (or 23 if in full-time education), or a mentally or physically handicapped child. (Note: 'dependent' is the adjective; 'dependant' is the noun)

Deponent: person who swears an affidavit or deposition

Descendant: persons born of, or from children of, another. Grandchildren are descendants of their grandparents, as children are descendants of their natural parents. The law distinguishes between collateral descendants, such as nephews and nieces, and lineal descendants, such as sons and daughters

Desertion: intentional separation and termination of cohabitation

Devise: transfer or conveyance of real property by will. The person who receives such property is called the devisee

Discovery: sworn disclosure of documents and records. Certain types of document which are "privileged" need not be discovered, but they must be identified to the other side

District Court: lowest court in the judicial system, with power to deal with most day-to-day family law proceedings, such as maintenance and access, and award damages up to €15,000

District Judge: judge of the District Court, addressed as "Judge"

Divorce: a court order ending a valid marriage and permitting the former spouses to marry again in a civil ceremony

Domicile: a person's fixed and permanent residence; a place to which he intends to return, even if he is temporarily absent. Legally, a person may have many residences or several nationalities, but only one domicile

*Duces tecum***:** (Latin: bring with you) type of *subpoena* which requires a person to appear before a court with specified documents or other evidence

Duress: threats or force preventing, or forcing, a person to act other than in accordance with free will. Duress may invalidate a marriage

Emergency care order: an order putting a child into the care of the HSE for up to eight days if there is a serious risk to the child's health or welfare

Evidence: testimony of witnesses at a trial, or the production of documents or other materials to prove or disprove facts. Evidence may be direct or circumstantial (that is evidence from which a fact may be presumed). The best evidence available—such as original, rather than copy, documents—must generally be presented to a court

*Ex aequo et bono***:** (Latin: in justice and fairness) most legal cases are decided on the strict rule of law. But, where a case is decided *ex aequo et bono*, the judge may make a decision based on what is just and fair in the circumstances

*Ex parte***:** (Latin: on the part of) court application made without notice to the other side. One party is therefore neither present nor represented

Examination-in-chief: questioning of witnesses under oath by the party who called those witnesses (also called direct examination). After the examination-in-chief, the other side's lawyer may question the witnesses in cross-examination. Thereafter, the first party may re-examine them, but only about issues raised during the cross-examination

Executor: person appointed by a testator to administer a will. The executor is a personal representative whose duties include proving the will, collecting in the estate, paying any debts and distributing the balance according to the wishes of the deceased

Exhibit: document or object produced as evidence in a trial

Family home: house in which a married couple usually live

Family law civil bill: a document filed in the Circuit Court office to start proceedings for a divorce or judicial separation

Family law summons: a document filed in the Central Office to start family law proceedings in the High Court

Fraud: dishonest conduct designed to persuade another person to give something of value by lying, repeating something that is or ought to have been known by the fraudulent party to be false or suspect, or by concealing a relevant fact from the other party

Guardian: person with the right and duty to be involved with a child's physical, religious, intellectual, social and moral welfare

Hearsay: evidence of which a witness does not have direct knowledge from his own senses but which is based on what others have said. Hearsay evidence is normally admissible in court proceedings only to show that a statement was made, not to prove the truth of the contents of the statement

High Court: court above the Circuit Court with full jurisdiction to decide all matters of law and fact. High Court judges are normally addressed as "Judge"

Illegitimate: status of child born outside marriage, abolished in 1987

Impotence: inability to have sexual intercourse

In camera: (Latin: in the room) in private. Family law proceedings are generally heard *in camera* or in private, but the Civil Liability and Courts Act 2004 and the Courts and Civil Law (Miscellaneous Provisions) Act 2013 amended the *in camera* rule to allow lawyer and press access to the family courts, subject to not identifying the parties or children involved[2]

In loco parentis: (Latin: in the place of a parent)

---

[2] But see the judgment of Keane J in *AB v CD* [2013] IEHC 578.

Injunction: court order that forbids someone to do something (prohibitory injunction) or compels him to do something (mandatory injunction). It may be enforced by committal to prison for contempt

Interim: temporary

Interim barring order: an immediate order requiring a violent person to leave a property, pending the hearing of a barring order application

Interim care order: an order that a child be placed in the care of the HSE when an application for a care order has been, or is about to be, made

Interlocutory injunction: an injunction which lasts only until the end of the trial during which the order was sought, when it may be replaced by a permanent injunction

Inter partes: Latin: between the parties

Intestate: person who dies without making a valid will

Intestacy: death without a valid will

Jactitation: false claim to be married to someone

Judgment in default: a ruling in favour of an applicant where the respondent has failed to appear or issue a defence within the time limits

Judicial separation: a decree relieving spouses of the obligation to live together

Junior counsel: barrister who has not "taken silk" or been called to the Inner Bar

Jurisdiction: power of a judge or court to act, limited by a defined territory, by the type of case or to certain persons

Kin: relationship by blood

Lay litigant: non-lawyer who brings a legal action without the assistance of a barrister or solicitor. The Supreme Court has said that a court will normally extend latitude to litigants in person[3]

Legal aid: state scheme providing advice or assistance from a solicitor or barrister at a reduced rate

Legal professional privilege: confidential communications between a lawyer and client may not be revealed in court unless the client, expressly or impliedly, waives the privilege. The communications must relate to court proceedings or intended litigation

Liability: any legal obligation or duty, now or in the future. If a court finds a person to be contributory liable, he bears part of the responsibility for the act or omission

---

[3] *McMullen v Kennedy* [2013] IESC 29.

Lineal descendant: direct descendant; for example, the child of his natural parent

Lis Pendens: Latin: notice of a pending legal action

Lump sum: money often paid to spouse in lieu of (or as well as) maintenance

Marriage: the voluntary union for life of one man and one woman to the exclusion of all others

Maintenance: periodic payments by one spouse to the other

Mediation: form of alternative dispute resolution involving an agreed mediator acting as a facilitator to help the parties negotiate an agreement. The mediator does not adjudicate on the issues or force a compromise; only the parties involved can resolve the dispute. The result of a successful mediation is called a settlement

Minor: person under the age of 18 who is not married or has not been married. An Irish resident under the age of 18 may not legally marry without the permission of the court, even if the ceremony takes place somewhere (such as Northern Ireland) where the minimum age for marriage is under 18

Mitigation: facts which, while not negating an offence or wrongful action, tend to show that the defendant may have had some excuse for acting the way he did

Moiety: Half[4]

Motion: an application for a court order, usually on notice to the other side

Natural justice: the requirement for application of the tenets *audi alteram partem* (hear the other side) and *nemo judex in sua causa* (no-one may be a judge in his own case). The principles of natural justice were derived from the Romans, who believed that some legal principles were self-evident and did not need a statutory basis

Nemo judex in sua causa: (Latin: nobody may be a judge in his own case) principle of natural justice. A judge must be seen to be free of bias and may not have any interest—personal, pecuniary or otherwise—in a case he is deciding

Next of kin: person's nearest blood relation

---

[4] *Sheehy v Talbot* [2008] IEHC 207.

Nullity: a court ruling that a valid marriage does not exist. Decrees of nullity may be granted by the civil courts or Church courts and have different effects

Obiter dicta: (Latin: sayings by the way) observations by a judge on law or facts not specifically before the court or not necessary to decide an issue. Such opinions are not binding in future cases

Order: formal written direction by a judge. Once a final order is made, it may only be amended if there has been an accidental slip in the judgment

Orse: (Latin: otherwise) otherwise known as

Out-of-court settlement: agreement between two litigants to settle a matter privately before a court has heard the matter or given its decision

Parent: father or mother of a child, whether married or not

Partition: division of jointly-owned land or property between the owners

Paternity: fatherhood, which may be established by DNA testing

Pension adjustment order: order for payment of all or part of one spouse's pension to the other spouse

Per stirpes: (Latin: by stocks) inheriting *per stirpes* means the division of a deceased's estate among his descendants, with the children of a deceased son or daughter dividing their parent's share equally among themselves

Periodical payments: maintenance

Perjury: deliberate lie under oath or in a sworn affidavit

Petition: written application to the court for judicial remedy, such as nullity

Petitioner: person issuing a petition

Pleadings: written allegations or claims delivered by one claimant to another which formally set out the facts and legal arguments supporting his position

Precedent: court judgment which is cited as an authority in a later case involving similar facts. Precedent cannot bind a higher court (for example, a Circuit Court decision cannot bind a High Court judge). A Supreme Court judgment binds all courts; although it does not bind the Supreme Court itself in future cases

Prima facie: (Latin: at first sight) a *prima facie* case is one which, at first sight, seems to support the allegation or claim made. If a *prima facie* case is not made out in the early stages of proceedings, the other side may apply to the court to dismiss the action without hearing the rest of the evidence

Privilege: special legal right, such as a benefit, exemption, immunity or power

Property adjustment order: court order transferring property from one spouse to another or varying ownership of property

Protection order: temporary court order, granted when an application for a safety/barring order has been made, preventing a person from threatening, molesting or pestering another, pending a barring application

Pro tempore (pro tem): (Latin: for the time) temporary or for the time being

Probate law: that part of the law which regulates wills and other subjects related to the distribution of a deceased person's estate

Quid pro quo: (Latin: something for something) giving something in exchange for something else

Rebuttable presumption: presumed fact based on the proof of other facts. Most presumptions are rebuttable, which means that the person against whom the presumption applies may present evidence to the contrary, thus nullifying the presumption

Record number: the number given to a case by the court office and quoted at the top right hand side of all documents

Rent: money or other consideration paid by a tenant to a landlord in exchange for the exclusive possession and use of land, buildings or part of a building

Reply: answer by a plaintiff to a defence or counterclaim

Reserved costs: apportionment of legal costs to be decided at a later stage

Reserved judgment: decision to be given at a later date

Residence: place where someone usually, but not necessarily permanently, lives

Respondent: person against whom a summons is issued, or a petition or appeal brought

Safety order: an order prohibiting a person from committing acts of violence or threatening to do so in the family home, or molesting or frightening the applicant

Sanction: to ratify, to approve or to punish

Secured payment: court order ensuring payment of maintenance by one spouse to the other

Senior counsel: barrister who has 'taken silk' or been called to the Inner Bar

Separation agreement: a voluntary agreement between two spouses to live apart

Sequestration: temporary confiscation of property by court order until the owner purges his contempt by obeying an earlier court order

Service: delivery of court documents by one party to the other, personally or by registered post. An affidavit of service is usually sworn

Settlement: agreed compromise of proceedings. Anyone drafting a settlement should note the difference between 'liberty to apply' and 'liberty to re-enter'[5]

Solicitor: general lawyer who may deal directly with the public and handle money

Spouse: husband or wife

Stare decisis: (Latin: to stand by decisions) policy whereby, once a court has made a decision on a certain set of facts, lower courts must apply that precedent in subsequent cases with the same facts

Stay (of execution): suspension of the operation of a court order until such time as the judge thinks fit

Subpoena: (Latin: under penalty) court order requiring a witness to attend at a certain time and place or suffer a penalty

Substituted service: if someone appears to be avoiding service of legal documents, the court may be asked to direct that, instead of personal service (that is, giving the documents directly to the person), they should be served in a different way, perhaps by posting them to the person's home or office, or leaving them with a member of his family

Successor: person who takes over the rights or property of another

Summons: written command to a person to appear in court

Supervision order: an order allowing the HSE to monitor a child at risk in the home. The order is for a fixed period, initially up to one year

Supreme Court: final court of appeal in Ireland, headed by the Chief Justice (to be supplemented by a civil Court of Appeal). Most appeals are on matters of law or procedure. The Supreme Court will not normally reverse a finding of fact by a lower court, unless the decision was perverse

Supreme Court judge: addressed as 'Judge'

Testamentary capacity: legal ability to make a will

Testator: person who dies after making a valid will

---

[5] *McMullen v Kennedy* [2013] IESC 29.

Testatrix: female testator

Testimony: verbal presentation of evidence in court

Trust: property given by a donor or settlor to a trustee, for the benefit of another person (the beneficiary or donee). A trustee manages and administers the property

Trustee: person who holds property rights for the benefit of another through the legal mechanism of a trust. A trustee usually has full management and administration rights over the property, which must be exercised to the advantage of the beneficiary

***Ultra vires*:** (Latin: beyond the powers) an action which is invalid because it exceeds the authority of the person or organisation which performs it

Undertaking: enforceable promise given to court

Undue influence: unfair pressure which may invalidate a contract or will

Variation: alteration of term of court order

Void: without legal effect. A document that is void is worthless. A 'marriage' involving a person under the age of 18 without prior court approval would be void in Ireland

Voidable: some marriages have such a fundamental defect that they are said to be void. Others have more minor defects and are voidable at the option of the innocent party

Waiver: renunciation of a right or benefit. Waivers are not always in writing. Sometimes actions can be interpreted as a waiver

Year: when used without any other qualification, a 12-month period beginning on January 1

INTRODUCTION TO FAMILY LAW

Introduction

This book deals with many of the aspects of the breakdown of relationships, marital and non-marital.

The first question it asks is whether a formal relationship existed, whether in a traditional marriage, an informal or 'common law' marriage or a civil partnership. Did the couple obey the rules governing registration of their relationship, for example? Were they both over 18, or did they have court permission to marry if under that age? Was there an issue of mental illness or sexual dysfunction before the marriage?

If there was a valid formal relationship, it may be rescued or it may be formally ended. If not, then the spouses or partners may not avail of marital or partnership legislation.

The book goes on to consider the ancillary remedies which may be sought by spouses or partners in a failed relationship, ranging from maintenance or the fate of the family home to remedies against threatened or actual violence.

Children may be an important part of any relationship, so the topics of custody and access, guardianship and even child abduction are dealt with. The area of adoption is touched on, but adoption is a specialised topic more suited to a separate work.

The vexed question of the recognition, or otherwise, by the Irish courts of pre-nuptial agreements is addressed. For everyone, the question of pensions, tax and inheritance is also important, especially in the case of relationship breakdown, and the rules and regulations governing these are comprehensively considered.

For those who can't afford to pay the hefty costs of a solicitor or barrister, there's a section on the rules governing legal aid.

For many of those involved in relationship breakdown, the thought of a day (or more) in court can be very frightening, so the alternatives to a legal solution are canvassed. But if you can't avoid going to court, this book explains what happens in the courtroom. There is also an explanation of how the new case progression system works.

If you end up in the divorce court, included is a synopsis of the 1996 legislation, plus draft legal forms. If you aren't seeking a divorce, there's information about all the Irish family law legislation which applies today, with links to where you will find the full Acts.

A section regarding useful websites and contacts includes information about rules, regulations and reports. Finally, there are some real-life questions culled from the author's website, with the answers to the queries.

The History of Family Law in Ireland

Until the end of the Middle Ages, Irish couples in failed marriages could divorce by mutual consent under Brehon Law. A woman might divorce her husband for gossiping about their marital relations, being sterile, failing to maintain her or beating her. A husband could divorce his wife for bad housekeeping, persistent illness, barrenness or if he wanted to go on a pilgrimage or become a monk.[1]

Gradually, Christian teaching on the indissolubility of marriage spread throughout Europe. But, in recent times, Christian rules have been

---

[1] 'Ireland's Brehon laws were before their time', *IrishCentral.com.*, available from http://www.irishcentral.com/roots/Irelands-Brehon-laws-were-before-their-time-118762389.html, accessed 27 January 2014.

increasingly ignored and marital breakdown has become more widespread. Most countries have now legislated for civil divorce.

Civil Divorce

In 1995, Ireland was the only country in the European Union to forbid civil divorce. Article 41.3.2° of the 1937 Irish Constitution said: "No law shall be enacted providing for the grant of a dissolution of marriage."

(Malta, which joined the EU in 2004, introduced divorce following a referendum on 28 May 2011 in which 122,547 people voted in favour, while 107,971 voted against.)

The ban in Ireland reflected the Catholic views of the majority of the people—and the judiciary—of the new Irish Republic.

Even as late as the 1950s, there was strong public opposition to divorce. In 1958, a woman who had already obtained an English divorce sued her ex-husband in the Irish courts to recover stg£339 1s 5d in legal costs awarded by the English Court. The judge in *Mayo-Perrott v Mayo-Perrott*[2] said the Irish courts would not give "active assistance to facilitate in any way the effecting of a dissolution of marriage in another country".

Irish courts will normally enforce a valid foreign court judgment but, in this instance, the Supreme Court said that the Irish judiciary "would fail to carry out public policy if, by a decree of its own courts, it gave assistance to the process of divorce by entertaining a suit for the costs of such proceedings".[3]

By 1962, however, attitudes in society had begun to change. When the High Court refused an order for the examination of an Irish witness in a foreign divorce case, the Minister for External Affairs appealed to the Supreme Court, which granted the application.

In 1978, a woman who had obtained a divorce in England applied to the Irish High Court for the enforcement of a maintenance order.[4] The judge said that providing maintenance for a spouse could not be regarded as

---

[2] [1958] IR 336.
[3] *ibid.*
[4] *NM v EFM*, unreported, High Court, July 1978.

contrary to public policy as it did not give active assistance to the process of divorce.

In 1986, the Irish government tried to remove the ban on divorce, but the electorate rejected the proposals. The defeat was put down to the influence of the Catholic Church[5] and the fear of farmers and house owners that divorce would affect their property rights.

The following year, in the case of *Johnston v Ireland*,[6] a couple complained to the European Court that the Constitutional ban on divorce was a breach of their human rights.

But the Court of Human Rights in Strasbourg held that the guarantee of the right to marry in the European Convention on Human Rights did not imply an equal right to divorce. The court also said that Article 8 of the Convention, on the respect due to family life, did not require Ireland to introduce divorce.

Pro-divorce campaigners pressed for another vote. The second referendum, in 1995, proposed to replace Article 41.3.2° with the formula:

> A court designated by law may grant a dissolution of marriage where, but only where, it is satisfied that:
>
> 1. at the date of the institution of proceedings, the spouses have lived apart from one another for a period of, or periods amounting to, at least four years during the preceding five years;
> 2. there is no reasonable prospect of a reconciliation between the spouses;
> 3. such provision as the Court considers proper having regard to the circumstances, exists or will be made for the spouses, any children of either or both of them and any other person prescribed by law; and
> 4. any further conditions prescribed by law are complied with.

In the period leading up to the second referendum, successive governments enacted extensive legislation to deal with the issue of property rights,

---

[5] 'Love is for Life: Pastoral Letter of the Irish Bishops', *Irish Hierarchy of Bishops,* available from https://www.ewtn.com/library/bishops/lovelife.htm, February 1985, accessed January 2014.

[6] [1986] ECHR 17.

which were seen as key to the loss of the first referendum. The major piece of legislation was Fine Gael TD Alan Shatter's 1989 Judicial Separation and Family Law Reform Act, which was substantially amended by the 1995 Family Law Act.

By 1995, a series of scandals had rocked the Catholic Church, such as clerical abuse and paternity cases involving a well-known bishop and media priest, and trust in Church leaders was at an all-time low. As the campaign reached its peak, the late Mother Teresa of Calcutta and Pope John Paul II urged the Irish electorate to vote against divorce, but their voices went unheard.

The pro-divorce campaign won by a whisker. At the final count, the electorate had voted in favour of divorce by a majority of slightly over 9,000 votes in a poll of 1.6 million: just over half of one percent.

A divisional High Court rejected a legal challenge to the result by anti-divorce campaigners, ruling that the Court could not interfere with the democratic process.

Five Supreme Court judges unanimously rejected an appeal. They criticised the government's decision to spend half a million pounds promoting a Yes vote as a breach of the constitutional right to equality and of the democratic process but said there was no proof that the campaign had materially affected the outcome of the poll.[7]

The Catholic Bishops issued a statement[8] reminding Catholics that Church teaching on the indissolubility of marriage had not changed—the valid and consummated marriage of a baptised man and woman excluded marriage to anyone else while both spouses were still alive.

Marriage Breakdown Statistics

In the event, the expected rush for divorces never materialised. Claims by the *Irish Times* that 80,000 people were in broken marriages and just waiting to divorce[9] proved to be gross exaggerations. In the five years

---

[7] [1995] 2 IR 10.
[8] 26 October 1995.
[9] 'Introducing divorce', *The Irish Times* archive, 26 September 1996; 'Divorce decision', *The Irish Times* archive,13 June 1996.

after the introduction of the Divorce Act, a little over 10,000 divorces were granted in the Circuit Court, with fewer than 100 in the High Court.

In 2012, according to the Courts Service annual report, there were 3,482 divorce applications and 1,290 for judicial separation.

Most of the applications were brought by women, reflecting a growing perception among men that the family law courts are biased against them. While female applicants only just outnumbered male applicants for divorce decrees, the figure for judicial separations was almost three to one in favour of women.

But the introduction of divorce does not appear to have contributed to the stability of marriage in Ireland. More than quarter of a century after divorce became available, the increasing incidence of relationship breakdown is reflected in the growing number of court applications in family law matters.

Between 1990 and 2012,[10] the number of District Court applications rose more than fivefold, from 8,028 to 40,669, including:

- 5,299 maintenance cases;
- 3,033 guardianship cases;
- 8,761 custody and access cases;
- 12,655 domestic violence cases;
- 9,315 childcare cases; and
- 1,636 other cases.

The number might have been even greater except for the fact that the rate of marriages has been falling. In the Republic of Ireland, the number of marriages dropped from a high of 20,778 couples in 1970 (7.1 marriages per thousand people) to 19,879 (4.3 marriages per thousand people) by 2011.

---

[10] Courts Service statistics

Divorce in the EU

Today, married Irish couples may obtain a divorce more easily than ever. Under a European Directive, a divorce obtained in any other EU country except Denmark will be recognised in Ireland. This has undermined the requirement in Irish law for a four-year separation, even though the Irish courts have ruled that separation does not necessarily mean living in separate houses.

Divorce has become an accepted part of life in 21st century Ireland, to the point where, in the 2002 case of *T v T*,[11] former Chief Justice Ronan Keane hinted that "clean break" divorces were now a real possibility.

---

[11] [2002] 3 IR 334.

CHOICES

Introduction

The first question which must be addressed is whether family law applies in a particular situation. Opposite-sex married couples can avail of the full panoply of family legislation, from nullity to divorce, judicial separation and incidental reliefs, such as laws relating to maintenance, domestic violence and the family home.

Unmarried opposite-sex couples may avail of a limited range of legislation, including that relating to children, maintenance and the home, but clearly cannot seek to end a relationship by the use of divorce legislation, as there was no marriage in the first place. However, they may seek a decree of nullity in relation to the civil partnership.

Same-sex couples who have their relationship registered can thereafter avail of the rights and obligations contained in the Civil Partnership and Certain Rights and Obligations of Cohabitants Act 2010. However, despite the changes in society, most couples in Ireland today are married, and may therefore avail of family law legislation.

Clearly, couples should not separate at the first setback. Whatever the difficulties—financial problems, infidelity, alcohol, gambling, drugs, sexual incompatibility—there are organisations which can help.

But, if after trying to resolve their differences, a couple still decide to part, they should carefully consider a range of important options.

Civil and Religious Elements

There are two elements to a marriage: civil and religious. For many couples, the main consideration is their legal or contractual relationship, brought about by a valid civil marriage. For others, the religious aspect of marriage can be more important.

In relation to the civil contract, there are three possible avenues for married couples who choose to split up: nullity, separation or divorce. For civil partners or cohabitants, there's the option of dissolution, separation or a redress order.

If there was no valid marriage from the start, either partner is entitled to apply for a decree of nullity—even if they have been together for many years and have a number of children.

If there *was* a valid civil marriage, the two options are separation—in which case the partners remain married and may not remarry—or divorce, after which the state permits civil remarriage.

In relation to the religious aspect of marriage, all the main Christian Churches except the Catholic Church permit the remarriage of divorced people in church. The Catholic Church also does not recognise the moral validity of same-sex partnerships.

Non-Catholics, therefore, may divorce and remarry in church without any difficulty. Catholics who have been validly married may not remarry in church unless their spouse dies. Catholics who wish to marry a new partner in church while the first partner is still alive must first obtain an ecclesiastical (or Church) nullity, which is a ruling by the Church authorities that the earlier supposed 'marriage' never existed.

Validity

The first issue to be addressed by any couple wishing to separate has to be: is our marriage or partnership legally valid?

That may seem an odd question to ask, particularly if the couple went through a marriage or civil partnership ceremony, have been together for many years and perhaps even have children. But it's not as straightforward as that. There may be a number of reasons why the relationship was void from the beginning—perhaps because of a problem with the ceremony or with the couple themselves.

If the couple discover that their marriage or partnership is not valid, that has wide-ranging implications for them. Either partner may then marry someone else or enter a civil partnership. However, they may not avail of constitutional protection for the family if they are not husband and wife. They may not be able to seek other reliefs if their civil partnership is declared void.

Any children of an opposite-sex couple, while not illegitimate, become 'non-marital' children. Any agreement entered into on the basis that the couple were married, such as a separation agreement, would be null and void.

If a couple do decide to seek a civil nullity, they may decide—at any time—to validate their marriage or partnership, if it is possible to do so. If, for example, one of the partners was under age at the time of the marriage or partnership ceremony, the couple may choose to marry or register a civil partnership with one another, assuming that both parties are over 18 and capable of giving consent at the time of that decision.

Separation Agreements

If there is no doubt about the validity of the marriage or partnership, and the couple want to split up formally without recourse to the courts, and do not wish to remarry or formally partner someone else, the simplest solution is probably a separation agreement. Such an agreement may be negotiated even before the couple separate and no statutory pre-conditions are required.

The main matters dealt with by a separation agreement are:

- an agreement to live separately;
- a 'non-molestation' clause, which means spouses will not interfere in the life of the other;
- arrangements for children, including custody, access, holidays and foreign travel;
- ownership of any property;

- maintenance and lump sum payments;
- indemnity from the debts of the other spouse;
- taxable status; and
- succession rights.

Separation agreements are private contracts and accepted as a way of allowing a couple to make their own arrangements for separation without the necessity for a court battle. Pre-nuptial agreements, however, are still not officially recognised in Ireland, as the courts consider they may destabilise the marriage contract.

Separation agreements must be drawn up voluntarily and may be set aside if there is any suggestion of duress, undue influence or misrepresentation. The agreement, which formally ends the duty to cohabit, should be drawn up with the benefit of legal advice.

In *VW v JW*,[1] the judge refused to set aside an agreement where the wife deliberately did not seek legal advice because, she claimed, she was an alcoholic.[2]

In *O'M v O'M*,[3] where the wife sought a divorce, Judge Alan Mahon ruled that an 18-year-old separation agreement was not a comprehensive and final agreement because it lacked a maintenance provision, had no custody and pension clauses and was not described as being in "full and final settlement". The judge said that the relevant value of property was the value at the date of the hearing, and he ordered the husband to pay his wife €400,000 because the value of the family home had risen substantially.

Most issues can be resolved in the separation agreement, though the law does not permit a spouse or civil partner to contract out of future maintenance payments. The 1964 Guardianship of Infants Act allowed parents to specify in a separation agreement who should have custody of the children. After the agreement has been drawn up, it may be "ruled" by the court, giving it the force of a court order.

---

[1] Unreported, High Court, 10 April 1978.
[2] Initials are normally used in reports of family law cases, in order to protect the anonymity of those involved.
[3] Unreported, Circuit Court, 5 May 2004.

The courts will not look favourably on anyone who, after independent advice, freely enters into a separation agreement and later tries to disclaim it. In *Hyman v Hyman*,[4] the court said a separation agreement should be drawn up, construed, dissolved and enforced on exactly the same principles as any other commercial agreement.

A separation agreement may be varied by the court if there are substantial changes in a person's circumstances. In *MG v MG*,[5] a couple signed a separation agreement in which the husband had agreed to transfer his interest in the family home to the wife in return for a payment of IR£20,000. The house was then worth IR£200,000. Later, the husband lost his job and asked the court to vary the original agreement. At that stage, the family home was valued at IR£800,000.

Judge John Buckley said:

> Where the parties are well-educated intelligent persons who have had the benefit of competent legal advice before entering into a recent separation agreement, it seems to me that the Court should be slow to make any radical alterations to the terms of such agreement unless there have been sufficient changes in the situations of the parties.
>
> Making any significant alterations to the arrangements may well cause further distress to the children, who may well see themselves as vulnerable pawns in a renewed conflict between their parents.

But the judge said that, if the couple could have foreseen the "remarkable increase in residential property values", he doubted whether the husband would have "so readily surrendered all his interest in the family home".

The judge ruled that the husband should continue to pay maintenance but should receive 10 percent of the proceeds of any future sale of the family home, though he was not given any equitable right to the property.

Property

If a separating couple disagree about the ownership of property, the court may decide the issue under the 1957 Married Women's Status Act.

---

[4] [1929] AC 601.
[5] Unreported, Circuit Court, 25 July 2000.

A claim under the 1957 Act is not like a claim to a property adjustment order under the Judicial Separation, Family Law or Divorce Acts, where the court takes many more factors into consideration. For a spouse to be entitled to some share in the other spouse's property, there must have been some direct or indirect financial contribution. However, as Geoghegan J said in *AS v GS*,[6] proceedings for a property adjustment order in judicial separation proceedings are registrable as a *lis pendens*, even where the applicant spouse has no interest in the specific property, but merely a claim to it.

Mr Justice Thomas Finlay said in *W v W*[7]:

> Where a wife contributes by money to the purchase of a property by her husband in his sole name, in the absence of evidence of some inconsistent agreement or arrangement, the Court will decide that the wife is entitled to an equitable interest in that property approximately proportionate to the extent of her contribution...

> Where a wife contributes either directly towards the repayment of mortgage instalments or contributes to a general family fund, thus releasing her husband from an obligation which he otherwise would have to discharge liabilities out of that fund and permitting him to repay mortgage instalments, she will—in the absence of proof of an inconsistent agreement or arrangement—be entitled to an equitable share in the property...approximately proportionate to her contribution.

> Where a wife expends monies or carries out work in the improvement of a property which has been originally acquired by—and the legal ownership in which is solely in—her husband, she will have no claim in respect of such contributions unless she established by evidence that, from the circumstances surrounding the making of it, she was led to believe—or, of course, that it was specifically agreed—that she would be recompensed for it.

> Even where such a right to recompense is established—either by an express agreement or by circumstances in which the wife making the contribution was led to such belief—it is a right to recompense in monies only and cannot and does not constitute a right to claim an equitable share in the estate of the property concerned.

---

[6] [1994] 1 IR 407.
[7] [1981] ILRM 202.

In *McC v McC*,[8] Henchy J said: "[w]hen the wife's contribution has been indirect (such as by contributing, by means of other earnings, to a general family fund) the courts will, in the absence of any express or implied agreement to the contrary, infer a trust in favour of the wife, on the ground that she has to that extent relieved the husband of the financial burden he incurred in purchasing the house."

In *CD v WD and Barclays Bank*,[9] CD claimed a beneficial interest in a 26-acre Co Kilkenny farm, which was held in her husband's sole name. WD had been full owner of the lands since 1972, 11 years before the couple married. In 1989, Barclays Bank registered a charge over the land, which did not include the family home.

The wife said she had contributed about IR£25,000 towards the building of the family home in Co Laois, which was also held in the husband's sole name. She also used her income as a nurse to pay day-to-day household expenses. She said that her husband had promised to put the Kilkenny land into their joint names, though nothing was ever done.

The bank obtained an order for possession in 1991 and served all the papers on the wife, but she made no claim to the land before the issue of the 1995 proceedings. She said she was unaware that she had any rights, but the judge said that was not the attitude of a joint owner.

The judge said the wife's action was "more a last ditch effort to rescue some form of asset from the bank than a true dispute between herself and her husband".

Although the wife had made a substantial direct contribution to the family home, she did not claim any share in the house. Her claim applied only to the Kilkenny land, towards which she had made no direct contribution.

The court ruled that her indirect contribution to the "general family fund" could not have given her any interest in the Kilkenny land between the marriage in 1983 and the date of the bank's charge, since the husband was already the full owner.

---

[8] [1986] ILRM 1.
[9] McGuinness J, High Court, 5 February 1997.

Judicial Separation and Divorce

Not all couples, married or not, are willing to negotiate separation terms amicably. The emotions which accompany the end of a relationship may make it impossible to negotiate an agreement. The alternatives for married couples are usually either judicial separation or divorce.

A decree of judicial separation does not give a right to remarry; merely to live apart. The couple remain married, so if both partners subsequently decide to give the relationship another chance, they may resume living together without the necessity for a remarriage, and without having to return to court.

Until February 1997, when divorce became available in Ireland, the only way to end a valid civil marriage finally and irrevocably was to establish a domicile abroad and obtain a divorce there. While this may have been an option for couples with no family ties in Ireland, it was not a realistic possibility for most people.

Even where one partner did obtain a foreign divorce, the decree might not always be recognised in Ireland because of problems of domicile. Until 1986, a foreign divorce would only be recognised in Ireland if granted in the country where both spouses were domiciled, not just resident.

The High Court expressed differing opinions in *McG v W*[10] and *MEC v JAC*[11]. In *McG v W*, McGuinness J held that one year's residence was enough to satisfy the domicile requirement of a pre-1986 English divorce, but in *MEC v JAC*, Kinlen J refused to recognise a 1980 English divorce because neither spouse was domiciled in England.

However, the decision of McGuinness J has not been followed in cases such as *BO'M v BO'M*[12] where Judge Olive Buttimer accepted the argument of counsel for the Attorney General that a 1981 English divorce should not be recognised, as neither spouse was domiciled in England at the time.

---

[10] [2000] 1 IR 96.
[11] [2001] 2 IR 399.
[12] Unreported, Circuit Court, July 2005.

The Oireachtas changed the domicile rules in the 1986 Domicile and Recognition of Foreign Divorces Act. That Act says that a foreign divorce obtained after 2 October 1986 will now be recognised if granted in the country where *either* spouse is domiciled.

In *CM v TM (No 2),*[13] the High Court held that the common law rule that a married woman's domicile depended on that of her husband had been abolished by the principles of equality before the law and equal rights in marriage enshrined in the Constitution. This decision was upheld by the Supreme Court in *W v W*[14] which said that a pre-1986 divorce would be recognised in Ireland if only one of the spouses was domiciled in the jurisdiction where the divorce was granted.

The problem of recognition for foreign divorces continues to be an issue for the courts. For example, in *PK (orse C) v TK,*[15] an Irish husband and his American wife who married in New York in 1963 had later moved to Ireland.

In 1977, the marriage broke down and the wife returned to New York, leaving the children with the husband in Ireland. The husband obtained an uncontested divorce in New York in 1980. The wife did not seek any maintenance.

Twenty years later, the wife sought a divorce in Ireland, claiming that the New York decree was invalid because neither spouse was domiciled in New York at the time. She maintained that she had only lived in New York because of economic necessity and had always intended to return to Ireland.

The High Court ruled that the husband's domicile was New York State, so the decree of the New York court would be recognised in Ireland and the couple were not married here. The wife appealed the decision.

The Supreme Court said it was clear that the wife wanted an Irish divorce so she could seek maintenance. But the Court said the overwhelming evidence was that the wife had either reverted to her domicile of origin or

---

[13] [1990] 2 IR 52.
[14] [1993] 2 IR 476.
[15] [2002] IESC 15.

had chosen New York as a domicile of choice by living there for 22 years. It therefore recognised the US divorce.

Under the 1996 Divorce Act, when the courts grant a divorce, the valid, subsisting civil marriage is dissolved. If the man and woman later decide they want to live together again as husband and wife, they have to go through the whole marriage procedure again.

ANNULMENT

Introduction

Annulment may apply to marriage or to civil partnership. A decree of nullity states that a valid marriage or partnership does not exist, although a voidable marriage or partnership continues to exist until a court declares otherwise.

Because of the relative newness of the legislation, there is no case-law on nullity of civil partnerships, so this chapter deals mainly with nullity of marriage, though the grounds for nullity of marriage may also apply in some cases of civil partnership.

Before divorce became available, annulment (or nullity—the terms are interchangeable) was one of the few ways of ending a 'marriage'. However, with the passing of the Divorce Act, nullity has become a less significant concept in the family law courts.

The number of civil nullity decrees had been rising steadily before divorce was introduced. In 1990, the courts granted 30 annulments. By 1995/6, that figure had nearly trebled, to 86. But following the introduction of divorce, the number of nullity applications almost halved to 48 in 1997. In 2012, there were only 28 Circuit Court applications for nullity, and none at all in the High Court.

The grounds for nullity have been somewhat developed in the past 50 years, but cannot be extended by the courts. In *MM v PM*,[1] McMahon J rejected the suggestion that the Constitution gave the High Court an inherent jurisdiction to create new grounds for nullity. He said the jurisdiction of the High Court:

> clearly must be exercised upon grounds to be determined by the legislature. For the courts to add new grounds would be to engage in legislation.

But nullity may be a preferable option for some people who believe that their marriage never validly existed. A decree of nullity may be sought in conjunction with a divorce or judicial separation application. If the court decides that a valid marriage does not exist, the couple may not continue with their judicial separation or divorce application, and any further court proceedings will be subject, not to family law, but to ordinary civil law, including the Civil Partnership and Certain Rights and Obligations of Cohabitants Act 2010.

Definition of Marriage

Marriage was defined by Lord Penzance, in an English judgment relating to a polygamous Mormon marriage,[2] as "the voluntary union for life of one man and one woman to the exclusion of all others".

---

[1] [1986] ILRM 515.
[2] *Hyde v Hyde and Woodmansee*, LR 1 P&D 130.

In Ireland, Murray J referred to marriage in *DT v CT*[3] as:

> A solemn contract of partnership entered into between man and woman with a special status recognised by the Constitution.

He said that, in principle, marriage was for life (even though divorce had been available in Ireland for six years at this stage).

In *LB v Ireland and the Attorney General and PB*,[4] Hogan J said marriage involved "mutual giving and sacrifice. In practical terms, this means the sharing of outgoings, expenses and, in some respects, at least, the capital assets of the parties".

To contract a valid marriage in the Republic of Ireland, the parties must:

1. have the capacity to marry each other;
2. freely consent to the marriage; and
3. observe the formalities required by Irish law.

If, for example, the union is not voluntary or the parties are not male and female, the relationship may never have been a marriage. In *Zappone and Anor v Revenue Commissioners and Ors*,[5] Dunne J said: "I do not see how marriage can be redefined by the Court to encompass same-sex marriage."

Until the late nineteenth century, the established Church—the Church of Ireland—had exclusive jurisdiction to deal with matrimonial causes. But, with the disestablishment of the Church, the civil courts took over. The courts now have jurisdiction to rule whether a civil marriage is valid or whether it is null and void.

This jurisdiction of the Irish courts to deal with matrimonial matters dates back nearly 150 years. The 1870 Matrimonial Causes and Marriage Law Act said the principles and rules of civil nullity should approximate to Church rules. As late as the 1930s, the courts were still citing the Church's grounds for nullity. In *McM v McM*,[6] the judge referred to the "principles of the ecclesiastical law as administered in our matrimonial courts".

---

[3] [2003] 1 ILRM 321.
[4] [2012] IEHC 461.
[5] [2006] IEHC 404.
[6] [1936] IR 177.

That is still the case today, and the grounds on which a civil court will grant a decree of nullity are much the same as the grounds for a Church nullity. Henchy J, in *N (orse K) v K*,[7] said the 1870 Act did not fossilise the law, but the civil doctrine of nullity nevertheless remained largely unchanged until recently.

A petitioner for a nullity decree must prove his case with a high degree of probability, and must "remove all reasonable doubt".[8] There is a presumption in law that a marriage is valid, so the petitioner has a "heavy burden" to prove that a marriage is invalid.[9]

Lack of Capacity

A marriage or a civil partnership may be annulled because the parties were not capable of marrying each other or registering a civil partnership. This lack of capacity may be because they were under age and had no court permission to marry, were already married or in a registered partnership, or were within the forbidden degrees of kindred, either by consanguinity (blood or kindred relationship) or affinity (relationship by marriage).

For example, siblings may never validly marry, even if they are unaware that they are siblings. In Britain, twins who were adopted by separate families as babies later married each other without realising they were brother and sister, the House of Lords was told during a debate on the Human Fertility and Embryology Bill in December 2007. Lord Alton said the pair did not realise they were related until after their marriage. A court annulled the union after the couple discovered their true relationship.[10]

Marriage between people who are related by marriage may also be prohibited. The Deceased Wife's Sister's Marriage Act 1907, which permitted a man to marry his dead wife's sister, and the Deceased Brother's Widow's Marriage Act 1921, which allowed a woman to marry her dead husband's brother, did not permit the marriage while the wife or husband were still alive.

---

[7] [1985] IR 733.

[8] *S v S*, unreported, Supreme Court, 1 July 1976.

[9] *Per* Denham J in *S v K*, unreported, High Court, 2 July 1992.

[10] 'Parted-at-birth twins "married"', *BBC News*, available from http://news.bbc.co.uk/2/hi/7182817.stm; accessed 7 January 2014.

But the High Court ruled in *O'Shea v Ireland and the Attorney General*[11] that there was no rational basis for the affinity restrictions. The restriction on the constitutional right of the couple to marry was not necessary to support the constitutional protection of the family, the institution of marriage or the common good, so was inconsistent with the right to marry under Article 40.3.1° of the Constitution. That right to marry was first recognised as an unenumerated personal right under the Constitution in *Ryan v Attorney General*.[12]

Other Grounds for Annulment

If the formalities of a marriage or civil partnership were not observed, such as signing the register or giving adequate notice to the Registrar of Marriages or Civil Partnerships under s 46 of the Civil Registration Act 2004, the relationship could also be annulled.

In 2008, the Circuit Court granted a decree of nullity because the spouse's sibling "stood in" for him at the wedding abroad. However, in *Hamza & anor v Minister for Justice, Equality & Law Reform*,[13] the Supreme Court said the minister was not entitled to disregard a Sudanese marriage just because it was conducted by proxy.

In *Hassan & anor v Minister for Justice, Equality & Law Reform*,[14] the Supreme Court said the minister could not be entitled to refuse family reunification to an applicant who claimed he went through a religious marriage ceremony in Somalia, though Murray J said he would:

> find it difficult to envisage that a marriage ceremony, in whatever form, performed in Somalia, where the common law has no application whatsoever, could in itself be the basis for its recognition as a common law marriage.

If either party didn't give full, free and informed consent to the marriage or civil partnership—for example, if they were threatened, pressurised or suffering from a mental illness—the relationship may be void or voidable.

---

[11] [2007] 1 ILRM 460.
[12] [1965] 1 IR 294.
[13] [2013] IESC 9.
[14] [2013] IESC 8.

A marriage may be annulled because the relationship could not be consummated due to physical or psychological impotence, or if one party is unable to enter into and sustain a normal marital relationship, for example because of mental illness or homosexuality.[15]

In *UF (orse UC) v JC*,[16] the judge refused a nullity to a wife on grounds of her husband's homosexuality, as it would add new grounds under the 1870 Act. On appeal, the Chief Justice said the incapacity to enter into and sustain a proper marital relationship could arise "from some inherent quality or characteristic of an individual's nature or personality which could not be said to be voluntary or self induced". Incapacity by virtue of the husband's "inherent and unalterable" homosexuality, of which the petitioner was unaware, was grounds for nullity. Incapacity is a ground for nullity, comparable to impotence.

Nullity relates to the moment one party said "I do", not to any subsequent event, such as having children or living together for many years. For example, in *AC (orse J) v PJ*,[17] a mother of five children was granted a decree of nullity. A country girl from a strict religious background, she was so afraid to tell her family when she became pregnant at the age of 21 that she was admitted to a psychiatric hospital suffering from acute anxiety. She was discharged from hospital the day before the wedding. The High Court judge said the woman's consent to the marriage was not a full and free exercise of her independent will.

Approbation

It is possible to approbate (or confirm) a marriage, so therefore it is important to take legal advice before starting any action which could prejudice an application for a nullity decree by approbation, such as the use of family law legislation.

In *OB v R*, for instance, the petitioner's second husband claimed that she had approbated the marriage by applying for social welfare payments as a deserted spouse.[18]

---

[15] *F v F* [1991] 1 IR 348.
[16] [1991] 2 IR 330.
[17] [1995] 2 IR 253.
[18] [1999] 4 IR 168.

In *D v C*,[19] Costello J referred to the case of *G v N*[20] and said that a person who had "taken advantages and derived benefits from the matrimonial relations" might be said to have approbated the marriage.

Where the case involved a lack of consent by the petitioner, the question of approbation did not arise, as such a marriage would be void, rather than voidable, and a void marriage could not be approbated. The judge granted a decree of nullity, even though the petitioner had previously sought a barring order against the respondent.

Basis for Nullity Application

A person who has recently married, and believes he or she may have been pressurised into marriage or was incapable of giving proper consent, may wish to obtain a civil nullity decree, rather than wait the required four years for a divorce.

Equally, for a spouse who wishes to avoid the financial implications of a divorce, a nullity, if available, may be a much more attractive option. If the marriage is annulled the couple would both be treated as single persons from the perspective of tax and other matters, and the issue of joint marital property or the Family Home Protection Act 1976 would not arise.

Although a couple is not legally required to obtain a decree of nullity where a marriage is void from the outset, it would be sensible to obtain the High Court's recognition of the *status quo* in case of legal difficulties later, when attempting to remarry or if there is an issue about the validity of the subsequent marriage. Anybody with an interest in the matter, not just the couple themselves, may apply for a nullity decree in the case of a void marriage.

Void Marriages

The five grounds which will render a marriage void are:

- an existing previous marriage, including remarriage after a divorce not recognised in Ireland, or after a Church nullity without a civil decree;

---

[19] [1984] ILRM 173.
[20] 10 App Cases 171.

- where either party was resident in Ireland and under 18 at the time of the marriage and did not have a court exemption;
- failure to observe the formalities, such as the three months' notice required by statute (although minor flaws are not necessarily fatal);
- absence of consent, including duress, undue influence, fraud and mental illness; and
- where parties are within the forbidden degrees of relationship (see page 103) or are the same sex.

A couple whose marriage is void cannot avail of marital property legislation. In the case of *MC v BS*,[21] the High Court found in 1998 that the couple's 19-year 'marriage' was void because of duress and lack of consent.

The couple had jointly bought a home in 1993. But Mr Justice Daniel Herbert said they would never have done so if they had known that they were not lawfully married. "The just and correct approach for this Court to adopt is to regard the property as having been purchased by strangers," he said.

The mother, MC, left the house at the end of 1994 and BS was left to bring up the children there. MC later tried to force BS to sell the property. Herbert J said there was no evidence that her motive in seeking the sale was vindictive, but he was satisfied that it was "wholly mercenary".

He found that MC was entitled to 10 percent of the property, and BS to 90 percent. MC was not entitled to insist on the sale of the house under the Partition Acts because she did not own at least half of the property.

Same-Sex 'Marriages'

The validity of same-sex 'marriages' has been considered by the courts in a number of cases, notably by the High Court in *Murray v Ireland*[22] and the Supreme Court in *TF v Ireland*[23] and *DT v CT*.[24]

In *Zappone and Gilligan v Revenue Commissioners, Ireland and the Attorney General*,[25] the judge said that, under the Irish Constitution, marriage was

---

[21] [2008] IEHC 463.
[22] [1985] IR 532.
[23] [1995] 1 IR 321.
[24] [2003] 1 ILRM 231.
[25] [2008] 2 IR 417.

"confined to persons of the opposite sex". That had been reiterated as recently as 2003, so this could not be said to be "some kind of fossilised understanding of marriage". The judge said she found it "very difficult to see how the definition of marriage could, having regard to the ordinary and natural meaning of the words used, relate to a same-sex couple".

The High Court also confirmed in *Foy v An tArdChláraitheoir*[26] that transgender individuals could not register their new gender, so a marriage between a person born a man and another man would probably be void. McKechnie J said: "[m]arriage as understood by the Constitution, by statute and by case-law refers to a union by a biological man with a biological woman."

In the English case of *Corbett v Corbett (orse Ashley)*,[27] a 40-year-old transvestite left his wife and family and married 25-year-old transsexual George Jamieson, who'd had a sex-change operation in Casablanca in 1960. After the operation, Mr Jamieson lived as a woman and called himself April Ashley. He was courted by Arthur Corbett (Lord Rowallan) and they married in Gibraltar in 1963.

They split up after a fortnight and Lord Rowallan petitioned for a declaration of nullity on the basis either that Ashley was a castrated man or because of Ashley's inability or refusal to consummate the marriage. Nine doctors gave evidence in what the judge called a "pathetic but almost incredible story". The court ruled that the respondent was always male, so the marriage was void.

The European Court of Human Rights disapproved of the *Corbett v Corbett* decision in the case of *Goodwin v UK*[28] which concerned a post-operative male-to-female transsexual.

In another English case, *S-T v J*,[29] the defendant had been born a female but underwent a partial sex change before the marriage. For 17 years, the wife remained unaware of her 'husband's' true gender until the production of the birth certificate at a divorce hearing. As a result, the wife applied for and was granted a decree of nullity.

---

[26] [2002] IEHC 116.
[27] [1971] P 83.
[28] [2002] 35 EHRR 447.
[29] [1998] 1 All ER 431.

The husband said his wife knew about his cross-dressing tendencies before the marriage, but she said she was only 18 and "very ill informed about cross-dressers". The marriage quickly turned into a "platonic friendship". His wife had a regular boyfriend, while S kept his own supply of female clothing.

The judge granted a declaration of nullity on the grounds that there was a lack of consent by the wife, not only because of her husband's cross-dressing, but also because of his concealed gynephilic transvestism.

In the case of *B (formerly known as M) v L*,[30] the wife of a 56-year-old man who had undergone a sex change in 1994 petitioned for nullity. The couple had been granted a judicial separation in 1993 and the husband applied for a divorce in 2005.

The wife said she was "very ill informed about cross dressers" when she met her husband at the age of 18. During their marriage, she had a regular boyfriend while the husband kept his own supply of female clothing.

Abbot J said there was a lack of consent by the wife, not only on the basis of the transvestism which she learned about during the marriage, but also in relation to the "gynephilic transvesticism" which the husband concealed. This lack of consent rendered the marriage void, rather than voidable.

Duress

For a marriage to be valid, any consent must be a "fully free exercise of the independent will of the parties". In *N (orse K) v K*,[31] the petitioner, who had been a 19-year-old virgin, became pregnant after a short and casual relationship. Her parents said she should marry the baby's father and she agreed, but later sought a decree of nullity on the grounds of duress.

The High Court refused a decree because it said the parties had intended to marry anyway, but the Supreme Court allowed an appeal. It said duress was not restricted to physical threats or other harmful consequences. If the decision to marry was:

---

[30] [2009] IEHC 623.
[31] [1986] ILRM 75.

caused by external pressure or influence, whether falsely or honestly applied, to such an extent as to lose the character of a fully free act of that person's will, no valid marriage had occurred.

In *DB (orse O'R) v NO'R*,[32] the judge said a marriage was invalid if induced by "fear of threats, intimidation, duress or undue influence". Fraud may also negative consent where it relates to a fundamental feature of the marriage (*S v O'S*).[33] The High Court said there was no freedom of will when one party was in the "emotional bondage" of the other.

In *Griffith v Griffith*,[34] a 19-year-old was told he'd be sent to jail if he didn't marry a pregnant girl. He realised later he couldn't have been the child's father. He was granted an annulment, as his consent was obtained by fear and fraud.

In *B v D*,[35] the judge said the "forceful arrogance" of the husband amounted to duress and the marriage was therefore invalid. In *CO'K (orse CP) v WP*,[36] the judge said attempts by a violent and domineering 18-year-old youth to obtain the consent of a quiet 16-year-old girl amounted to duress and undue influence.

In *PW v AO'C (orse W)*,[37] the petitioner husband had married in a Catholic Church in London in 1956 after his fiancée threatened to throw herself under a train if he did not marry her immediately. In 1979, the husband obtained a Catholic Church nullity and, in 1981, he went through a ceremony of marriage with another woman. He was charged with bigamy but subsequently acquitted. He was granted a decree of nullity on the grounds of duress.

The judge in *MK (orse MMcC) v FMcC*[38] said the will of a reluctant 19-year-old bride and a resentful 21-year-old husband was overborne by their parents.

---

[32] [1991] 1 IR 289.
[33] Unreported, High Court, 10 November 1978.
[34] [1944] IR 35.
[35] Unreported, High Court, 20 June 1973.
[36] [1985] IR 279.
[37] [1992] ILRM 536.
[38] [1982] ILRM 277.

If a person marries after obtaining a Church nullity but not a state annulment, there may no question of bigamy if the original 'marriage' is subsequently declared void by the courts.[39]

Pre-Existing Pregnancy

In *EP v MC*,[40] the judge refused a decree where a pregnant girl had threatened to have an abortion unless her boyfriend married her.

But pre-existing pregnancy is not, in itself, sufficient to invalidate a person's free consent. In *ACL v RL*,[41] the judge said a couple aged 28 and 32 with a baby had intended to marry at some stage and he refused a decree. And in *KW v MW*,[42] where the petitioner claimed he was pressured into marrying his 17-year-old pregnant girlfriend, the judge said he was satisfied that the couple had contemplated marriage at some stage, and refused a decree.

Mental Illness

Pre-existing mental illness might be grounds for dissolving a marriage. In *R v R*,[43] Costello J granted a decree of nullity to a woman whose husband had been suffering from paranoid schizophrenia for five years before their marriage. But the judge added:

> It does not follow from the decision I have reached on the facts of this case that every unfortunate sufferer from paranoid schizophrenia is, as a matter of law, incapable of entering into a valid ceremony of marriage.

In *RSJ v JSJ*,[44] where the husband petitioned after an eight-month marriage because of his schizophrenia, the judge said the husband had understood the nature, purpose and consequences of marriage. If it were voidable, it would only be on the wife's application. But if, through illness at the date of marriage, a petitioner lacked the capacity to form a

---

[39] *OB v R* [1999] 4 IR 168.
[40] [1985] ILRM 34.
[41] Unreported, High Court, 18 October 1982.
[42] Unreported, High Court, 19 July 1994.
[43] Unreported, High Court, 21 December 1984.
[44] [1982] ILRM 263.

caring and considerate relationship, the judge might consider it grounds for nullity.

Indeed, in *D v C*,[45] the judge said a husband's manic depression before, during and after marriage severely impaired his capacity to form and sustain a normal marriage.

The judge said: "It should be recognised that there have been important scientific advances in the field of psychiatric medicine since 1870 and that it is now possible to identify psychiatric illness, such as for example manic depressive illness, which in many cases may be so severe as to make it impossible for one of the partners to the marriage to enter into and sustain the relationship which should exist between married couples if a lifelong union is to be possible."

In *DC v DW*,[46] the judge granted a decree to a schizophrenic wife on her own petition.

In *BD v MC (orse MD)*,[47] Mr Justice Donal Barrington accepted a wife's emotional immaturity as grounds for nullity. In *W v P*,[48] the judge allowed the petition of the wife of a suicidal farmer who had an emotional age of five.

For a marriage to be dissolved on the grounds of mental illness, the illness must have existed at the time of the marriage. In *SC v PD (orse C)*,[49] SC was seeking a decree of nullity after 22 years of marriage and three children. A month before the first baby was born, the wife had an episode of hypermania. She showed the same symptoms during her second and third pregnancy, with "bizarre ideas".

Mr Justice Brian McCracken said that the wife's manic depression did not affect her ability to have marital relations unless triggered by some event. He said a person could not be granted a decree of nullity if suffering from a latent illness which did not affect the ability to enter into marriage, but which might subsequently affect the ability to sustain the marriage.

---

[45] [1984] ILRM 173.
[46] [1987] ILRM 58.
[47] [1984] ILRM 173.
[48] Unreported, High Court, 7 June 1984.
[49] Unreported, High Court, 14 March 1996.

Polygamy

A polygamous marriage is not valid in Irish law. In *Akram v Minister for Justice, Equality and Law Reform*,[50] the court upheld the minister's decision to refuse to recognise Akram's post-nuptial declaration of citizenship because he had polygamously married an Irish woman and a Pakistani.

In the Supreme Court case of *Conlon v Mohamed*,[51] Mohamed was a citizen of South Africa and domiciled there. Conlon was a citizen of Ireland with a domicile in Ireland. Conlon was seeking possession of a house which belonged to Mohamed. He claimed that he had validly married her, so the house was the marital home and he was entitled to remain in it.

The couple had gone through an Islamic marriage ceremony in a South African mosque six years earlier. Conlon did not attend, but a male friend of Mohamed represented her. Later, the couple exchanged rings and vows at a separate ceremony.

Mohamed said the exchange of rings and vows showed that the couple intended the mosque marriage to be monogamous. The couple planned to marry in a register office on their return to Dublin but never did so.

South African law did not recognise an Islamic marriage in a mosque or a marriage by proxy, and the marriage was also banned under South Africa's apartheid laws. The Supreme Court ruled that the couple had never been married, so the house was not a family home.

In the case of *HAH v SAA*,[52] the High Court refused to recognise a polygamous marriage performed in Beirut in Lebanon. The judge said that, if she were to construe the word "marriage" as including polygamous marriages, she would be re-writing the understanding of marriage in Ireland. "That is something I cannot do."

Article 4.4 of the European Council Directive on Family Reunification states:

---

[50] [2004] IEHC 33.
[51] [1989] ILRM 523.
[52] [2010] IEHC 497.

> In the event of a polygamous marriage, where the sponsor already
> has a spouse living with him in the territory of a member state, the
> member state concerned shall not authorise the family reunification
> of a further spouse.

But the High Court later said there was a distinction between recognising
a potentially polygamous marriage for family reunification reasons and
recognising it for reasons of matrimonial reliefs and related remedies.

In *DM v CF*,[53] the Attorney General appealed against a Circuit Family
Court decision that a traditional or customary marriage in Zimbabwe was
valid. A handwritten letter from the local headman confirmed that the
bridegroom had paid the bride price and that the subsequent marriage
was recognised in Zimbabwe.

The applicant said that, although he and his wife were Christians, they
respected their families' beliefs by having a traditional marriage in
accordance with Shona traditions. As Christians, neither he nor his wife
intended to take another spouse.

Mrs Justice Maureen Clark said that the decision in *Conlon v Mohamed*[54]
was not relevant because it did not deal with the issue of family
reunification. She was "firmly of the view" that reference to the Circuit
Court to decide whether a refugee's marriage was valid according to
Irish law was "misconceived and gives rise to unnecessary delay in
family reunification".

"Polygamy is unlawful in the UK and Ireland, and polygamous marriages
are not recognised as valid marriages according to our laws," she said.
"There is no dispute about that."

Voidable Marriages

More commonly, a marriage is not void *ab initio* (from the beginning), but
is 'voidable', which means that it remains valid until a competent tribunal
declares otherwise.

---

[53] [2011] IEHC 415.
[54] [1989] ILRM 523.

In *B (formerly known as M) v L*,[55] Mr Justice Henry Abbott, citing Costello J in *D v C*[56] said:

> In essence, a voidable marriage is one where only the parties have an interest, and a void marriage is one which society has an interest and which rests on grounds of public policy.

The two grounds for voidable marriage are:

- physical impotence; and
- inability to enter into and sustain a normal marital relationship.

A marriage is voidable where, for example, one of the partners was psychologically incapable at the time of the marriage of forming "a caring or considerate relationship".[57]

In *G v G*,[58] a wife said she had an "invincible repugnance" to her husband, and the judge said he should use a "little bit of gentle violence" on her!

Repudiation

Where a marriage is 'repudiated' by one spouse who claims that the marriage never existed, the other spouse may rely on his or her own mental, physical or emotional incapacity when seeking a decree of nullity.

In *W v W*,[59] the wife was granted a decree based on her own psychological incapacity. The High Court said the husband had repudiated the marriage by seeking a Church nullity, and it granted a decree of civil nullity.

In *OK v OK*,[60] the petitioner husband had gone through a marriage ceremony in Dublin in 1994, but separated from his wife five years later. The husband said he was incapable of entering into and sustaining a normal marital relationship because of depression, bipolar disorder and emotional immaturity. He said his wife also did not give her full, free and informed consent because of her own emotional immaturity.

---

[55] [2009] IEHC 623.
[56] [1984] ILRM 173.
[57] *RSJ v JSJ* [1982] ILRM 263.
[58] [1924] AC 349.
[59] [1981] ILRM 202.
[60] [2005] IEHC 384.

The wife initially denied the husband's claims and said he had approbated the marriage by his conduct, so the proceedings were an abuse of process. Later in the proceedings, she withdrew her objection.

Mr Justice O'Higgins said it would be wrong for a court in any case to

> accept uncritically the evidence of medical experts, no matter how distinguished. To do so would, in effect, be to substitute the opinion of the medical person involved for the decision of the Court itself.

The judge said that bipolar illness itself did not mean that a person could not enter into and sustain a marital relationship. "Very many people subject to this illness are capable of contracting and sustaining rich enduring marital relationships," he said.

He said that a petitioner could rely on his own incapacity where the other party had repudiated the marriage. He cited *McM v McM*,[61] where it was held that a spouse could rely on his own impotence to nullify a marriage only if the other party had previously repudiated the marriage. This decision was followed in many cases, including *J v J*[62] and *DC v DW*.[63] The judge said he had no doubt that the petitioner was incapable of sustaining a marital relationship because of the effects of his illness on his personality.

However, in *PC v VC*,[64] O'Hanlon J ruled that, even when one party strongly affirmed the marriage contract, the other party could rely on want of capacity which existed on both sides. If it were impossible for both parties to sustain a normal marriage relationship for any length of time, "the petitioner should not be denied a decree of nullity because the respondent wishes to hold him to the marriage bond".

O'Hanlon said the Court of Appeal in England in *Harthan v Harthan*[65] had decided that, even where there was incapacity resulting from physical impotence unknown to the impotent spouse at the time of the marriage, a decree of nullity should be granted on his or her application, without requiring repudiation of the marriage by the other spouse.

---

[61] [1936] IR 177.
[62] [1982] ILRM 263.
[63] [1987] 1 ILRM 58.
[64] [1990] 2 IR 91.
[65] [1949] P 115.

Quirke J followed the O'Hanlon decision in *PMcG v AF*.[66] He said it was "not necessary for the petitioner to prove repudiation of the marriage by the other party, even in cases based on the incapacity of the petitioner". He granted the petition on the grounds that the husband was incapable of sustaining a normal marital relationship, because of his own serious mental illness and its effect on someone with the personality traits set out in the psychiatric evidence.

Sexual Infidelity

In *MJ v CJ*,[67] a wife was granted a decree of nullity because her husband admitted days after the wedding that he had been involved with a mother-of-two until just before the marriage. He had previously denied the relationship.

On the other hand, in 1999, the High Court refused a decree of nullity to a man whose wife had an affair with her employer shortly after the marriage.[68] The man claimed that, if he had known she was having an affair, he would not have married her. He said his consent to the marriage was not "full, free and informed".

Mr Justice O'Higgins concluded that the allegations were true, but said the "nondisclosure of inappropriate behaviour" before or during courtship was not a ground for nullity.

"It is not incumbent on the parties to give a history of their good or bad behaviour prior to getting married in order to contract a valid marriage," he said:

> In this case, the parties had a courtship which lasted several years. They knew prior to getting married the nature of the contract they were undertaking.

The Supreme Court agreed and dismissed his appeal.

Even flagrant sexual infidelity by one spouse is not always sufficient for a nullity decree. In *PC and CM (orse C)*,[69] PC was seeking a decree of nullity

---

[66] Unreported, High Court, 7 May 2003.
[67] Unreported, High Court, 21 February 1991.
[68] *PF v GO'M (orse GF)*, unreported, High Court, 25 March 1999.
[69] [1996] 3 Fam LJ 78.

after six years of marriage. His wife, CM, claimed the marriage was valid but had irretrievably broken down.

When the couple met, she already had a baby. PC and CM saw each other regularly, but eventually broke up and CM continued her sexual relationship with the child's father. Later PC bought a house, took CM to see it and asked whether it would be "all right", which she took as a proposal of marriage.

They married in 1989, but a year later, she said she wanted to end the marriage. She left home for four days and had sex with the boy's father again. When she returned, the couple tried to sort out their difficulties and saw a counsellor, but in 1993, CM started a sexual relationship with the counsellor.

In 1994, the husband petitioned for nullity. A consultant psychiatrist said the wife had an immature personality disorder at the time of the marriage.

Mrs Justice Laffoy said the wife had been "flagrantly unfaithful" to her husband, but was able to understand the nature, purpose and consequence of the marriage contract and had entered into the marriage with good intent. She refused a decree of nullity.

Immaturity

In *LB v TMacC*,[70] the husband was "undoubtedly feckless, irresponsible and immature", and was not the man the wife thought she was marrying. But "one may regretfully observe that the same could be said of many marriages", said Kearns J, rejecting the appeal against the High Court refusal of a decree of nullity.

However, emotional or psychological immaturity at the time of the marriage may be grounds for a nullity decree. In *PC v VC*,[71] the judge said a marriage was doomed from the outset by reasons of the couple's immaturity. He said there was lack of emotional capacity and psychological weakness on both sides. Delay was not evidence of approval of the marriage, but of confusion. Temperamental incapacity alone was

---

[70] [2009] IESC 21.
[71] [1990] 2 IR 91.

insufficient for a decree, but in this case there was also lack of capacity, so the judge declared the marriage null and void.

Informed Consent

In *N (orse K) v K*,[72] the Supreme Court had ruled that for, a marriage to be valid, the consent of each spouse—in addition to being freely given—must be informed.

In *PF v GO'M (otherwise GF)*,[73] the petitioner claimed that he had not given full free and informed consent to the marriage because his wife was having an affair when she became engaged to him. He claimed that, if he had known of this relationship, he would not have married her. The High Court refused to grant the nullity and, on appeal, the Supreme Court said that not being fully informed about the other person's conduct or character before the marriage was not enough to make the marriage void.

Although consent could not be considered informed where one party withheld information about their inherent disposition and mental stability, this was not the case where the misconduct or other misrepresentation was hidden. Also, while adultery was a ground for judicial separation, it had never been a ground for nullity. The Supreme Court said there was a constitutional necessity for certainty in marriage.[74]

In the case of *MO'M (orse O'C) v BO'C*,[75] a wife appealed against the High Court's refusal to grant her a decree of nullity. Before the marriage, her husband had been a priest. After ordination in 1972, he worked for four years as a curate but found the life lonely and difficult and consulted a psychiatrist from 1976 to 1982, when he was laicised.

He married his wife in 1985 when he was 37 and she was 32. They had two children and separated in 1989, though they were still living in the same house when the wife brought her petition in 1994.

---

[72] [1986] ILRM 75.
[73] [2001] 3 IR 1.
[74] *LB v TMacC* [2009] IESC 21.
[75] [1996] 1 IR 208.

The wife told the High Court she was "completely stunned" when she learned that her husband had been attending a psychiatrist for six years. But the judge said both parties were capable of entering into, maintaining and sustaining a proper marriage relationship. He also found that the wife gave full, free and informed consent to the marriage. He refused a decree and the wife appealed.

In the Supreme Court, Mr Justice John Blayney said:

> A person's mental health or mental stability is obviously a matter of great importance and anything which might throw doubt upon it calls for serious consideration.

> The test is subjective. It is possible that another person would not have reacted in the same way, but this was the wife's evidence of how she would have reacted if she had known.

He allowed the appeal and declared the marriage null and void because the wife's consent was not informed.

Finality

If a nullity petition is brought in the Circuit Court and the result is appealed to the High Court, that is normally the end of the matter.[76]

The courts have constantly stressed the need for finality in all proceedings As Lord Simon said in the 1977 *Ampthill Peerage* case in England, the appellate courts "do their own fallible best to correct error. But in the end you must accept what has been decided. Enough is enough".[77]

But in *DT v CT*,[78] the judge said that marriage was "in principle for life" and, even after a divorce, "many, if not most, states required that the divorced spouses continue to respect and fulfil certain obligations", usually financial.

He said:

> If the law permitted a spouse to cut himself or herself adrift of a marriage on divorce, without any continuing obligation to the former

---

[76] Courts (Supplemental Provisions) Act 1961.
[77] House of Lords, [1977] 1 AC 547.
[78] [2003] 1 ILRM 321.

> spouse, it would undermine the very nature of the marriage contract itself and fail to protect the value which society has placed on it as an institution, ... Hence the constitutional imperative of proper provisions for spouses.

In the case of *P v P*,[79] the appellant husband argued that he had been denied a fair hearing in the High Court, so should be allowed a further appeal.

His wife had initiated Circuit Court proceedings relating to the custody of the children, access, right of residence in the family home and maintenance. The Circuit Court heard the case in 1999 and the husband appealed the decision to the High Court.

The appeal came before the High Court a year later. After hearing opening submissions from counsel, but before hearing any evidence, the judge said: "Without making any final conclusions because I have not heard the evidence, but from what little I have heard about this case, it seems to me that this is the classic situation where the family budget is too small."

The husband said that, based on the judge's remarks, he did not wish to proceed with his appeal. In the Supreme Court, his counsel argued that the Court could set aside a final High Court order where there had been a fundamental breach of the constitutional right to a fair and proper hearing.

But the Chief Justice said the husband should first have brought a High Court application to have the judge's order set aside. He dismissed the appeal on the grounds that the Supreme Court had no jurisdiction to hear it.

There should be no delay in pursuing a nullity application once it is lodged, as this may lead to the case being dismissed.[80]

Nullity in Civil Partnerships

A decree of nullity may also be granted to civil partners where either or both partners lacked the capacity to register the civil partnership for any reason, including that either or both partners was:

---

[79] [2001] IESC 76.
[80] *LM v Judge Ó Donnabháin & AM (Notice Party)* [2011] IESC 22.

a) under the age of 18;
b) already validly married; or
c) already in a recognised and undissolved registered relationship with someone else.

A decree of nullity of a civil partnership may also be granted where:

a) registration formalities were not observed;
b) either partner did not give free and informed consent for any reason, including:
    (i) duress;
    (ii) undue influence;
    (iii) one or both partners did not intend to accept the other as a civil partner at the time of the registration; or
    (iv) a consultant psychiatrist attests that either was unable to give informed consent,
c) the partners were too closely related[81]; or
d) the partners were not of the same sex.

Civil nullity is rarely a straightforward matter and it may be difficult to assess whether a case will succeed or fail because of the wide disparity in the case law. In the *PF* case,[82] a Supreme Court judge called on the government to clarify the law on nullity.

Mrs Justice Catherine McGuinness said that, at the time when divorce was unavailable in Ireland, there might have been some advantage in allowing the courts to develop the law of nullity. But now that judicial separation and divorce were both available, the Oireachtas should provide a clear statutory code setting out the grounds for nullity and its consequences for the couple and any children.

Ecclesiastical Nullities

While other Christian Churches all accept the ideal of marriage as a union in which the couple swear lifelong fidelity, only the Catholic Church refuses to accept the remarriage of divorced people in church, unless the 'marriage' has first been annulled by the Church.

---

[81] s 26, Civil Partnership and Certain Rights and Obligations of Cohabitants Act 2010.
[82] *PF v GO'M* [2001] 3 IR 1.

The overwhelming majority of church marriages in the Republic of Ireland are Catholic Church marriages—although, of the 3.8 million Catholics in the Republic of Ireland in the 2011 census, 64,798 were divorced.

Most religions permit the remarriage of divorced people in a church, mosque or synagogue, but Catholics are not permitted to remarry in church while a validly-married spouse is still alive. Many Catholics therefore seek ecclesiastical decrees of nullity which permit them to marry (or remarry) in church.[83] This should not be confused with a state annulment, granted by the courts, which permits civil remarriage.

Civil partnership is not considered a marriage in the eyes of the Catholic Church, so civil partners may not apply for a Church nullity in respect of their civil partnership.

A Catholic Church nullity decree (or 'ecclesiastical nullity') may only be obtained if there was a serious problem from the start of the marriage. Such problems include lack of full consent, impotence, a forbidden degree of relationship between the spouses (such as a godparent marrying an unrelated godchild before 1983) or where one or both the parties is unbaptised.

The ecclesiastical decree affects *only* the religious element of the marriage. Catholics who have been granted a Church nullity, but who have not been divorced or been granted a state nullity, may not remarry in a civil ceremony. Anyone who does so could be committing the crime of bigamy.[84]

Catholics who have been granted an ecclesiastical decree of nullity (without a civil decree or divorce) may marry in church without the need for a dissolution of a pre-existing valid civil marriage, but the marriage is valid only in the eyes of the Catholic Church. The state will not recognise the second marriage as valid.

In the case of *People (Attorney General) v Ballins*,[85] Mrs Christina Ballins had gone through a civil marriage with William Ballins in a register office in Cornwall in 1954. They had one daughter. Soon afterwards, she returned to Ireland where she went through a Catholic Church wedding to John

---

[83] As in *CF v JDF* [2005] IESC 45.
[84] *PW v AO'C (orse W)* [1992] ILRM 536.
[85] [1964] Ir Jur Rep 14.

Kenny in 1960. The Catholic Church allowed the ceremony as it does not recognise the validity of a register office wedding alone where either partner is a Catholic.

The judge said there was a serious conflict between the civil law and canon law. Normally he would impose an 18-month prison sentence for bigamy, but in this case, he bound over Mrs Ballins to keep the peace for two years.

In Ireland, the number of nullity decrees granted by the Catholic Church rose dramatically after the introduction of divorce. In 1981, 67 couples were granted ecclesiastical nullity decrees in the 32 counties. Almost ten times that figure — 582 annulments — were granted in 1997 after divorce was introduced. The figures have now dropped to less than half that, with 255 decrees granted in 2011.

The largest number of applications was to the Dublin Regional Marriage Tribunal (169), followed by Armagh (117), then Galway (71) and Cork (51).

Catholic Church Nullity Procedure

A Church nullity decree, despite some misconceptions, is not available only to the rich. While the lawyers' bill in a civil nullity action (without legal aid) could, in some cases, run to tens of thousands of euro, a Church nullity may cost only a fraction of that.

The cost of the nullity procedure is subsidised by the Catholic Church, but the parties will be asked to make a financial contribution to the process. Costs vary from tribunal to tribunal, but nobody will be refused the services of a tribunal because they are unable to pay.

In practice, only a minority pay the full fee. The number of petitioners paying nothing in 2011 varied from 10 percent in the Armagh region to 56 percent in the Cork and Ross region. Full fees were paid in between 12 percent (Cork and Ross) and 51 percent (Galway) of cases.

If the case is accepted for hearing, both spouses will be invited for an interview. Each has to give a statement on oath and may be asked to undergo psychological assessment. If one party refuses to co-operate, the tribunal may decide the case on the evidence of the other spouse and witnesses alone. The hearing is in private—not even the spouses are allowed to be present. The representatives of each spouse put the arguments to a court of three Church judges, who decide the matter.

The defect in the marriage contract can be due to a pre-existing impediment (such as consanguinity or affinity, one spouse being underage, etc), a defect in the capacity to consent (such as deceit, simulation or psychological incapacity) or a defect in the form of marriage (the priest had no faculties, the ritual was not followed, etc).

Where a Church nullity decree is granted on psychological grounds, one or both of the parties may not be allowed to remarry because the Church considers that the defect which caused the nullity still exists and would put any future marriage in danger. The veto may be lifted by the local bishop if he is satisfied, after an investigation, that the person is fit for marriage in all essential respects.

Before a decree is granted, the case must be judged by two independent tribunals—one of the four regional marriage tribunals (Dublin, Cork, Galway or Armagh) and the National Appeals Tribunal. Both tribunals must establish with moral certainty (probability is not enough) that there was a fundamental defect in the marriage contract.

As with a civil nullity, there is a presumption of validity and it is up to the applicant to prove otherwise. The process of obtaining a Church nullity decree in Ireland may take two years or more from start to finish.

The jurisdiction of the Catholic Church to grant ecclesiastical decrees of nullity is set out in the Code of Canon Law. The code also sets out the Catholic understanding of the sacrament of matrimony and the procedures to be followed in an application for a Church nullity.

JUDICIAL SEPARATION

Introduction

Before the Reformation, marriage was regarded by the law as a sacrament, and the duty of cohabitation—the main duty arising from the marriage contract—was enforced by the Church with spiritual punishments *pro salute animae* (for the health of the soul). Voluntary separations were forbidden by law, and contracts for voluntary separations were invalid.

Under King Henry VIII, Church law was subordinated to the common law and voluntary separations became permissible.

Pursuant to the Matrimonial Causes Act 1870, the only grounds on which a divorce could be granted were adultery, cruelty and unnatural practices.

The ancillary relief was limited to orders for alimony and custody. The decree deprived the guilty spouse of the right to a share in the estate of a deceased spouse, either as a legal right or on intestacy.

The procedure for a divorce *a mensa et thoro* did not alter the status of the husband and wife. The only effect of the order, apart from the ancillary reliefs, was to relieve the petitioning spouse from the duty to cohabit with the other. Although called divorce, it was effectively a decree of judicial separation and did not allow remarriage.[1]

In *N v K*,[2] the judge said marriage was a civil contract which created reciprocating rights and duties between the spouses. He said:

> One of the reciprocating rights and duties is obviously that of cohabitation. It is an important element in marriage that the spouses live together.

In the overwhelming majority of cases, the parties were already living apart, so the decree was frequently of little significance. These proceedings were normally brought solely to obtain ancillary relief or to remove the succession rights of the spouse described as the "guilty party".

Modern Legislation

In 1989, the Judicial Separation and Family Law Reform Act removed the courts' jurisdiction to grant a divorce *a mensa et thoro*. Instead, the High Court and Circuit Court were given power to grant decrees of judicial separation.

Separation nowadays may be by agreement or by order of the court (a decree of judicial separation). Judicial separation allows a married couple to live apart and make formal arrangements for separate lives. However, the couple remain married so it is inaccurate to refer, for example, to 'my ex-husband' or 'my ex-wife'.

A judicial separation is available only to married couples, and the 1989 Act allows a decree of judicial separation on six grounds:

---

[1] Conversely, as well as the power to allow a couple to live separately, the courts could also theoretically require a couple to live together as man and wife. The jurisdiction to order the restitution of conjugal rights was removed by the Family Law Act 1981.

[2] [1985] IR 733.

- adultery;
- unreasonable behaviour;
- one year's continuous desertion;
- one year's separation (with consent);
- three years' separation (without consent); or
- no normal marital relationship for at least a year.

The 1989 Act significantly extended the grounds on which a judicial separation could be granted. It also widened the range of ancillary reliefs to include periodical payments and lump sum orders, property adjustment orders, orders extinguishing succession rights and miscellaneous ancillary orders, such as financial adjustment and pension orders, maintenance and custody and access.

A judicial separation, apart from giving the couple the right to live apart, may deal with incidental matters which arise when a marriage breaks down, such as children, property, the family home, maintenance and succession rights.

Validity of 1989 Act

The constitutional validity of the 1989 Judicial Separation and Family Law Reform Act was challenged in the case of *TF v Ireland and MF*,[3] before Article 41.3.2° of the Constitution came into force. MF had obtained a Circuit Court decree of judicial separation from her husband, TF, on the grounds that a normal marital relationship had not existed for at least a year. She also obtained a permanent barring order against her husband and was awarded custody of the children.

The husband said the Act didn't allow enough time for a reconciliation and set too low a threshold for an order which would negatively affect his constitutional marital rights. He also claimed that sections of the Act which granted his wife the right to live in the family home for life and which provided a dependent spouse with accommodation after a judicial separation were an attack on his constitutional property rights.

The High Court refused to hear evidence from theologians in relation to natural moral law or the essential features of a Christian marriage, and the

---

[3] [1995] 1 IR 321.

judge dismissed the husband's claim. He said that, while the concept of marriage referred to in Article 41.3.1° might be derived from the Christian concept of marriage, it was up to the courts, rather than the Churches, to interpret those rights.

The judge said all the basic rights in a marriage, such as the right to have children, to live together, to give and receive moral and financial support and to make decisions relating to family property were protected by Article 40.3 of the Constitution. He said those rights were not unqualified and their exercise could be regulated by the Oireachtas in the interests of the common good.

Any interpretation of the Constitution should take account of changing ideas and values, and therefore a married woman no longer had to live in "an unacceptable state of bondage".

The judge said the one-year separation rule was justified, particularly as the separation proceedings could be adjourned by consent. There were serious difficulties in trying to provide an objective measurement of success or failure in reconciliation therapy. It depended on whether the husband and wife were sincerely trying to be reconciled or just attending as a matter of form.

The breakdown of a marriage meant there was no physical capacity to consummate the marriage and no emotional and psychological relationship between the spouses. If one party was implacably opposed to the continuation of the marriage, the fundamental relationship would be destroyed.

The judge declared a decree of judicial separation merely meant that the husband and wife no longer had to live together. It did not affect the bond of marriage or prevent the couple getting back together again. The grant of a decree based on the absence of a normal marital relationship was little more than a recognition of an existing, and usually tragic, state of affairs.

On the issue of the family home, the courts had long recognised that the home had a psychological value as a point of unity around which the children of a broken marriage might preserve or rebuild some of the relationships on which a family's development depended.

An order giving a spouse the sole right to live in the family home merely conferred a right of residence, not a right of ownership, and it could be balanced by a reduction in maintenance. The power to grant a right of residence to one spouse was not an unjust attack on the property rights of either party, but just one feature of the "difficult and unhappy task" of trying to balance the best interests of both spouses and their dependent children.

On appeal, the Supreme Court said it had to decide whether the balance of the legislation was so unreasonable and unfair as to be an attack on constitutional rights.

The five judges said the Constitution protected the institution of marriage because of its contribution to the welfare of the nation and the state. The state's guarantee to protect the family was given to every married couple.

The concept and nature of marriage in the Constitution were derived from the Christian notion of partnership based on an irrevocable personal consent given by both spouses, which established a unique and very special lifelong relationship, as stated by Mr Justice Declan Costello in *Murray v Ireland*.[4] That definition was adopted by the Supreme Court in *TF v Ireland*.[5] Marriage was also a civil contract which created reciprocal duties and rights between the couple and established a status which affected both parties to the contract and the community as a whole.

One of those rights and duties was cohabitation, without which the "unique and very special lifelong relationship" could not be developed. But, in many cases, the common good required that the spouses should be separated, despite the nature of the indissoluble bond of marriage between them. If one spouse withdrew consent to cohabitation, it could not be enforced. Where such consent was withdrawn, an important ingredient of the normal marital relationship was removed, although the bond of marriage remained.

The party in breach of the marriage contract was entitled to seek a judicial separation, but in view of the numerous other rights safeguarded by the Act, the entitlement to a decree in such circumstances was not a failure to protect

---

[4] [1985] IR 532.
[5] [1995] 1 IR 321.

the institution of marriage. The legislation made every effort to protect the family after a marriage broke down.

The judges said that the provision of grounds for judicial separation did not mean that the state had failed to "guard with special care the institution of marriage or protect it against attack".[6]

The court said that anyone who claimed that the one-year separation requirement in the Act was inadequate had to prove that was the case.

The right of one spouse to occupy the family home had to be seen in the context of that part of the Act which aimed to ensure that, as far as practicable, provision was made for the whole family, so the right of sole residence in the family home and the provision of proper accommodation for the dependent spouse and children were not an unjust attack on the property rights of the spouse who was excluded from the home. The Supreme Court dismissed the appeal.

Effect of Judicial Separation Decree

The principal effect of a decree of judicial separation—to free the spouses from their duty to cohabit—is often the least of their worries, as the problems which have led to the couple consulting lawyers may often have already resulted in a cessation, to a greater or lesser degree, of normal marital relations.

The decree does not *compel* the couple to separate, and a different order is required to exclude one of the spouses from the family home.

A decree under the 1989 Act (and the 1995 Act) gives the spouses access to a wide range of secondary remedies, including financial provisions, property adjustment and the occupation of the family home.

Family Law Act 1995

The 1995 Act changed much of the 1989 Act dealing with financial, property, custody and other orders. Under the 1995 Act, there is no limit to the number of occasions on which the court can grant a property

---

[6] Art 41.3.1°, Bunreacht na hÉireann.

adjustment order, except that it can't be granted after the death or remarriage of the other spouse.

In *CO'C v DO'C*[7] for example, the couple were judicially separated and their 2008 settlement included various property adjustment orders. The husband asked the court to set aside, vary or discharge the original settlement on the grounds that the property crash meant his financial circumstances had changed so much that he could not comply with it.

The High Court judge accepted that the properties were "not worth what they were previously worth by reason of the economic downturn and the reduction in property prices generally". The judge acknowledged that, in the husband's "critical" financial position, he could not service the borrowings on the properties.

The judge in *Benson v Benson (deceased)* said that, while the Irish courts would "uphold agreements freely entered into at arm's length by parties who were properly advised",[8] it "may well be appropriate" to consider allowing an extension of time for appealing even a consent order on the basis of new events. But she held that, under s 18(1)(e) of the Family Law Act 1995, a property adjustment order made under s 9(1)(a) cannot be varied, although such a property adjustment order can be made more than once.

Accordingly, the court made a new, further property adjustment order in favour of the wife. Dunne J said the proper approach was to appeal the original order, rather than seek a variation.

Previous Relief

A court is barred from considering an application for a judicial separation if the couple had earlier been granted a decree of divorce *a mensa et thoro*.

In the case of *F v F*,[9] a wife had sought a decree of divorce *a mensa et thoro* and a barring order against her husband in 1986. The proceedings were settled by agreement, on the basis that the husband would stay away from the family home and neither party would interfere with the other.

---

[7] [2009] IEHC 248.
[8] [1996] 1 FLR 692.
[9] [1995] 2 IR 354.

Six years later, the wife tried to bring proceedings for judicial separation and claimed a permanent barring order, a property adjustment order and the removal of her husband's rights to succeed to her estate.

The Supreme Court ruled that the earlier proceedings barred the wife from bringing a new action under the 1989 Act. The Chief Justice said the court would not support an action where a separation was sought merely as a way of obtaining other reliefs.

Separation Agreement

A couple may also not seek a judicial separation if they already have a separation agreement in force. In *PO'D v AO'D*,[10] the couple had signed a separation deed in 1979. Later, the husband claimed a judicial separation but the wife said the court could not grant a judicial separation where the husband and the wife were no longer obliged to live together because of the separation agreement.

Her solicitor said it was not open to the husband to issue proceedings seeking a relief which he did not need (i.e. a decree of judicial separation) just so that he could obtain a property order to which he would not otherwise be entitled.

Counsel for the husband said the 1989 Act did not prevent parties to separation agreements from applying for a judicial separation. He said the situation would be different if the husband and the wife had agreed not to take any further proceedings.

The Supreme Court said the separation agreement was a comprehensive disposal of the issues that had arisen between the husband and the wife, and she was entitled to rely on the agreement as a bar to the judicial separation proceedings.

Judicial Separation Procedure

If a person consults a solicitor about the possibility of a judicial separation, the solicitor must first discuss the possibility of reconciliation and give the applicant a list of names and addresses of qualified marriage counsellors.

---

[10] [1998] 1 ILRM 543.

If there is no prospect of reconciliation, the solicitor must advise about mediation and provide a list of qualified mediators. If the couple finally decide to separate, the possibility of a separation agreement must also be discussed.[11]

The solicitor must file a certificate to confirm that he has complied with the Act. If he fails to do so, the court may adjourn the proceedings until the certificate has been filed.

Judges and lawyers do not wear wigs or gowns in family law proceedings. Judicial separation proceedings are heard in private and are as informal as practicable, consistent with justice. However, if a judge makes remarks which would suggest to a reasonable person that he is objectively biased, either party may ask him not to hear the rest of the case.[12]

An application for judicial separation need not be restricted to a single ground. Frequently claims of unreasonable behaviour and the absence of a normal marital relationship are included in a single application.

An applicant may not allege adultery as a basis for a decree of judicial separation if the couple have lived together for a year after the alleged adultery became known to the other spouse. Unreasonable behaviour may not be pleaded if the couple live together for more than six months after the last alleged incident of such behaviour.

Conduct

One of the grounds for judicial separation is "that the respondent has behaved in such a way that the applicant cannot reasonably be expected to live with the respondent".[13]

Under the old ground of cruelty for a decree of divorce *a mensa et thoro*, an applicant had to prove conduct which made it unsafe for him or her to live with the other spouse.[14,15] That is no longer necessary, but the applicant

---

[11] s 5, Judicial Separation and Family Law Reform Act 1989.
[12] *P v Mc Donagh* [2009] 316 JR.
[13] s 2(1)(b) Judicial Separation and Family Law Reform Act 1989.
[14] *Carpenter v Carpenter* Milward 159.
[15] *McA v McA* [2000] 2 ILRM 48.

now has to show that, as a result of the other spouse's behaviour, it is no longer reasonable to expect the couple to live together.

In the case of *Murphy v Murphy*,[16] the President of the High Court said the husband's conduct had resulted in a situation "where common life became impossible". The judge said that, while individual incidents were trivial in themselves, their cumulative effect could be serious. In *BL v ML*,[17] the husband's behaviour included violence, verbal abuse and false allegations about his wife.

Adultery

In *ES v DS*,[18] Abbott J granted a decree of judicial separation on the grounds of the husband's adultery, rather than the absence of a normal marital relationship for one year before the proceedings. However, he added:

> In the post-divorce age, it is not appropriate for a Court to penalise either party for adultery and, in this case, it would be unjust on the husband to have any penalising consequences attached to his adulterous relationship.

Relationship Breakdown

A further ground for judicial separation is that the marriage has broken down to the extent that the court is satisfied that a normal marital relationship has not existed between the spouses for at least one year immediately before the date of the application.

In *K v K*,[19] a decree was granted on this basis, but the Circuit Court didn't order the husband to leave the family home. The judge refused to grant the wife a barring order but gave her the sole right to occupy the family home for life because s 10(2)(a) of the 1995 Act says the court must take into consideration that, "where a decree of judicial separation is granted, it is not possible for the spouses concerned to continue to reside together".

---

[16] [1962] Ir Jur Rep 77.
[17] [1989] ILRM 528.
[18] [2010] IEHC 474.
[19] Unreported, Circuit Court, 1990.

There is no need for proof of *irretrievable* breakdown. The court will require evidence that the couple's relationship is so different from a reasonably normal relationship that the court may conclude that the marriage has broken down. The situation must have continued for at least a year before the application. Fault, under this ground, is irrelevant and there is no requirement for proof of 'intolerable behaviour' by the respondent spouse.

Issuing Proceedings

The document which is issued to begin judicial separation proceedings is called an application. The person seeking the separation is the applicant and the other spouse is the respondent.

Once the judicial separation application has been issued, and before the court rules on the case, a spouse may seek preliminary orders to ensure proper financial provision for her and the children until the hearing of the action.

Before the full hearing of the judicial separation case, a spouse may also seek orders including a barring order (preventing the other spouse entering the family home), a custody (or access) order in relation to any dependent children and orders for the protection of the family home, furniture and personal belongings.

The court will not grant a judicial separation unless it is satisfied that arrangements have been made for the welfare of any dependent children, including custody, access and matters relating to the children's "religious and moral, intellectual, physical and social welfare".[20] Custody will generally be left to the parents to decide but, if they can't agree, the court will make a decision. That decision "is never final but evolves with the child, retaining in changing times the fundamental concept of the welfare of the child".[21]

The courts encourage written open offers before the hearing of separation and divorce proceedings because they:

---

[20] Art 42.1 Bunreacht na hÉireann.
[21] *Per* Denham J in *C v B* [1996] 1 ILRM 63.

- provide certainty and save the costs of a hearing;
- provide leverage on costs if a protracted hearing does not significantly improve the offer;
- show the court the points of disagreement, from which the issues may be examined; and
- allow the parties to defend their view about how provision might be made.[22]

Once a judicial separation has been granted, the court may make an order for periodical payments (or maintenance) in favour of the dependent spouse and children up to the age of 18 (or 23 if in full-time education), or mentally or physically disabled dependants. Such provision must be "adequate and reasonable, having regard to all the circumstances".[23]

Factors Taken into Account

Before making any order, the court must consider

> the income, earning capacity, property and other financial resources which each of the spouses concerned has, or is likely to have in the foreseeable future.[24]

In almost all cases, the court accepts that the standard of living of both spouses will be reduced following a separation or divorce.

The maintenance order may be backdated to the date of issue of the judicial separation application. If the husband is employed and there have been problems with payment of maintenance, there could be an attachment of earnings order, whereby payments will be deducted at source by his employer.

The court will take into account both spouses' salaries and any children's allowance or social welfare. It will also consider the length of the marriage, the spouses' ages and their future earning capacity. The maintenance order in respect of each child stops automatically when the child ceases to be dependent.

---

[22] *GB v AB* [2007] IEHC 491.
[23] Judicial Separation and Family Law Reform Act 1989, s 20(1).
[24] *ibid*, s 20(2).

The court may also order a spouse to pay a lump sum for expenses and liabilities and may direct that periodical and lump sum payments be secured, possibly by the transfer of the property to trustees.

The court may also make property adjustment orders to achieve a fair distribution of property, including the family home. "Proper and secure accommodation"[25] should, where practicable, be provided for a spouse who is wholly or mainly dependent on the other spouse, and for any dependent child.

Family Home

Frequently, the court will grant the wife and children the right to occupy the family home, at least until the children have all ceased to be dependent. The husband's ability to provide a home for himself would be taken into account.

Thereafter, the court could consider the contributions each of the spouses had made to the home and might well come to the conclusion, as the English Court did in *Wachtel v Wachtel*,[26] that the family home should be regarded as the joint property of both.

The court may later vary the order relating to the occupation of the family home and order its sale and division of the proceeds.

If a couple are subsequently reconciled, the court may rescind the separation decree by consent, if the judge is satisfied that a reconciliation has taken place and the couple want to resume (or have already resumed) cohabitation as man and wife.

Division of Assets

The assets of a marriage are widely construed and may include money, property, pensions, inheritances, goods, shares and trust funds.

The division of assets in Ireland on separation or divorce differs from the way assets are divided in England. For many years, the English courts

---

[25] *ibid*, s 19(b).
[26] [1973] Fam 72.

operated what was known as "the one third rule",[27] whereby the wife received about one third of the husband's income as maintenance plus about one third of the capital assets of the family.

But, as Lord Denning said in *Wachtel v Wachtel*[28]:

> This proposal is not a rule. It is only a starting point. It will serve in cases where the marriage has lasted for many years and the wife has been in the home bringing up the children. It may not be applicable where the marriage has lasted only a short time, or where there are no children and she can go out to work.

The Supreme Court confirmed that the "one third rule" should only be used as a rough guide. In *T v T*,[29] Mrs Justice Susan Denham said:

> The concept of one third as a check on fairness may well be useful in some cases, however it may have no application in many cases.

> It may not be applicable to a family with inadequate assets. It may not be relevant to a family of adequate means if, for example, such a sum could only be achieved by a sale of assets which would destroy a business, or the future income of a party or parties, or if it related to property brought solely by one party to the marriage, or any other relevant circumstance. It may not be applicable to a situation where a party has wealth from his or her own endeavours to which the other party has no claim except under s 20 [of the Family Law (Divorce) Act].

Source of Assets

The court is entitled to consider all the assets of a couple, including those obtained before marriage or by inheritance.

In *M v M*,[30] a wife sought a share in the IR£1.4 million proceeds of sale of a farm which had been inherited by the husband and had been leased out during the marriage. The husband said the proceeds did not form part of the "matrimonial property" and he should keep the full amount.

---

[27] *Ackermann v Ackermann* (1972) 2 WLR 1253.
[28] *ibid.*
[29] [2002] IESC 68.
[30] Unreported, High Court, 2001.

But the judge held that there was no concept of "matrimonial property" in Irish law, as there was in other legal systems. He said there was nothing in the legislation which limited the extent of the spouses' assets which the court could consider when making orders.

The husband had been awarded custody of the children and would need to buy a suitable house. The judge said an equal division of the sale proceeds would be unfair, so he awarded the wife IR£350,000, to include the proceeds of the sale of the family home, of which she was half owner.

In *C v C*,[31] O'Higgins J said the applicant husband had a strong claim to the family home because he had inherited it and had family connections with it for a very long time. The wife had not contributed directly or indirectly to the acquisition of the property.

In this case, the concept of giving the wife one third of the assets was not useful. Proper provision required that the wife have enough money to buy a suitable home and a proper level of maintenance. He awarded the wife €3 million to buy a new house, plus €240,000 a year maintenance and €20,000 for each of the four dependent children.

The judge in *CED v AD*[32] also referred to the importance of the source of assets.

In *TM v TM*,[33] the parties had been married for 35 years and most of the assets were in a discretionary trust, the Repus Trust, which had been established by the husband in the US after the marriage. Apart from a period home, the trust included 750 acres of land which had been in the husband's family for generations. As well as the property value of €11.2 million, the husband and wife also had independent assets worth €14.5 million.

McKechnie J held that the trust was a post-nuptial settlement so could be varied. He said the concept of non-variation of trusts did not apply in family law cases where the trust instrument was "entered into after contracting, and during the occurrence of, a valid marriage".

---

[31] Unreported, High Court, 25 July 2005.
[32] Unreported, High Court, 13 December 2005.
[33] Unreported, High Court, 2 June 2004 and 14 March 2006.

McKechnie J also said that the term "settlement" in family law proceedings had a broader meaning than under taxation law. If one party could control property in a trust in some way, whatever the legal setup of the trust, it would come within the remit of family law proceedings.

In the substantive case, Abbott J considered contributions by both spouses to the family assets, but noted that the house and lands were the ancestral family home of the husband. The court ruled that the main house and lands should go to the husband, but that a further house on the estate would be allocated to the wife. The assets were divided roughly two thirds to the husband and one third to the wife. The judge said that, if the husband could not accept this division, the entire property could be sold and the assets divided between the spouses.

However, with property brought into the marriage or acquired by inheritance or gift, the duration of the marriage was very relevant. This is evidenced by the fact that a Supreme Court appeal in *TM v TM* was finalised by way of a consent order in 2011.

In *CF v JDF*,[34] the parties had two dependent children when they applied for judicial separation. The husband was a banker and the wife operated a beautician's, but the husband's job was terminated and the wife's business ran into problems. They then started running a stud farm in Wicklow. The husband used 22 acres of land which belonged to his father, but the father retained ownership of the land. In 2001, the wife claimed that her husband and father-in-law either held the lands jointly or that they were held on trust for the husband, who was likely to inherit the land.

In the High Court, the husband's father produced his will and said he had no intention of transferring the land to his son. Even after his death, he would only be willing to bequeath him a life interest. But after considering a number of authorities,[35] the High Court judge decided that, while he could not make a property adjustment order in relation to the 22 acres, it was unlikely that the father would try and take the land back, so he took into account the value of this property as an asset available to the husband.

---

[34] [2005] IESC 45.
[35] *Gillett v Holt & anor* [2000] 2 AER 289; *Re Brasham (deceased)* [1987] 1 AER 504; *Felix Smyth and John Joseph Halpin & anor* [1997] 2 ILRM 39; *Inwards and Baker* [1965] 1 AER 446 and *Cullen v Cullen* [1962] IR 268.

However, in the Supreme Court, the judge ruled that the father did not intend to leave the 22 acres to his son in his will. The judge said there must have been at least some clear evidence of an actual promise, inducement or representation by the father that he intended the son to be the owner of the land. Without it, the doctrine of promissory or proprietary estoppel could not operate and the land could not be held to be an asset of the husband.

However, in *HP v FP*,[36] where a Circuit Court judge had concluded that three properties were owned by the respondent's father, MacMenamin J in the High Court said the respondent was estopped from asserting this because all the legal documents indicated that the respondent (not his father) was the legal owner of the property. He said the respondent's wife was entitled to a 25 percent interest in the three properties.

In *SD v BD*,[37] an inheritance by the husband made a large contribution to the joint assets. Abbott J said:

> While there is no doubt that the efforts of the husband and indirectly of the wife greatly augmented the value of these inherited assets, considerable weight should be given to this aspect of the case.

Although assets are evaluated at the time of the hearing, as Denham J said in *T v T*[38]:

> The fact that a considerable sum of money was acquired by the spouse after their separation, the basis for such a new acquired sum, or the existence of a deed of separation, may be very relevant.

If one spouse has disposed of assets within three years before a judicial separation or divorce application is brought, the other spouse may challenge that disposition. Alternatively, a spouse may apply to the court to prevent such a disposition. There is a presumption that such dispositions are intended to deprive a spouse of relief.

Even the sale of shares may be affected. In *LO'M v NO'M (orse NMcC)*,[39] the High Court ruled that shares in a number of building companies

---

[36] [2010] IEHC 423.
[37] [2007] IEHC 492.
[38] [2002] 3 IR 334.
[39] [2003] 1 ILRM 401.

which were developing and selling houses constituted personal property, and a spouse could be prevented from selling them. A business may also qualify as a marital asset.[40]

Statistics

In 1990, there were 636 applications for judicial separation. Within four years, the number of applications had risen more than four-fold to 2,847. The numbers began to fall after the introduction of divorce, with only 1,208 applications in 1997, but that number stayed fairly steady, with a total of 1,269 judicial separation applications to the Circuit Court in 2012. Women brought 73 percent of the judicial separation applications in 2012—almost three quarters of the total.[41]

Although the High Court can also grant a judicial separation, only 18 of 858 judicial separation orders were granted by the High Court in 2012.

---

[40] *BD v JD* [2005] IEHC 407.
[41] Courts Service Annual Report 2012.

DIVORCE

Introduction

Divorce was introduced to Ireland by the Family Law (Divorce) Act, which came into force on 27 February 1997.

Since the introduction of divorce, the number of applications has risen steadily. In the first full year, 2,725 people applied to the Circuit Court for a divorce. In 2012, almost 3,462 applications for divorce were received by Circuit Courts around the country, 1,622 of them by husbands. There were

20 High Court applications for divorce. The total number of divorce applications was up about 3.5 percent on the previous year.[1]

Once a divorce is granted, both parties are free to remarry. A court has no power to restrict the remarriage of a divorced person, no matter what the grounds for divorce. Respondents may not refuse to be divorced as long as:

- the parties have lived apart (not necessarily in separate houses) for four of the five years before the start of proceedings;
- there is no reasonable prospect of reconciliation; and
- proper provision has been made (or will be made) for both spouses and any dependants.

A solicitor consulted by someone seeking a divorce must first discuss with the client the prospect of reconciliation and provide a list of people qualified to help resolve the couple's problems. He must also discuss the possibility of mediation to help the couple agree the terms of the separation or divorce and give the client a list of qualified mediators. Thirdly, the solicitor must discuss the alternatives of judicial separation or a written separation agreement. A register of professional organisations qualified to help couples in difficulty was supposed to be compiled under the provisions of the 1996 Divorce Act, but this was never done.

If divorce proceedings are issued anyway, the other spouse must be given the same information about reconciliation, mediation, judicial separation or a separation agreement as soon as he or she instructs a solicitor. Both solicitors must certify that they have given their clients the required information before the case begins, otherwise the judge may adjourn the proceedings.

Ancillary Orders

Before the court decides whether or not to grant a divorce, it may make a number of temporary orders, including:

1) a protection order;
2) a safety order;

---

[1] Courts Service Annual Report 2012.

3) an interim barring order;
4) a barring order;
5) a child custody order;
6) an access order;
7) a maintenance order; or
8) an order preserving the family home, its contents or the proceeds from its sale.[2]

If a spouse disposes of cash or property to try and prevent the other spouse obtaining his or her rightful share, the court may set aside a transaction carried out up to three years before the divorce application, even if the asset has been transferred out of the State.

Maintenance and Lump Sums

Once a divorce has been granted, the court may order one spouse to pay the other:

1) maintenance;
2) secured maintenance; or
3) a lump sum.

Maintenance payments may be secured against property, or the court may order that they be deducted at source from a spouse's salary—though the judge must take account of that spouse's views about whether he would make the payments without a so-called attachment order. Alternatively payment may be made directly to the other spouse or through the District Court clerk. All payments, other than pensions are made without deduction of income tax.

Maintenance payments may be backdated to the beginning of proceedings and the court may order that any retrospective payments (allowing for voluntary payments already made) be paid in a lump sum by a certain date. Alternatively, a spouse may be ordered to pay a lump sum towards the reasonable expenses of the other spouse before the application for maintenance.

Maintenance payments for a child end when the child ceases to be dependent or dies. If the dependent spouse remarries, her own maintenance payments cease, except for any outstanding arrears.

---

[2] The meaning and extent of the domestic violence orders are explained in the chapter on domestic violence.

Property

At any time after being granted a divorce, either spouse may ask the court to:

1) transfer property from one spouse to the other (or in favour of a dependent child);
2) settle any property for the benefit of the other spouse or any dependent child;
3) vary any agreement or bequest settling property on either spouse or a dependent child; or
4) reduce or extinguish the interest of either spouse under a settlement.

At any time after the court makes a secured maintenance, lump sum or property adjustment order, it may also order the sale of any property in which either spouse has an interest, although it won't order the sale of a family home where one spouse has been given the right of sole occupation.

The court may specify the conditions of sale of any property, including who should be offered the property and when, and may decide on the division of the sale proceeds. Any maintenance paid out of the sale proceeds ceases on the death or remarriage of the dependent spouse, except for any arrears. Before making any such orders, the court must hear representations by anyone who has an interest in the property or the proceeds of its sale, such as a building society or bank.

If the court orders one divorcing spouse to transfer property to the other, stamp duty is not payable. The Divorce Act also makes special provision for the payment of capital gains, capital acquisitions and probate tax. The tax situation can be complicated after a divorce and solicitors may recommend the spouses to see a specialist tax accountant.

If the judge orders one of the spouses to sign over property and he or she fails to do so, the court may authorise someone else to sign the document on behalf of the defaulting ex-spouse.

When the court is considering the question of the family home, it must take into account that a couple cannot live together after a divorce and that dependent spouses and children need proper accommodation. If a spouse has remarried and lives with a new partner, the court will not make an order affecting their home.

In the English case of *Cordle v Cordle*,[3] the Court of Appeal said a judge should always look first at the housing needs of the spouses and provide a home for the primary carer and children. If there were enough assets available, he should then provide accommodation for the other parent. A court should also attempt to ensure that at least one of the parties could work and earn a living.

Either spouse may also ask the court to make an order relating to:

1) the exclusive right to live in the family home for life;
2) the sale of the family home and division of the proceeds;
3) the ownership of any property;
4) dispensing with the consent of the other spouse to the sale of the family home;
5) protection of the family home;
6) arrears of rent or mortgage;
7) restriction of the sale or disposal of household goods;
8) partitioning of property;
9) child welfare, custody and access; or
10) a protection, safety, interim barring or barring order.

Where divorce proceedings are issued after judicial separation proceedings, the court can hear both matters as a divorce action. In *GB v AB*,[4] the wife initiated judicial separation proceedings in 2001 and the husband began divorce proceedings in 2006. Both sets of proceedings were heard as a divorce action.

Even after the proceedings have started, if both spouses wish to attempt reconciliation at any stage, the judge will adjourn the proceedings although, if the talks break down, either spouse can ask the court to resume the case. Where proceedings have started, the cost of any mediation or counselling is at the court's discretion.

Any communication between the spouses—or with anyone else—aimed at trying to resolve the couple's differences may not be used in evidence if the case does go ahead. Even if the judge believes the couple can't be reconciled, he may still adjourn the case to give them a chance to agree on any of the outstanding issues, such as property, finances and children.

---

[3] [2002] 1 FLR 207.
[4] [2007] IEHC 491.

Choice of Court

Divorce proceedings may be brought in the High Court or the Circuit Family Court, although the Circuit Court must transfer the matter to the High Court on the application of any interested party if it concerns land with a rateable value of more than €254. The Circuit Court may assess the rateable value of any land which does not already have a rateable valuation.

The decision whether to bring proceedings in the Circuit Court or High Court is of fundamental importance. It depends on a number of matters, including the value of the family's assets and the right of possible appeal.

In *OR v OR*,[5] solicitor Alan Shatter (later Minister for Justice) argued that, according to the Rules of the Superior Courts, where neither party in family law proceedings had applied to remit a case to a lower court, the High Court had no power to remit it.[6] But Murphy J, citing the judgment of Gannon J in *R v R*,[7] said the High Court would decline to hear the case and the parties should be left to "pursue their remedies in those courts on which the Oireachtas has expressly conferred jurisdiction".

Proceedings are heard in private, generally in different courts (or on different days) from non-family law proceedings, and are as informal as possible. Even though a couple may have applied for a divorce, the court has the power to grant a judicial separation or decree of nullity instead, though this would be unusual.

Living Apart

The meaning of 'living apart' was established in the case of *MMcA v XMcA*.[8] The High Court ruled that, where a couple were living in the same household and one of them applied for a divorce, it was up to the court to decide whether the couple were in effect 'living apart from one another' for the purpose of the Divorce Act.

Mr Justice Brian McCracken said the matrimonial relationship could not be dictated purely by reference to the location of the couple or by whether

---

[5] Unreported, High Court, 3 December 1984.
[6] *MTT v NT*, unreported, Supreme Court, May 1984.
[7] Unreported, High Court, 16 February 1984.
[8] [2000] 2 ILRM 48.

they lived under the one roof. He said the court also had to consider the mental and intellectual attitude of the spouses.

In this case, the couple had married in 1968 and had two grown up children. The wife claimed a decree of judicial separation. The husband counterclaimed for a decree of divorce, which was opposed by the wife.

In 1988, the husband left the family home when the wife discovered he was having an affair. In 1991, the husband ended his relationship and returned to live in the family home because, he said, he wanted to develop a better relationship with his son.

The couple slept in separate bedrooms, even on holiday, and never resumed sexual relations. They had a 'civilised relationship' at home, were polite to each other and would even take their meals together occasionally. The husband said he would tend to go early to his 'apartment' and watch television. He had a separate telephone line installed in his room. He would be away for three weekends out of four and would only see his wife for two or three hours a week.

In 1995, while the couple were still living in the same house, the wife had a sexual relationship with another man and, in 1996, the husband began a relationship with a woman with whom he was still living at the time of the court case. The husband finally left the family home in 1997.

The judge said:

> The fact that the section in effect allows the parties to live together for one year out of five and then separate again without affecting the rights under the section, seems to me to make it quite clear that it was the view of the legislature that it was necessary to make such provision, as otherwise parties who attempted but did not attain reconciliation would not be able to avail of the Act if they lived together for a short time during the preceding five years.

> Marriage is not primarily concerned with where the spouses live or whether they live under the same roof, and indeed there can be a number of circumstances in which the matrimonial relationship continues even though the parties are not living under the same roof – as, for example, where one party is in hospital or an institution of some kind, or is obliged to spend a great deal of time away from home in the course of his or her employment. Such separations do not necessarily constitute the persons as living apart from one another.

Clearly there must be something more than mere physical separation, and the mental or intellectual attitude of the parties is also of considerable relevance. I do not think one can look solely either at where the parties physically reside, or at their mental or intellectual attitude to the marriage. Both of these elements must be considered, and in conjunction with each other.

Just as parties who are physically separated may in fact maintain their full matrimonial relationship, equally parties who live under the same roof may be living apart from one another. Whether this is so is a matter which can only be determined in the light of the facts of any particular case.

The judge said he was satisfied that, from the time the husband first left home in 1988, he considered the marriage at an end. When he returned in 1991, he did not intend to return to a marriage, but only wanted to have a better relationship with his children.

The judge gave the wife the family home, an apartment in Tenerife, a business which she had been managing for many years, the neighbouring house and a house in Dublin. The husband was given the second home and the apartment in which he was living.

The husband also paid IR£1.2 million for the wife's share of a joint business and was ordered to pay IR£4,500 a month maintenance and a lump sum of IR£300,000. The judge said the wife should also benefit from the husband's pension fund and life assurance policies.

Proper Provision

This emphasis on 'proper provision', rather than 'proper division' and the 'clean break' principle[9] practised by the English courts, is at the heart of Irish jurisprudence on divorce. The meaning of the phrase 'proper provision'—or providing properly for both parties—was explained by the Supreme Court in *T v T*.[10] That case involved a country solicitor who left his wife after he had a series of affairs.

For some years after they married, the wife had worked as unofficial receptionist in the husband's practice, acted as secretary and furnished

---

[9] See the judgment of Denham J in *T v T* [2002] 3 IR 334.
[10] *ibid*.

and cleaned his office. The wife, who had had seven pregnancies, said she felt "demeaned and ridiculed" when the husband admitted in 1996 that he was having an affair with a member of his staff.

The High Court estimated that the solicitor was worth between IR£14 million and IR£20 million. Most of his fortune was based on property which he bought after leaving his wife. His annual income was estimated at over IR£1 million.

In December 2001, the High Court granted the husband a divorce and ordered him to pay his wife a lump sum of IR£5 million. The husband had been paying IR£400 a week for maintenance of the couple's three children. The High Court ordered him to pay IR£800 a week to maintain the youngest boy.

The judge said the wife had been "appalled by the husband's behaviour" and the "anguish suffered by [the youngest child] was enormous". He had intended to give the wife 51 percent of the husband's pension but, in the light of her husband's behaviour, he had increased this to 55 percent. The husband was also ordered to pay his wife's legal costs.

The husband appealed to the Supreme Court against the size of the lump sum, the pension adjustment and the costs order. By a four-to-one majority, the appeal on the lump sum and costs was dismissed. The pension appeal was allowed.

Counsel for the husband said the wife should have received less than IR£5 million because:

1) she could return to court at any time because of the lack of finality in Irish divorce law;
2) she had her own income and earning capacity;
3) at the time of the separation, the husband had transferred to her a third of his assets, worth IR£1.5 million;
4) 80 percent of the husband's assets were acquired in the two years after the separation;
5) she did not have exceptional needs, the children were substantially provided for and the husband had new obligations; and
6) her standard of living before the separation could be achieved with less than IR£5 million.

On behalf of the wife, counsel argued that:

1) the court should apply the statutory criteria set out in the Divorce Act;

2) the traditional role of women in the home should not be valued at less than the role of the breadwinner;

3) the assets should be assessed at the date of trial, except where there was deliberate or reckless wastage; and

4) the lack of a maintenance order for the wife should be reflected by payment of a large lump sum.

Former Chief Justice Ronan Keane said that in "big money" cases—which he preferred to call "ample resources" cases—equal division of the assets was "emphatically not mandated by the [Irish] legislation". Provided that was borne in mind, he thought there should be no difficulty with the Irish courts adopting a broadly similar approach to *White v White*.[11]

Mrs Justice Susan Denham, giving another of the majority verdicts in the Supreme Court, said the Divorce Act did not seek to establish a fault system and the court should not have reduced the solicitor's share of his pension just because of what was formerly regarded as guilt or blame. "To do so would be to impose a fine for supposed misbehaviour in the course of an unhappy married life," she said.

Denham J said the High Court was correct to value the husband's assets at the date of trial, since that was consistent with the wording of the statute. However, the fact that a spouse had acquired a considerable sum of money after separation, the basis for the acquisition or the existence of a deed of separation might be very relevant.

In this case, the husband's assets had benefited greatly from the increase in property prices, but the funding of the property was assisted by his legal practice, which had benefited directly from the wife's work as receptionist and cleaner and, indirectly, by her work as home-maker.

The judge said the Divorce Act provided for "proper provision, not division", and it was not a question of dividing the assets on a basis of percentage—though a figure of one third of the assets might be a "useful benchmark to fairness".

---

[11] *ibid.*

She said:

> 'Proper provision' is a proper provision based on the constitutional and statutory recognition of the family. The special place of the family and of family duties are recognised. The Court must look at both aspects of a spouse's role in the family, two sides of the coin. Thus the Court must have regard to the role of the spouses in relation to the welfare of the family, to their contribution in looking after the home or caring for the family.
>
> On the other side of the coin, the Court must have regard to the effect on the earning capacity of each of the spouses of the marital responsibilities assumed by each, and the degree to which the future earning capacity of a spouse was impaired by reason of the spouse having relinquished or foregone the opportunity of remunerative activity in order to look after the home or care for the family.
>
> A long-lasting marriage, especially in the primary childbearing and rearing years of a woman's life, carries significant weight, especially if the wife has been the major home and family carer.
>
> The concepts of certainty and consistency are subject to the necessity of fairness. Consequently, each case must be considered on its own facts, in light of the principles set out in the law, so as to achieve a just result. Thus, while the underlying constitutional principle is one of making proper provision for the spouses and children, this is to be administered with justice to achieve fairness.

The judge said the High Court had not failed to consider the income and earning capacity of the wife, but it would help if such factors were considered "in an express manner, and reasons for decisions given".

The judge said the absence of a 'clean break' principle in Irish law did not exclude a lump sum order, and payment of a lump sum could bring "a fair financial decision and certainty to the financial affairs of the family".

As Abbot J said in YX v XY[12]:

> A proper exercise of such jurisdiction involves, not the division of assets between the spouses to the exclusion of the creditors, but the provision of necessities such as living accommodation, basic maintenance and, in appropriate cases, security therefor, or property transfer orders in lieu thereof.

---

[12] [2010] IEHC 440.

In this case, the husband's income before the collapse of Lehman Brothers was €6 million a year. His properties were worth €1.4 billion in a fire sale, but he had total borrowings of €2.3 billion.

The family home was worth €4.4 million, with a mews which could bring in an annual rent of €20,000, and the wife had €600,000 in cash as well as owning a building worth €300,000.

Annual household expenses were said to be almost €700,000. At €40,000 per annum the wife would probably "survive with a very modest standard of living", said the judge. The couple enjoyed

> a luxurious home, a choice of private air flights, good holidays and a good social life generally. However, notwithstanding their generous lifestyle, it could not be said that they led the life of the idle rich.

He granted a judicial separation and gave the wife an exclusive right of residence for life in the family home. He ordered the husband to pay the wife €60,000 a year maintenance, with a 100 percent pension adjustment order, a lump sum of €7,000 and 20 percent of the family assets after payment of all debts.

But in *JD v DD*,[13] Mrs Justice Catherine McGuinness said that, in a marriage which was "a lengthy partnership of complementary roles", there should be a reasonably equal division of the accumulated assets.

In *SD v BD*,[14] Abbott J said the caring role of the mother and the father had lasted 29 years, "a very long commitment" which led to "strong considerations of parity of esteem in deciding the division of assets in this ample resources case".

Factors to be Considered

Judges must decide what constitutes proper provision by looking at the legislative guidelines and previous case law. According to s 20(2) of the 1996 Act, the court must consider:

- the income, earning capacity, property and other financial resources of both spouses;

---

[13] [1997] 3 IR 64.
[14] [2007] IEHC 492.

- the spouses' financial needs, obligations and responsibilities now or in the future;
- the family's past standard of living;
- the spouses' ages, duration of the marriage and the length of time they lived together;
- any physical or mental disabilities of either spouse;
- contributions either spouse made to the welfare of the family in terms of income, property, financial resources, looking after the children or looking after the home;
- how each spouse's earning capacity was affected by family responsibilities and whether either left paid employment to look after the home or family;
- any income or benefits to which either spouse is entitled by law;
- conduct which it would be unjust to disregard;
- both spouses' accommodation needs;
- the value of any benefit (such as a pension) to which either spouse would be entitled if they stayed married; and
- the rights of anyone else, including a new spouse.

These matters have been considered in some detail by the High Court and Circuit Court, including cases where large sums of money were involved, such as *JD v DD*[15] and *McA v McA*.[16]

Not every judge will give the same weight to every factor in s 20. Hoffman LJ said in *Piglowska v Piglowski*[17]:

> There are many cases which involve value judgments...on which reasonable people may differ. Since judges are also people, this means that some degree of diversity in their application of values is inevitable.

Section 20(2)(a)—which requires a judge to take note of any financial resources a spouse is "likely to have in the foreseeable future"—has been interpreted as allowing a judge to consider property which, strictly speaking, belongs to third parties.

In the English case of *Thomas v Thomas*,[18] the Court of Appeal said a court did not have to limit its orders exclusively to resources of capital or income

---

[15] [1997] 3 IR 64.
[16] [2000] 2 ILRM 48.
[17] [1999] UKHL 27.
[18] [1995] 2 FLR 668.

which were actually shown to exist. It might infer from the evidence that other, unidentified resources were available. The court said a judge need not totally disregard the potential availability of wealth from sources owned or administered by others.

In *LB v Ireland*,[19] MacMenamin J said proper provision should be based on all the circumstances, including:

1) the financial resources and needs of both spouses and dependants;
2) their present and future obligations and responsibilities;
3) the standard of living of the parties before the breakdown of the marriage,
4) the respective ages of the parties;
5) the duration of the marriage;
6) the terms of any separation agreements;
7) the role of the spouses in relation to the welfare of the family;
8) their contribution to looking after the home or caring for the family;
9) the effect on their earning capacity as a result of the marital responsibilities they assumed;
10) the degree to which future earning capacity was affected because of a spouse staying home to care for the family; and,
11) where one spouse contributed to the resources of the other, the detriment suffered by that spouse.

Proper provision can only be calculated by taking into account a series of factors, including the tax consequences of any order. In *BD v JD*,[20] a husband in a judicial separation action appealed against a High Court order that he should pay his wife €4 million over two years, plus a €100,000 contribution towards her costs.

By far the largest asset in the case was the husband's business which the High Court judge decided was worth €10 million. He rejected the wife's claim that she was entitled to a half share in the companies.

Counsel for the husband said proper provision could not be calculated without considering the effect of the tax burden on the husband of taking money from his companies. But counsel for the wife said the judge had

---

[19] [2008] 1 IR 134.
[20] [2004] IESC 101.

simply left it up to the husband to extract the money from his companies "in the most fiscally and commercially effective fashion".

Tax on the lump sum could vary between €800,000 and €1,680,000, "clearly very substantial sums in the context of the total worth of the parties", said Mr Justice Adrian Hardiman in the Supreme Court. The lump sum, plus the cost of buying the wife out of the family home, transaction costs and tax liability "substantially exceeds one half of the value of the company".

Hardiman cited *DT v CT*,[21] where Fennelly J said the realisation of assets "necessarily entails the incurring of realisation costs and expenses in the form of legal and other professional expenses and tax liability, in particular capital taxes".

The Supreme Court said the tax consequences must be considered, and sent the case back to the High Court to consider the tax effects of withdrawing funds from the company.

Similarly, in *MK v JPK*,[22] Mr Justice Brian McCracken said a judge assessing a lump sum payment should take into account:

> the costs of realising the lump sum, such as capital gains tax or professional fees. However, one-off costs of realisation, which normally can be calculated fairly accurately in advance, are very different from fluctuating values which differ from day to day.

In *BC v MC*,[23] a husband said that he could get a bank loan to pay his ex-wife a €50,000 lump sum, but could not take the money from his company's profits without incurring a substantial tax liability. Peart J reduced the lump sum to €35,000.

Proper provision may change if circumstances change before the order has been complied with. In *NF v EF*,[24] the court ordered the husband to secure maintenance and a lump sum by the auction of property with a €600,000 reserve. The money was to be used to pay for the wife's nursing

---

[21] [2002] IESC 68.
[22] [2006] IESC 4.
[23] [2012] IEHC 602.
[24] [2007] IEHC 317.

home care. But, following the "dramatic fall" in property prices, the husband appealed to the High Court to vary the orders.

In the appeal,[25] Abbott J said that, if parts of an order made in the divorce decree became impossible, the Court had to consider alternatives to ensure proper provision. The court had to take into consideration the assets, income and financial requirements of the parties in light of the changed circumstances.

The judge accepted that, in this case, due to the "dramatic and unforeseen turmoil in the financial and credit markets", the value of the property had halved. He said:

> If the circumstances of the case have fundamentally changed through a dramatic and unforeseen drop in property values, short of the impossibility of a sale of some crucial asset available for the provision in the order, then, on the test of *Thwaite v Thwaite*,[26] there may be circumstances where the Court might not enforce that part of the order relating to the sale of such property, unless alternative arrangements may be made for provision to ensure the balance and symmetry of the order previously made.

He said the property should be sold for not less than €300,000 and the proceeds paid to the wife, in which case the husband need not pay the lump sum.

In *U v U*,[27] a judge said a High Court order in a divorce case had become impossible to perform because of the impact of "the great recession and disastrous fall in Irish property prices following Lehman's collapse in 2008".[28]

In *JD v DD*,[29] dealing with proper provision and reviewable dispositions, the applicant wife and her husband had been married in 1966 and separated after 30 years. The husband's affidavit of means failed to disclose that he had transferred money to the Isle of Man to establish a trust after the proceedings were issued.

---

[25] [2008] IEHC 471.
[26] [1982] Fam 1.
[27] [2011] IEHC 228.
[28] See *AK v JK* [2008] IEHC 341.
[29] [1997] 3 IR 64.

The statutory concept of 'reviewable dispositions', introduced by s 29 of the Judicial Separation and Family Law Reform Act 1989, was replaced by s 35 of the Family Law Act 1995 and continued in s 37 of the Family Law (Divorce) Act 1996. To prevent a transaction being set aside by the court, the purchaser must prove that there was 'valuable consideration', and that the purchaser acted in good faith, not knowing that the vendor intended to defeat a claim for relief.

McGuinness J held that, while the court couldn't put pressure on the trustees, the existence of the trust should not be ignored in calculating maintenance. She held that the trust was a reviewable disposition because it was an effort by the husband to reduce the money available for distribution. She set aside the husband's disposition.

In *MP v AP*,[30] O'Higgins J said that proper provision was not necessarily the same as 'adequate and reasonable' provision, which was the criterion under the Judicial Separation Act. However, provisions which were adequate and reasonable could also constitute 'proper provision' under the Divorce Act.

Proper provision can even include the period after a party's death. In *BC v MC*[31] on appeal from a Circuit Court divorce decree, Peart J refused to make a s 18(10) blocking order against the ex-wife, thus allowing her to claim against her ex-husband's estate after his death.

The judge said that there should be proper provision for the period after the husband had died, insofar as circumstances then permitted, and not simply during his lifetime. He said he would not make a blocking order unless satisfied that proper provision had been made for the wife's maintenance after her ex-husband's death.

'Reasonable Needs'

Irish law on the division of assets differs from English law and common law generally. Until the turn of the century, the basis for the division of assets in the English divorce courts was a spouse's 'reasonable needs'. Where there were extensive family assets and a clean break solution was

---

[30] [2005] IEHC 326.
[31] [2012] IEHC 602.

considered desirable, the courts used to grant the wife a lump sum large enough to provide for her 'reasonable requirements' until her death. The rest of the family assets went in general to the husband. This was the general rule where a wife had been a stay-at-home wife and mother.

However in the case of *White v White*,[32] a farmer's wife who sought an equal share of the family farm argued that it was not fair that her husband should retain most of the family property.

White v White[33] marked a turning point in the English approach to the division of matrimonial property in 'big money cases'. The House of Lords rejected the 'reasonable requirements' guideline and said a judge should depart from equality only where there was good reason for doing so.

The Lords said financial needs should not be regarded as the only factor in deciding an award, particularly when the couple's financial resources exceeded their needs. They particularly stressed the value of a woman's work in the home as a wife and mother.

The Lords said there should be no presumption that assets should be equally divided between spouses, but equality of division should be used as a yardstick against which the final division should be checked.

The Lords said the courts were also entitled to take into consideration that property had been acquired before marriage or had been inherited. Mrs White was awarded €2.5 million—40 percent of the total assets.

The English courts were subsequently at pains to reiterate that *White v White* did not introduce a requirement for equal division of assets. In *Cowan v Cowan*,[34] Lord Justice Thorpe said the decision

> clearly does not introduce a rule of equality. The yardstick of equality is a cross-check against discrimination. Fairness is the rule.

But the court said that, if one spouse had made an exceptional contribution, that could justify a departure from the principle of equality.

---

[32] [2000] 2 FLR 981.
[33] [2000] UKHL 54.
[34] [2001] 2 FLR 192.

However, the judgment established the general principle that the courts should no longer discriminate between husbands and wives. It said the contribution of a home-maker should be considered equal to that of the breadwinner.

But when the High Court in Ireland attempted to follow the *White* judgment in *MK v JK*, it was overruled by the Supreme Court which said that the concept of a single payment to meet a wife's reasonable requirements had never been part of Irish family law.[35]

McGuinness J, in her judgment, said that such a payment would have to be part of a clean break divorce settlement, which was "neither permissible nor possible" in Ireland. She said the 1996 divorce legislation required a judge to make "proper provision" for both spouses according to a set of mandatory guidelines.[36]

In 'ample resources' cases, the dependent spouse of a long marriage will normally be entitled to between one-third and half of the family assets. But there is no such thing in Irish law as a clean break divorce.

In *GB v AB*,[37] even though the net assets of the husband and wife totalled more than €6 million, Abbott J said it was "not possible to view the case as an ample resources case", hence a clean break as envisaged by the Supreme Court in *T v T*[38] was not possible. But he said that, in five years or so, the husband's assets could be profitable in terms of liquidity and saleability, and then the case could easily become an ample resources case.

In *Goodbody Stockbrokers v Allied Irish Banks plc*,[39] where the wife claimed that all assets of the marriage were to be held on a 50:50 basis, the High Court ruled that the wife was not entitled to funds in her husband's stockbroker account which he had pledged as security for a loan. Birmingham J said that, while discussions between the spouses might potentially be relevant to the distribution of the assets "in the context of marital disharmony", that did not create an interest by the wife.

---

[35] *MK v JK (orse SK) (No 2)* [2003] 1 IR 326.
[36] Family Law (Divorce) Act 1996, s 20(2).
[37] [2007] IEHC 491.
[38] [2002] 3 IR 334.
[39] [2013] IEHC 155.

Division of Assets

Assets comprise income and all related matters, including the family home, family income, individual incomes, businesses, savings—whether in a spouse's sole name or joint names—pensions, holiday homes, bonds, potential succession rights, tax benefits, social welfare benefits and personal possessions, including stocks and shares.

While a spouse may not normally insist on a share of the assets owned by the other spouse, that does not necessarily apply in family law matters. In *W v W*,[40] the High Court said that, where assets were the proceeds of sale of an inherited property, that should be taken into account.

In that case, a wife had sought some of the proceeds of the sale of a farm which had been inherited by her husband. The couple were in their 50s and the wife had made a substantial contribution to the family as primary carer of the children.

The court awarded a wife a lump sum of IR£4.7 million, giving her a total of IR£4.9 million out of total assets of approximately IR£17 million.

In the case of *MK v JK (orse SK) (No 2)*,[41] a High Court judge said that he was "happy that, in current phraseology, the Court may use the term 'equality'". He awarded the wife half the assets of her husband and his new partner, and the husband appealed to the Supreme Court.

The couple, who had married in England in 1963, had six children and separated in 1980. In 1982 they signed a deed of separation. The wife remained in the family home with the children, while the husband paid maintenance.

A clause in the separation agreement allowed for variation of maintenance if there was a fundamental change in the circumstances of either spouse.

In 1995, the husband obtained a divorce in Haiti and went through a ceremony of marriage with MB in Massachusetts. He and MB later married in a civil ceremony in Ireland in 2001 after his divorce.

---

[40] Unreported, High Court, 2001.
[41] [2003] 1 IR 326.

After the separation, the husband obtained a very good job with a US company and became very well off, though most of his property was held jointly with MB. He was paid very handsomely, and received a bonus of up to 100 percent of his salary.

The wife applied for a divorce in Ireland in 1998. In his judgment at the end of the five-day hearing in November 2000, the High Court judge criticised the husband as a man of "corporate mentality" whose attitude towards his wife was determined by "the questionable morality emanating from this mid-American company".

The judge condemned the way the husband had obtained the Haitian divorce and remarried in the United States, and described him as having "driven a coach and four through Irish legislation". He said the marriage in the United States was bigamous.

The judge said he intended to adopt the fundamental rules that had been in existence for nearly 200 years in deciding whether a wife was entitled to be maintained according to the lifestyle of her husband.

The judge ordered the husband to transfer the family home to the wife and pay her:

1) maintenance equal to half his annual salary (including bonuses) backdated to May 1999; and
2) a lump sum of IR£1.5 million, representing about half the assets held by the husband and his new wife.

At a later hearing, the judge also ordered the trustees of the husband's Irish pension fund to pay 80 percent of the husband's Irish pension to the wife when it became due. A counterclaim by the husband was dismissed and he was also ordered to pay his wife's costs, as well as his own.

The husband appealed on the grounds that the High Court judge had failed to pay due regard to the 1982 separation deed or to the fact that the couple had been separated for more than 20 years.

The Supreme Court criticised the way the High Court judge had come to his decision. Mrs Justice Catherine McGuinness said:

While I would, of course, accept that the wife of a rich man (or the husband of a rich woman) could always expect a substantially greater award both in income and in capital than the parties to the average marriage, I very much doubt that a policy of equal division of assets between husband and wife has prevailed under common law rules since the beginning of the 19th century, or even the 20th century, either in this jurisdiction or in England.

The concept of a single capital payment to the wife to meet her 'reasonable requirements' for the remainder of her life has never in fact formed a part of Irish family law. There are two main reasons for this. Firstly, such a capital payment is inevitably a part of a 'clean break' settlement in divorce proceedings. In this jurisdiction the legislature has, in the Family Law (Divorce) Act 1996, laid down a system of law where a 'clean break' solution is neither permissible nor possible.

Secondly, the approach of the Irish courts, in accordance with both Article 41.2 of the Constitution and the statutory guidelines, has been to give full credit to the wife's contribution through her work in the home and as a mother to her children. In this jurisdiction, the overriding requirement of a fair outcome is governed by s 20(5) of the 1996 Act...

The provisions of the 1996 Act leave a considerable area of discretion to the Court in making proper financial provision for spouses in divorce cases. This discretion, however, is not to be exercised at large. The statute lays down mandatory guidelines.

The Court must have regard to all the factors set out in s 20, measuring their relevance and weight according to the facts of the individual case. In giving the decision of the Court, a judge should give reasons for the way in which his or her discretion has been exercised in the light of the statutory guidelines. In this case, the judge notably failed to do this.

The judge also said that, under s 20(3) of the Divorce Act, the court had to "have regard to the terms of any separation agreement which has been entered into by the spouses and is still in force".

The Supreme Court returned the matter to the High Court to consider the question of proper provision in the light of the mandatory provisions of the Divorce Act. The financial orders were varied at the second trial, but the husband was ordered to pay the costs of both trials. On appeal, the

Supreme Court upheld the financial orders but said each side must meet its own costs in the first trial.[42]

In *SD v BD*,[43] another ample resources case, the husband and wife had signed a deed of separation in 1985, which included £300 a week maintenance and the transfer of the family home. In 2003, the wife instituted divorce proceedings and claimed that the division of the assets under the separation agreement was inequitable.

The husband argued that, while the marriage had lasted 14 years, the couple had been separated for 22 years, during most of which time his wife had a relationship with another man. Abbot J ordered the husband to pay the wife a lump sum of €4 million—about quarter of the assets—plus maintenance of €1,500 a week.

In *MK v JPK*,[44] the High Court granted a decree of divorce and ordered the husband to pay his wife a lump sum of about half of his assets and maintenance of about half his annual income. The husband appealed to the Supreme Court, which ordered a retrial.[45]

At the retrial, the husband was ordered to pay his wife a lump sum of €450,000 plus €40,000 a year maintenance and his Irish pension, to transfer the family home to the wife and to pay the costs of both trials. The husband again appealed.

The value of the husband's assets at the time of the trial was about US$1.6 million and the judge gave the wife approximately one third of those assets. However, the husband said there had been a "sharp decline" in the value of the dollar which had led to a fall in US stock market values and a decline in the value of his assets.

But Mr Justice Brian McCracken said:

> If the husband chooses to invest his assets in the stock market, he must be prepared to accept the fluctuations in that market.

---

[42] *MK v JPK* [2006] IESC 4.
[43] [2007] IEHC 492.
[44] [2006] IESC 4.
[45] [2001] 3 IR 371.

Affidavit of Means

Details of the assets are set out in an affidavit of means. The punishment for deliberately omitting assets from the affidavit can be severe. In *LE v UF*,[46] Mrs Justice Mary Irvine said a lack of disclosure in the court process could bar a claimant from relief, though the court's power should be exercised very sparingly.[47] She said:

> If there has been a history of evasion and equivocation on the part of the spouse in respect of their financial affairs in family law proceedings, the courts are not prepared to permit the spouse to benefit from that conduct.

In *U v U*,[48] the husband failed to mention in his affidavit of means that he owned a "magnificent sports car" which cost €410,000. His wife sought his committal to prison as a result.

And in *SD v BD*,[49] Abbot J said a wife was not entitled to any arrears of maintenance because of her "positive lack of disclosure" of her employment and directorships,

> It is a fundamental aspect of family law proceedings that both parties would give at the earliest possible stage a full disclosure of income and assets … The route of this disclosure is paved with sworn affidavits.

Full and Final Settlements

The courts may take note of any previous judicial separation or separation agreement, but judges are free to vary this.

In *MP v AP*,[50] the terms of a 13-year-old separation order were said to be "of very great importance". After the breakup of the marriage "in circumstances of considerable acrimony and bitterness", judicial separation proceedings were settled in 1992 and orders made on agreed terms.

Maintenance was agreed at £1,800 a month net of income tax. The husband paid the wife a lump sum of IR£175,000, paid the VHI premium, all

---

[46] Unreported, High Court, 10 June 2009.
[47] See *O'Riordan v Ireland (No 5)* [2001] 4 IR 463, and *DK v AK* [1993] ILRM 710.
[48] [2011] IEHC 228.
[49] [2007] IEHC 492.
[50] [2005] IEHC 326.

medical, dental and education bills for the two children to third level and agreed to buy his wife a new car every four years.

But although the settlement was "intended to be long-term and lasting", the wife frittered away the "very considerable lump sum". The judge said that, if the wife "decided to dissipate the settlement monies, rather than manage them prudently, it would be wrong" for the husband to bear the consequences.

Since splitting up, the husband's earnings had far outstripped the wife's. In 2003, he earned €591,254 after tax, and was likely to earn another €1 million when he retired from his solicitors' partnership. The wife's income for the year was €31,717.

The wife's home was valued at €1.1 million. The husband owned a €1.75 million home, another €750,000 house, a time share property, a Spanish home worth €367,000, a IR£320,000 holiday home in Ireland and other properties held in trust. He had shares worth €66,642, while she had shares worth a tenth of that.

O'Higgins J said it would be wrong to ignore "the huge disparity in income" but, in the light of the earlier settlement, a property adjustment order was not "necessary or desirable". He increased maintenance from €28,800 to €38,000 after tax, ordered the husband to pay a lump sum of €100,000, and extinguished the succession rights of both parties.

In *WA v MA*,[51] Hardiman J also gave "very significant weight" to an 11-year-old separation agreement, but in *RG v CG*,[52] Finlay Geoghegan J ignored the provisions of a four-year-old judicial separation settlement, saying that proper provision must exist at the time of the divorce and be based on the value of the parties' assets at that time.

In *MS v PS*,[53] Mr Justice Garrett Sheehan said he attached "no significance" to "full and final" consent orders for the maintenance of five children in judicial separation proceedings in 1992 and 1997.

---

[51] [2005] IR 1.
[52] [2005] 2 IR 418.
[53] [2008] IEHC 448.

On divorce, the wife claimed maintenance of €193,556 a year, including all the cash in the husband's bank account, all his shares and all his pensions. But the judge said she had "weakened her financial position" in the two years before the divorce hearing by "considerable spending". She had won €243,000 in the lottery in 1998.

He ordered the husband to pay the wife a €60,000 lump sum plus €10,000 a year maintenance for each dependent child, to transfer pensions worth €133,000 and to top up the children's education fund.

In *SN v PO'D*,[54] a wife appealed a High Court order concerning proper provision on divorce. The couple separated in 1999 and a judicial separation decree was granted in 2001 based on the terms of a 'full and final' consent agreement. The wife was a successful businesswoman, and the husband had 'sufficient means'. The principal issue in the appeal concerned the extent to which the High Court had to take account of the settlement.

In 2003, the wife instituted divorce proceedings. The husband counterclaimed for property adjustment and lump sum payments. He said the wife had not fully disclosed her financial circumstances at the time of the settlement and had subsequently sold her interest in her companies for "a very substantial sum".

The High Court judge gave "very considerable weight" to the 2001 settlement. However he said the full and final settlement clause could show up "an embarrassing gap in wealth" between the husband and wife, which could result in the husband:

> suffering such loss of self-esteem, grieving or obsession with the litigation that he would easily lose the capacity to celebrate, enjoy and be bubbly with his children, as a father should.

The High Court judge awarded the husband €500,000 for the "information deficit loss". He also ordered the wife to pay the husband €1,648,800 from the sale of her business, for the husband's "comparative lack of success in business ... and his consequent loss of self-esteem", reduced the maintenance to €7,000 a year, and granted a divorce.

---

[54] [2009] IESC 61.

In the Supreme Court, Fennelly J said there had been "a significant failure of disclosure" by the wife. But the notion of proper provision did not provide for an award to compensate for loss of self-esteem.

While the High Court judge's calculation of €500,000 for "information deficit loss" was inadequate, it was in the interests of both parties that finality be brought to the litigation as far as possible. Rather than send the matter back to the High Court for assessment, Fennelly J substituted the €2,148,000 for the €500,000 lump sum as proper provision. He affirmed the lower maintenance order.

In *BC v MC*,[55] because the couple had formerly been granted a judicial separation and there was no separation agreement with a full and final settlement clause, the arrangements could be revisited when the courts were considering ancillary orders in a divorce.

In *GB v AB*,[56] Abbott J ordered the husband to pay the wife €120,000 a year index-linked and insured maintenance, buy her a car, pay her VHI and car insurance and provide a lump sum of €1.75 million. The husband's pension was transferred to the wife. The wife also got 90 percent of the husband's shareholding in a retail company. If she sold the shares within five years, the husband would no longer be required to make periodic payments and the wife would take the proceeds in full and final settlement.

Even where the terms of a divorce or separation are said to be full and final, the parties may reapply to the court for variations of orders if there is a substantial change in circumstances, such as one party losing their job or winning the Lotto.

In *SD v BD*,[57] Abbot J ordered the husband to pay the wife a lump sum of €4 million—about quarter of the assets—plus maintenance of €1,500 a week, but he stressed this was not a full and final settlement.

> I do not consider that the judgment of the Supreme Court in *T v T*[58] is authority for the proposition that the Court may make provision for the parties on the basis that it is to be in full and final settlement of all

---

[55] [2012] IEHC 602.
[56] [2007] IEHC 491.
[57] [2007] IEHC 492.
[58] [2002] IESC 68.

claims of the parties against each other. In my view, the judgment in *T v T* only permits or mandates the Court to do so in the event of the parties agreeing and requesting that it would.

The Supreme Court set out general principles to be followed in *YG v NG*.[59] The issue in that case, where there was an existing separation agreement, was what further provision should be made and under what circumstances.

"What weight is to be given to the previous separation agreement?" asked Denham CJ.

> Was the previous settlement a full or partial estoppel? What happens if there has been a change in circumstances? A windfall? A financial disaster? A serious illness? A change in needs? How relevant is it if a party has mismanaged his or her provision made in an earlier agreement?

She said that, in light of the law and the Constitution, a few general principles could be applied:

1) A separation agreement was a legal document, entered into by consent, and should be given significant weight, especially if it was agreed that it should be in full and final settlement of all matters.
2) Irish law does not establish a right to a clean break. However, it is a legitimate aspiration.[60]
3) The Constitution and Divorce Act give the Court a specific jurisdiction and duty.
4) The Divorce Act requires the court to make proper provision "in all the circumstances"; a deed of separation in full and final settlement is a significant factor.
5) If the circumstances have not changed since the separation agreement was signed, the provision ordered by the court could be the same, as long as it was proper provision.
6) If the circumstances of either spouse have changed significantly, the court must consider all the circumstances carefully, but is not required to redistribute wealth.
7) If a spouse has a new or different need, including an illness that may be a relevant factor.
8) The bursting of the property bubble may also make an earlier provision unjust.

---

[59] [2011] IESC 40.
[60] *DT v CT* [2002] 3 IR 334 and *F v F* [1995] 2 IR 354.

9) If a spouse acquires wealth after separation unconnected to any joint project during married life, that does not in itself give the other spouse a right to further money or assets.

10) If one spouse becomes very wealthy after concluding a separation agreement, there is no right for the other spouse to get more money or other assets.

11) The court has to look at all the circumstances and make proper provision, not redistribute wealth.

12) The facts to be considered will include the length of time since the separation agreement. The longer the time since the agreement, barring catastrophic circumstances, the less likely a court will be to alter arrangements.

13) The standard of living of a dependent spouse should be similar to that enjoyed when the marriage ended.

14) If a spouse has new needs, such as a debilitating illness, that will be a factor to be considered.

15) Inherited assets are not treated as assets obtained by both parties in a marriage. Each case should be considered specifically.

16) Spouses should not be compensated for their own incompetence or indiscretion to the detriment of the other spouse.

17) Any exceptional change in the value of assets, which was unforeseen at the time of the judicial separation or High Court hearing, is a relevant factor.[61]

In relation to the "bursting of the property bubble", the Supreme Court allowed an appeal in *MD v ND*[62]: because of the drop in the value of assets since the High Court order, farmland which was to be sold to pay a €2.9 million lump sum had fallen in value from €28,000 an acre to €7,800 an acre. The Supreme Court said this made the financial provision unfair and not in keeping with the intention of the High Court judge. Denham J said that not admitting the valuation evidence "would result in an injustice".

Before the bubble burst, the rise in property prices could also affect settlements or court orders. In *CF v JDF*,[63] McGuinness J said that the financial position of the parties might well have substantially altered because of the rise in the value of property in the counties around Dublin over the previous three years. She said the Supreme Court could not hear evidence of these matters on appeal, nor was it desirable for that court to

---

[61] *MD v ND* [2011] IESC 18.
[62] [2011] IESC 18.
[63] [2005] IESC 45.

try and readjust the High Court orders. She advised the only course open to her was to return the matter to the High Court to allow a fresh adjudication based on up-to-date financial and valuation evidence.

However, the courts are unlikely to revisit orders if:

- the settlement was recent;
- the settlement was reasonable or generous;
- one party frittered away their share; or
- the settlement was intended to be full and final.

The courts might take a different attitude if one party lied about their assets before the settlement or unforeseeable events occurred between the settlement and the judicial separation or divorce.

Family Home

For spouses, the 'family home' is protected by the Family Home Protection Act 1976. The home of civil partners is defined as a 'shared home' in the 2010 Act. A spouse or civil partner cannot sell, mortgage, lease or transfer the property without the other party's advance written permission, even if it is in that party's sole name.

Often the spouse who lives with the children will be allowed to stay in the family home until the youngest child is 18, or 23 if in full-time education. This legislation is not the same for same-sex couples.

A court can order one spouse or civil partner to transfer ownership of the property, it can order the house to be sold immediately or later and the proceeds divided in whatever proportions it considers proper—except where the property is in negative equity—or, in the case of a tenancy, it can transfer the tenancy.

Domicile

Either spouse must be domiciled in the Republic of Ireland when proceedings began, or have lived in the state for at least a year before that date.

The difference between domicile and habitual residence is that 'domicile' implies an intention to live in a country permanently. 'Habitual residence' simply refers to the country where a person usually lives.

In *PAS v AFS*,[64] Fennelly J said that, although a child's birthplace was of "prime importance in many cases", a child could even be habitually resident in a country where the child had not ever been. In *SR v MMR*,[65] the Supreme Court held that there must be joint consent by parents to the acquisition of a minor's new habitual residence. One parent could not unilaterally make that decision.

Different issues can be decided in courts of different jurisdictions. In *WD v SD*,[66] the couple—neither of whom was an Irish citizen—had six children. The husband was a tax exile and they moved frequently between their Irish home, a home outside Europe and a summer holiday hotel in France.

In 2008, the wife sought a judicial separation. The husband challenged jurisdiction but the High Court found[67] that the habitual residence of the family was Ireland. Divorce proceedings were heard in the non-European jurisdiction and Abbott J dismissed the judicial separation proceedings, but decided issues of child welfare.

Foreign Divorce

Formerly, foreign divorces were recognised in Ireland only in certain circumstances.

In *Mayo-Perrott v Mayo-Perrott*, the judge said that Irish courts would recognise a foreign divorce only if the parties could establish that they were domiciled in the jurisdiction of the court granting the decree. In *KED v MC*,[68] the High Court ruled that a divorce granted by the English courts was not valid in Ireland as it was not based on the husband's domicile.

---

[64] Unreported, Supreme Court, 29 November 2004.
[65] [2006] IESC 7.
[66] [2011] IEHC 120.
[67] [2009] IEHC 579.
[68] Unreported, High Court, 26 September 1984.

In *K v K*,[69] the Supreme Court refused to recognise a 1982 Ohio divorce decree because the applicant was not domiciled in Ohio. The court ruled that the man was still validly married when he contracted a bigamous marriage in Dublin in 1983. Despite the fact that the man had been 'married' for almost 17 years, the Supreme Court said that he was entitled to deny that he was validly married to the applicant 'wife'.

The Domicile and Recognition of Foreign Divorces Act 1986 allowed the recognition of a divorce granted anywhere in Britain and Northern Ireland as long as either spouse was domiciled there. Thus Irish couples who are prepared to live abroad for a period may be able to circumvent the required four-year waiting period for an Irish divorce and obtain a divorce in another jurisdiction.

The Brussels II regulation requires the Irish courts to recognise a British divorce which was granted on the basis of 'habitual residence' in Britain or Northern Ireland.

A person who had been habitually resident in England or Wales for one year would be entitled to apply for a divorce on the grounds of adultery or unreasonable behaviour. Once the English Court had accepted jurisdiction and agreed to deal with the matter, under the new regulation, the Irish courts would have to decline jurisdiction if the English divorce application were challenged by the other spouse. The Irish courts would also be required to recognise the English decree.

If both spouses agree, they may seek a divorce after two years' separation. If they don't agree, the separation must be five years or more.

Dependent Children

In relation to any dependent children, the court must take into account:

1) their financial needs;
2) their property or financial resources;
3) any physical or mental disability;
4) any income or social welfare benefits to which they are entitled;
5) their accommodation needs;

---

[69] [2004] IESC 21.

6) the parents' proposed education or training of the children;
7) the parents' financial circumstances; and
8) any separation agreement.

Normally both parents remain joint guardians of their children after a divorce. However, the court may—after ordering probation, welfare or HSE reports—declare that one parent is unfit to have custody and award custody to the other spouse. A parent who is declared unfit by the court will not have an automatic right to custody of the children if the other spouse dies. Among the reasons for being declared an unfit parent would be violence, mental or physical cruelty, sexual assault, desertion, alcoholism or serious mental illness.

The court may also give directions about access to dependent children and about their general welfare. This may involve supervised access by the non-custodial parent.

A divorced spouse may also ask the court at any time to make a financial compensation order, requiring the other spouse to take out a life insurance policy, or assign the benefit of an existing policy, to improve the financial security of the dependent spouse or children or to make up for her loss of a benefit such as a pension.

The court won't make such an order where the applicant has remarried, and the order ceases once the applicant dies or marries again. The court may also make a pensions adjustment order.

If a divorced spouse dies without providing properly for a former spouse, the surviving spouse—if still single—may apply for a share of the estate of the deceased person. Normally, when granting a divorce, the court will also make an order preventing such an application in the future by one or both spouses.

The court won't grant a share in the estate if the surviving spouse had deserted the deceased spouse or behaved in such a way that it would be unjust to give the survivor a share. However, a spouse who leaves the home because of intolerable behaviour by the other spouse may not be considered guilty of desertion.

The personal representative of the deceased person, that is the executor or administrator of the estate, must make reasonable efforts to inform the surviving spouse of the death. If the survivor intends to apply or has already applied for a share of the estate, or an order has already been made in favour of the surviving spouse, that spouse must tell the personal representative within a month of being contacted, otherwise the representative may distribute the assets regardless.

Any application for a share in an estate must usually be made within six months of a grant of probate or administration being taken out. The judge will hear evidence from any relevant person, including any new spouse. The court will also take into account any property adjustment, lump sum payment or bequest already made to the surviving spouse and will not give the survivor—in total—more than their legal right under the 1965 Succession Act: half the estate, or one third if there are children.

Inheritances—or 'interests in expectancy'—may also form part of the assets which a judge will take into consideration.

The court also has to take account of any separation agreement still in force, as it did in the High Court cases of *JN v RN*[70] and *MG v MG*.[71]

The court may subsequently vary any order dealing with money or property in the light of changed circumstances or new evidence. The application may be made by either spouse, by a new spouse or, on the death of a spouse, by anyone who has 'a sufficient interest'[72] or is acting on behalf of a dependent child. Clearly this gives the court power to reduce maintenance—or even, in an extreme case, to order that property be handed back—if, for example, a remarried couple find themselves homeless or in financial difficulties because of the burden of maintenance payments.

Conduct

The conduct of a spouse will be relevant in certain circumstances, such as where one has deserted the other or has behaved so badly that the other spouse has been forced to leave home. The judge will disregard such

---

[70] Unreported, High Court, 1999.
[71] Unreported, Circuit Court, 2000.
[72] Family Law (Divorce) Act 1996, s 22(2)(b).

conduct when making orders relating to maintenance payments for children.

In *SD v BD*,[73] where the wife had already been refused arrears of maintenance because of her lack of disclosure, Abbott J said it would be:

> entirely confusing, unfair and unjust to equate misconduct under these criteria with the lack of notification and candour displayed in the proceedings in respect of which the wife has been substantially penalised.

In the case of *T v T*,[74] the Supreme Court approved the decision of Lord Denning in *Wachtel v Wachtel*[75] that, short of misbehaviour which was "obvious and gross", the Court should not reduce an order for financial provision merely because of what was formerly regarded as guilt or blame. "To do so would be to impose a fine for supposed misbehaviour in the course of an unhappy married life," said Denning LJ.

Earlier financial and property orders—made at the time of a divorce *a mensa et thoro* or a judicial separation—may be discharged if a spouse applies for a divorce. But if the orders are not discharged when the court grants a divorce, they remain in force.

Costs

In most family law cases, legal costs are not awarded, so each spouse has to foot his or her own legal bill. In the case of repeated applications to court and lengthy or complicated proceedings, these can run into tens of thousands of euros.

In *MK v JPK*,[76] McCracken J said that, in family law cases, the court must look at the affect of the award of costs on both parties. He said:

> If the husband has to bear the costs of both parties of the first trial, this is going to very considerably reduce the assets available out of which an award may be made to the wife.

---

[73] [2007] IEHC 492.
[74] [2002] IESC 68.
[75] [1973] Fam 72.
[76] [2006] IESC 4.

In *F v L*,[77] Barron J said that the practice of always allowing the wife her legal costs against the husband was "no longer justified".

Where costs are awarded, they are a matter for the judge. In *TF v Ireland and MF*,[78] the applicant had unsuccessfully sought a declaration that parts of the Judicial Separation and Family Law Reform Act 1989 were unconstitutional. The High Court judge refused to make any order for costs and the plaintiff appealed.

In the Supreme Court, Hamilton CJ held:

> The question of the costs of any proceedings before the Court is a matter for the discretion of the judge hearing and determining such matter.

In the case of *BD v JD*,[79] a Supreme Court judge set aside an order for a €100,000 contribution by the husband to the wife's legal costs. Hardiman J said the wife had lost her claim and, "bearing in mind that it is a family law action", he did not see any cogent reason why either party should contribute to the other's costs.

In *MK v JPK*,[80] the husband was ordered to pay the costs of two High Court trials, which lasted 12 days, and an appeal. He said the estimated costs of €880,000, would "eat up the balance of his assets".

Mr Justice Brian McCracken said:

> The general rule in actions for damages where a retrial has been ordered is that costs follow the event in relation to both trials, and the question of the costs of the first trial are dependent on the outcome of the retrial.

But he said that, in family law cases, there was a "pool of assets" of the husband and the wife, which were to be used to make proper provision for both spouses and any dependants and to pay the legal costs. Where there was no question of either party having further assets to pay costs, the general rule did not necessarily apply.

---

[77] [1991] 1 IR 40.
[78] [1995] 1 IR 321.
[79] [2004] IESC 101.
[80] [2006] IESC 4.

In the case of *YG v NG*,[81] Denham CJ said a High Court order that a husband should give his wife €1 million to buy another house plus €600,000 for her own use was not proper provision. She allowed the appeal and sent the case back to the High Court to make proper provision for both spouses.

YG v NG involved a couple who had married in 1977. They lived in a house which the husband inherited. The wife had £3,000 savings when they married and they ran a garage and farm at the start of their marriage. The husband built and sold houses. They separated in 1995.

Following a separation agreement in 1996, the husband paid the wife £100 a week for two years and £50 per week after that. He paid her health insurance, provided a house and a lump sum of £70,000. A 'full and final settlement' clause was a feature of the separation agreement. She then sought a divorce, and the husband argued he had made proper and permanent provision through the separation agreement.

Clean Break

Traditionally, judges have maintained that Irish divorce legislation does not permit a 'clean break' because, under the statutes, divorced couples can return to court to ask for variations in financial and property orders.

Mrs Justice Catherine McGuinness said in the case of *JD v DD*[82]:

> The Oireachtas has made it clear that a 'clean break' situation is not to be sought and that, if anything, financial finality is virtually to be prevented.

> The Court, in making virtually any order in regard to finance and property on the breakdown of a marriage, is faced with the situation where finality is not and never can be achieved. This also appears to mean that no agreement on property between the parties can be completely final, since such finality would be contrary to the policy and provisions of the legislation.

> The statutory policy is, therefore, totally opposed to the concept of the 'clean break'. This policy is not only clear on the face of the statutes

---

[81] [2011] IESC 40.
[82] [1997] 3 IR 64.

but was most widely discussed, referred to and advocated in the considerable debate that surrounded the enactment of divorce legislation.

Former Chief Justice John Murray stated that, while Irish law did not establish a right to a clean break,

> the objective of seeking to achieve certainty and stability in the obligations between the parties is a desirable one where the circumstances of the case permit.[83]

But if the circumstances have not changed and proper provision was made in the separation agreement, there should be no change at the divorce stage.

But finality in divorce may not be so far away, following the *T v T* decision. Former Chief Justice Ronan Keane accepted that, in some cases, "finality is not possible" and that the legislation "expressly provides for the variation of custody and access orders and of the level of maintenance payments".[84]

But he added that he did not believe that the Oireachtas intended that the courts should abandon any possibility of achieving certainty and finality and of avoiding further litigation between ex-spouses.

> I am satisfied that, while the Irish legislation is careful to avoid going as far as the English legislation in adopting the 'clean break' approach—not least because of the Constitutional constraints—it is not correct to say that the legislation goes so far as virtually to prevent financial finality ... On no view could such an outcome be regarded as desirable and I am satisfied that it is most emphatically not mandated by the legislation under consideration.

European Council regulation (EC) 1347/2000 on the jurisdiction, recognition and enforcement of judgements in matrimonial matters could also have implications for property rights. While Irish courts have the power to reopen financial matters, and a spouse does not have the legal right to contract out of future variations of maintenance, in England and Wales, all financial matters may be finalised once and for all on the granting of a divorce.

---

[83] *F v F* [1995] 2 IR 354.
[84] Family Law (Divorce) Act 1996, s 22.

Divorce Questionnaire

If you plan to consult a solicitor, it would help if you comp. this questionnaire first so that you have the answers to the questions y. are most likely to be asked:

1) Your full name, address and date of birth
2) Your spouse's full name, address and date of birth
3) Your occupation and your spouse's occupation
4) Date and place of marriage. (Please produce your marriage certificate.) Are you satisfied that the marriage was valid?
5) Names and dates of birth of any children. Is any of them still under 18, receiving full-time education or suffering from physical or mental disability?
6) Are you both Irish citizens? Are you domiciled here or have you been ordinarily resident in Ireland for more than one year?
7) When did you separate? Give a full list of the addresses at which you and your spouses have lived since you parted
8) Detail all residences owned by you or your spouse. In whose names are the properties registered? What is the value of each property? Give full details of any outstanding loans or mortgages
9) Does any of the property have a rateable value of more than €254?
10) Does either of you own any other land or premises? If so, is it registered or unregistered? If registered, what is the folio number?
11) What are your respective incomes? Please produce any financial statements, credit card statements or P60s for either of you
12) Have there been previous family law proceedings of any type? Give details, with certified copies of any previous court orders, deed of separation or separation agreement
13) Why has the marriage broken down? Who was to blame? Has there been unreasonable behaviour, violence or cruelty (mental or physical)? If so, give details and approximate dates. Bring any diary or notes with you. Has either spouse deserted the family home?
14) Is there any reasonable prospect of a reconciliation between you and your spouse?

Which the following orders will you be seeking, in addition to the decree divorce?

1. Maintenance or interim maintenance (possibly secured against income or property)
2. Discharge or variation of any previous maintenance order
3. A lump sum
4. Payment of earlier liabilities or expenses
5. An attachment of earnings order
6. Variation of any pre-marriage or post-marriage settlement
7. The transfer of the family home and contents into your name or that of a dependent child
8. Payment of arrears of mortgage or rent
9. Restrictions on the disposal of any property
10. The right to live in the family home without your spouse
11. Sale of the family home and division of the proceeds
12. Division of ownership of the family home
13. The right to sell the family home without your spouse's consent
14. The transfer into your name of any other property
15. Sole or joint custody of dependent children
16. Access to dependent children
17. A written social report in relation to the children
18. A safety, protection or barring order
19. An insurance policy to provide for you and any dependent children
20. A pension adjustment order
21. The preservation of your pension rights as a spouse
22. The extinction of your spouse's succession rights

CHAPTER SIX

Civil Partnership and Unmarried Couples

Introduction

Although this book deals mainly with the breakdown of relationships of married couples, since 2010 the state has recognised the civil partnership of same-sex couples and the duties of cohabitants to each other, so the law regarding relationship breakdown now also relates to couples who are not married to each other.

So-called 'common law marriage' was formerly not recognised in Ireland and unmarried couples could not generally claim the benefit of marital legislation. But now couples who live together for a specified length of time qualify as 'cohabitants' and can avail of many of the same reliefs as married couples.

Civil partnership for same-sex couples in Ireland was introduced by the Civil Partnership and Certain Rights and Obligations of Cohabitants Act 2010.

The legislation also made major changes to the rights and duties of cohabitants, formerly known as 'common law spouses'. Previously, when a relationship between cohabitants broke up, the parties were thrown back on the civil law when seeking many remedies. Now all that has changed.

In 2012, just 429 civil partnership ceremonies were carried out, compared to 20,694 weddings, therefore it will be a while before there is a body of case law which deals with all the issues relating to civil partnership, cohabitation and possibly 'marriage' (and break-up) between same-sex couples.

Since the start of 2011, the 2010 Act has allowed same-sex couples to register their relationships and have a ceremony like a marriage. Registered relationships in 33 other jurisdictions were recognised in Ireland by the Civil Partnership (Recognition of Registered Foreign Relationships) Orders 2010 and 2011.

Forbidden Partnerships

As with marriage, civil partnerships may not be within certain degrees of relationship. Forbidden relationships include relationships of the half-blood (for example a sibling includes a half-brother or half-sister), and all the relationships and former relationships include those by adoption.

A man may not enter a civil partnership with his:

- Grandfather or grandson;
- Grandparent's brother;
- Father or son;
- Father's or mother's brother;
- Brother;
- Nephew or grandnephew.

A woman may not have a civil partnership with her:

- Grandmother or granddaughter;
- Grandparent's sister;
- Mother or daughter;
- Mother's or father's sister;
- Sister;
- Niece or grandniece.

Anyone who registers a civil partnership under the Act obtains rights similar to those of married couples, including property and succession rights and joint treatment for pension purposes.

While tax and social welfare benefits for civil partners are nearly the same as for married couples, a civil partner can't apply for guardianship, adoption, maintenance, custody or access of children under a registered relationship. Only natural parents and opposite-sex couples have comprehensive rights and obligations in relation to children.

Civil partners can seek orders under maintenance and domestic violence legislation if the relationship breaks down. Civil partners may also formally end their relationship by dissolution after living apart for two of the previous three years—less than the separation requirements for divorcing spouses.

Proceedings

If a civil partner institutes legal proceedings against the other, under the Rules of the Superior Courts (Civil Partnership and Cohabitation) 2011, proceedings must be commenced by a civil partnership special summons if seeking:

a)   an order declaring the status of a civil partnership;
b)   a declaration that a conveyance is void;
c)   an order dispensing with the consent of a civil partner to dispose of an interest in a shared home;
d)   an order relating to the conduct of a civil partner that might lead to the loss of an interest in the shared home or make it unsuitable for habitation;
e)   a maintenance order;

f)   deciding a question about the title to, or possession of, property;
g)   a decree of nullity;
h)   a decree of dissolution;
i)   an order for provision out of the estate of a deceased civil partner;
j)   an order directing the sale of property;
k)   an order setting aside a disposition; and
l)   orders under the Partition Acts 1868 and 1876.

A notice of motion is required to begin civil partnership law proceedings relating to:

a)   an order making a written agreement for maintenance or other payments or disposition of property a rule of court; or
b)   an application by the personal representative of a deceased civil partner for permission to distribute the estate.

An application under (a) must be based on the affidavits of both civil partners, exhibiting the agreement. Both civil partners must verify that they have taken, or had an opportunity to take, independent legal advice.

If civil partners apply for a dissolution of their partnership, they must swear an affidavit which includes:

a)   the date and place of the civil partnership registration;
b)   the length of time the parties have lived apart and the address of both partners during that time, if known;
c)   the civil partners' ages, the length of their partnership and how long they lived together after the partnership registration;
d)   any physical or mental disability of either partner;
e)   details of any children of either partner (or children whom either partner is obliged to support), stating what provision has been made for them;
f)   whether there is any possibility of a reconciliation and, if so, on what basis;
g)   details of any previous partnership relief and any separation agreement (certified copies of any court orders or agreements should be exhibited);
h)   details of any previous matrimonial or family law relief obtained by either partner (and a certified copy of any court order or agreement);

i)   the domicile of each partner at the start of the proceedings, or where each partner has been ordinarily resident for the year before the application;

j)   details of the shared home(s) or other residences of each partner, including, if relevant, the occupation and ownership of any former shared homes;

k)   a description of any land or premises referred to, and whether it is registered or not;

l)   anything else relevant to 'proper provision'.

The forms and details about how to make other civil partnership applications—such as a decree of nullity, declaration of civil partnership status, property issues, provision out of the estate of a deceased civil partner or relief under the Partition Acts—are set out in statutory instruments numbers 348 of 2011 and 385 of 2011.[1]

An affidavit of means must be served with the verifying affidavit grounding the proceedings, after which either partner can ask the other to vouch the items in the affidavit within 21 days. If they fail to do so, the court can grant an order for discovery or adjourn the proceeding until the request is complied with.

Applications are made by notice of motion for orders relating to:

a)   conduct leading to the loss of a shared home;

b)   restrictions on the disposal of household goods;

c)   discharge or variation of a maintenance or earnings order;

d)   interim or secured maintenance orders;

e)   payment of maintenance through the District Court;

f)   an attachment of earnings order (and decision whether payments are earnings);

g)   a safety, barring, interim barring or protection order;

h)   conduct or removal of goods pending a dissolution application; and

i)   maintenance or lump sum payments pending a dissolution application.

---

[1] SI No 348 of 2011, Rules of the Superior Courts (Civil Partnerships and Cohabitation) 2011 *Irish Statute Book;* available from http://www.irishstatutebook.ie/2011/en/si/0348.html and SI No 385 of 2011, Circuit Court Rules (Civil Partnerships and Cohabitation) 2011 *Irish Statute Book;* available from http://www.irishstatutebook.ie/2011/en/si/0385.html.

After a decree of dissolution, any application for these reliefs is also by notice of motion:

a) an order to make or secure maintenance or lump sum payments, or an attachment of earnings order;
b) a property adjustment order;
c) the right to occupy the shared home, or an order for its sale;
d) a financial compensation order;
e) a pension adjustment order;
f) an order preventing either partner claiming from the estate of a deceased former partner; and
g) discharge or variation of various other orders under s 131(1) of the 2010 Act.

Any application under s 131 must be supported by an affidavit setting out how and when circumstances have changed or why the court should vary or discharge the order.

Either partner may, at any stage, ask the court for directions relating to:

a) dependent children of either partner whose welfare might be affected by the proceedings;
b) the sale of any property in which anyone else may have an interest;
c) an order which will affect the rules of a pension scheme; or
d) an application for provision out of the estate of a deceased civil partner.

An application for a redress order must made within two years of the end of the relationship, unless there are exceptional circumstances. Unlike a marriage, where the waiting period is four years, a civil partnership may be dissolved after two years.

Same-sex or opposite-sex adults who are not married or related and haven't registered a civil partnership but have been living together in an "intimate and committed" relationship (for at least two years if they have children and five years if they don't) can also apply to court for certain orders.[2]

---

[2] Civil Partnership and Certain Rights and Obligations of Cohabitants Act 2010, Part 15.

In *RC v Minister for Health & Children*,[3] Mrs Justice Mary Irvine said that the 2010 Act dealt with property rights, so it required more qualifying criteria than just living together in a committed relationship for any length of time.

Part 2 of the 2010 Act allows the courts to make declarations on the status of a civil partnership. It also empowers the Minister for Justice to decide what categories of relationship contracted in other jurisdictions will be treated as equivalent to civil partnership under Irish law.

For civil partners who are not Irish citizens, statutory instrument 569 of 2011 introduced a fee of €175 for all applications for a certificate of naturalisation, as well as changes to forms.

Registration

Extensive amendments to the Civil Registration Act 2004 are made by Part 3 of the 2010 Act, providing detailed arrangements for civil partnership registration. These include notice and information requirements, declarations, venues and the effects of civil partnership.

Three months' notice of an intended registration is required unless, for example, one of the parties is very ill, in which case a court exemption may be obtained. Registration takes place at the office of a registrar or another venue approved by the HSE, and a registration ceremony may be conducted if the couple so desire. The minimum age for civil partnership is 18.

Shared Home

Part 4 of the Act provides protection for the shared home of registered civil partners and prevents the sale of the home by one partner without the other's consent.

Maintenance

Under Part 5, a civil partner may apply to the court for maintenance from the other partner during the relationship where that partner has failed to

---

[3] [2012] IEHC 204.

maintain the applicant. An attachment of earnings order may be made under Part 6 to secure payment under a maintenance order.

Part 7 specifies that payments under maintenance orders are made without deduction of income tax, provides that certain property will be jointly held and says that any agreement which precludes the payment of maintenance by either civil partner will be unenforceable.

Succession

Succession by civil partners is dealt with by part 8, including legal right shares under the Succession Act 1965. Where there is a will, a civil partner is entitled to half of the estate if the deceased has no children, and one third of the estate if the deceased has children. An order for provision for a child from the estate of a person in a civil partnership may reduce the share of the estate available for the other civil partner. In an intestacy, the rules of distribution for civil partners operate in the same way as for spouses.

Domestic Violence

Civil partners have the same protections as spouses under the Domestic Violence Act 1996, according to Part 9.

Pensions

A pension scheme which provides a benefit for a spouse is also deemed to provide a benefit for a civil partner under Part 10.

Nullity and Dissolution

Decrees of nullity of civil partnership and the effect of a decree of nullity are dealt with by Part 11 of the Act. The grounds for nullity are that there was an impediment to the civil partnership at the time of its registration (such as one or both of the parties being under age), or one or both of the parties not having given informed consent.

Part 12 allows the dissolution of civil partnerships and sets out the effect of a decree of dissolution. To obtain a decree of dissolution, the partners must have lived apart for at least two of the previous three years, and proper provision must be made for both partners. The Circuit Court and the High Court have jurisdiction to dissolve civil partnerships and provide extensive ancillary relief, including financial, property and pension orders.

Civil partnership proceedings are heard *in camera* under Part 13, and are as informal as possible. The District Court has jurisdiction in domestic violence cases and in certain property disputes and maintenance matters.

Part 14 provides for amendments to other acts, including the Family Law Act 1995 and the Family Law (Divorce) Act 1996. These ensure that any ancillary relief granted to a former spouse who registers as a civil partner will lapse, just as it currently does on remarriage. The schedule to the Act confers certain property rights, rights of redress and other rights and responsibilities on civil partners following registration.

Unmarried Couples

Whether or not an unmarried opposite-sex or same-sex couple qualify as cohabitants depends on:

- the length of the relationship;
- the basis on which the couple live together;
- the degree to which the couple present themselves to others as a couple;
- each person's degree of financial dependence;
- any contributions made to acquiring property or other assets;
- whether there are dependent children; and
- whether one of the adults cares for and supports the children of the other.

Cohabitants, whether of the same sex or the opposite sex, must live together in an 'intimate and committed relationship' and must not be in a functioning marriage or an existing civil partnership. However, the Act does not define the meaning of 'intimate and committed relationship', 'living together' or 'financially dependent'.

Cohabitants who are married to someone else must have been living apart from their spouse for four of the previous five years, although they need not be divorced.

Qualified Cohabitants

The 2010 Act defines 'qualified cohabitants' as adults, same-sex or opposite-sex, who are not married to each other, not registered as civil partners (but could be) and living together in an intimate and committed relationship for at least five years, or two years if they have a child together. Note, an 'intimate' relationship is not necessarily a sexual one.

Rights of Cohabitants

Cohabitants do not have the same rights as married couples or civil partners, but they do have rights in relation to property, children, inheritance, maintenance and access to fertility services. A cohabitant whose relationship has broken down can apply for a redress order, usually within two years of the end of a relationship.

The court will take into account the financial needs and obligations of the cohabitants, the rights of former spouses, civil partners or dependants, the length and nature of the relationship and the financial and other contribution of each cohabitant to the relationship. Cohabitants can apply for orders relating to maintenance, property, pensions, attachment of earnings and provision to be made from the estate of a deceased cohabitant.

Cohabitants can also make voluntary financial agreements, where each cohabitant has had legal advice, or waived the right to seek legal advice. The agreement constitutes a contract when it has been signed by both individuals.

Under s 202 of the Civil Partnership Act, a 'cohabitants' agreement' may be drawn up to regulate their joint financial and property affairs. The cohabitants must each receive independent legal advice before entering into the agreement, or receive legal advice together and waive the right to independent legal advice in writing. The agreement must be in writing and signed by both cohabitants, and comply with the general law of contract. This option was not available to married couples at the time of writing.

A cohabitants' agreement may provide that neither cohabitant may apply for an order for redress, that is to say a compensatory maintenance order, a pension adjustment order or a property adjustment order. The court may vary or set aside a cohabitants' agreement only in exceptional circumstances where its enforceability would cause serious injustice.

It's not necessary to register a cohabitants' agreement; it will be considered by a court only if the relationship breaks up. There is no limit to the number of sequential agreements a person may make either with the same cohabitant or with a subsequent cohabitant.

The qualified cohabitants' redress scheme for unregistered or unmarried cohabiting couples is established by Part 15 of the 2010 Act. The scheme provides protection for an economically-dependent partner at the end of a long-term same-sex or opposite-sex relationship. It is available only to 'qualified' cohabitants, as defined by s 172 of the Act, and may be activated when the relationship ends, whether by break-up or death.

Relief available at the end of a cohabitant's relationship is at the court's discretion and includes compensatory maintenance and pension adjustment orders, property adjustment orders and provision from the estate of a deceased cohabitant.

Part 15 of the Act also extends certain statutory protections to cohabiting, unmarried, opposite-sex and unregistered same-sex couples. For example, the Residential Tenancies Act 2004 and the Civil Liability Act 1961 are amended so that they apply to same-sex couples, not just couples "living together as husband and wife".[4]

When making orders under the Act, the courts must take into account the rights of other people, particularly a spouse or former spouse, a civil partner or former civil partner.

The 2010 Act substantially changes the rules for unmarried couples. In *The State (Nicolaou) v An Bord Uchtála*,[5] Henchy J said:

> For the state to award equal constitutional protection to the family founded on marriage and the 'family' founded on an extramarital union would in effect be a disregard of the pledge which the state gives in Article 41 [of the Constitution] to guard with special care the institution of marriage.

---

[4] Civil Partnership and Certain Rights and Obligations of Cohabitants Act 2010, s 203 and s 204.
[5] [1966] IR 567.

That statement no longer applies in Irish law.

In the past, if an unmarried couple were to split up, even if they had children, there was no obligation on either person to support the former partner.

This was decided in the High Court case of *Bernadette Ennis v Colm Butterly*.[6] The couple were both married—but not to each other—and were separated when they met in 1984. The following year, they started to live together and bought a house in joint names. They agreed that when divorce was available in Ireland, they would seek a divorce from their current spouse and marry each other as soon as possible.

Ennis paid all the mortgage payments and household expenses, while Butterly gave her money for herself and her son. Butterly also paid his wife maintenance.

In 1993, Ennis learned that Butterly was occasionally living with his wife so she threw him out. Butterly begged her for forgiveness; he promised to marry her as soon as possible, gave her another engagement ring, asked her to live full-time at home, promised to pay all household outgoings, said she could have her own current account and access to his credit card account, said he would give her half of a IR£350,000 cheque, offered to make her a director of his company and promised he would be faithful to her.

In return, she agreed to marry him as soon as they were both free, and in the meantime she would give up work and stay at home full-time.

But in 1994, Ennis learned that Butterly was having an affair with another woman, and she told him to leave home. Butterly said he would still honour his financial commitments to her, but he failed to do so. Ennis claimed damages for breach of contract, as well as negligent and fraudulent misrepresentation.

The court said that the breach of contract related to an agreement to marry and an agreement to live together as man and wife until they could marry each other, in return for which Ennis had given up her business and lived as a full-time home-maker.

But Mr Justice Peter Kelly said that the Family Law Act 1981 abolished actions for breach of promise of marriage. In any case, Ennis and Butterly were each married to someone else. Even before the 1981 Act, their

---

[6] [1996] 1 IR 426.

agreement to marry each other would have been unenforceable as a matter of public policy.

Butterly said the proceedings were, in effect, a claim for "palimony" based on the decision of the Supreme Court of California in *Marvin v Marvin*[7] which said:

> The courts should enforce express contracts between non-marital partners, except to the extent that the contract is explicitly founded on the consideration of meretricious sexual services.

The High Court said it would not follow the US decision, but preferred the English case of *Windeler v Whitehall*,[8] in which the judge said:

> A husband has a legal obligation to support his wife, even if they are living apart. A man has no legal obligation to support his mistress, even if they are living together.

Kelly J said:

> Given the special place of marriage and the family under the Irish Constitution, it appears to me that the public policy of this state ordains that non-marital cohabitation does not and cannot have the same constitutional status as marriage.
>
> To permit an express cohabitation contract to be enforced would give it a similar status in law to a marriage contract...As a matter of public policy, such agreements cannot be enforced.
>
> Whether one calls it palimony or not, it is not capable of enforcement in this jurisdiction...If it is not a palimony claim, it is clearly an attempt to enforce a contract, the consideration for which is wifely services being rendered on the part of a mistress.

Such contracts are no longer so clearly unenforceable.

Children

The position regarding the children of unmarried couples also differs markedly from that of married couples. The offspring of an unmarried couple are now called 'non-marital children', rather than 'illegitimate'. They retain the same rights as marital children to the estates of both their parents—but unmarried fathers in Ireland have very limited rights to their children.

---

[7] 18 Cal 3d 660 (1976).
[8] [1990] 2 FLR 505.

First of all, an unmarried father may need to prove that he is the father of the children. Under the 1987 Status of Children Act, a court can order a blood test to confirm the parentage of a child. The 1987 Act also allows a child to seek a declaration by the Circuit Court that a person is his mother or father—even if the parent is dead.

In *JPD v MG*,[9] a man sought custody of two children, but his divorced wife said they weren't his and demanded a blood test. The High Court ordered a test on the basis that the importance of truth and justice outweighed the presumption of the children's legitimacy.

The husband appealed, claiming that the children's welfare was paramount and that he was presumed to be their guardian, as they were conceived within marriage. The Supreme Court unanimously agreed that the children's welfare should always be the primary concern and that a judge should use his discretion in ordering a blood test. But in this case, they said a test should be ordered, and they dismissed the appeal.

Where a couple are not married, the Supreme Court has ruled that the father has no automatic right to be guardian to his children.

The 1964 Guardianship of Infants Act requires the court to make the infant's welfare "the first and paramount consideration" in proceedings concerning the infant's custody, guardianship or upbringing, or the administration of any property belonging to, or held on trust for, an infant, or the application of the income of the property.

Adoption of Non-Marital Children

The Adoption Act 1952 permitted the adoption of a child born out of wedlock without the consent of the natural father or the right to be heard by the Adoption Board before an adoption order was made. The Supreme Court held in *The State (Nicolaou) v An Bord Uchtála*[10] that this did not discriminate against the natural father or infringe his constitutional rights. It held that the protection given to the family in Article 41 of the Constitution related only to the family based on marriage.

---

[9] [1991] 1 IR 47.
[10] *ibid.*

However, Irish law was changed following the judgment of the European Court of Human Rights in *Keegan v Ireland*.[11] The case was heard by the ECHR on 23 November 1993 and a decision given on 26 May 1994.

The court heard that Joseph Keegan had met 'V' in May 1986. They lived together from February 1987 and on Valentine's Day 1988 they became engaged.

On 22 February 1988, V confirmed that she was pregnant. Shortly afterwards, they split up. On 29 September 1988, V gave birth to a daughter of whom Keegan was the father. He saw the baby when it was one day old. Two weeks later, he visited V's parents' home but was not allowed to see either V or the child. During her pregnancy V had arranged to have the child adopted and in November 1988 the child was placed with prospective adopters.

Keegan subsequently instituted Circuit Court proceedings to be appointed guardian which would have allowed him to challenge the proposed adoption. He also applied for custody of the child. In May 1989, the Circuit Court appointed Keegan guardian and awarded him custody.

Following an appeal by V and the prospective adopters, the High Court ruled in July 1989 that Keegan was a fit person to be appointed guardian and that the welfare of the child did not require the denial of this right.

V and the prospective adopters then asked the judge to state a case to the Supreme Court. On 1 December 1989, former Chief Justice Tom Finlay stated that the High Court had incorrectly construed s 6A of the 1964 Act as conferring on the natural father a right to be a guardian. An unmarried father had "no constitutional right to guardianship". The Act gave him only a right to *apply* to be guardian, and his position could not be equated with that of a married father.[12]

The Chief Justice said the court's first and paramount consideration was the welfare of the child, and the blood link between child and father was merely one of "many relevant factors".

---

[11] 18 EHRR 342 1994.
[12] *JK v VW* [1990] 2 IR 437.

Finlay CJ said the extent of the rights of an unmarried father varied "very greatly indeed", ranging from a child

> conceived as the result of a casual intercourse, where the rights might well be so minimal as practically to be non-existent, to the situation of a child born as the result of a stable and established relationship and nurtured at the commencement of his life by his father and mother in a situation bearing nearly all of the characteristics of a constitutionally-protected family, when the rights would be very extensive indeed.

The Supreme Court said it was up to the judge to decide what was best for the welfare of the children. The matter was referred back to the High Court and, in his judgment of February 1990, Mr Justice Barron, in light of what was said to be a danger to the child's psychological health, allowed the appeal of the natural mother and the prospective adopters.

Keegan complained that there had been a violation of his right to respect for family life under Article 8 of the European Convention on Human Rights as his child had been placed for adoption without his knowledge or consent, and Irish law did not give him a right to be appointed guardian. He complained that he had no standing in the proceedings before the Adoption Board and, as the natural father, he had been discriminated against in the exercise of his rights compared to the position of a married father.

The ECHR said the idea of the 'family' was not confined solely to marriage-based relationships and could include other *de facto* family ties where the parties were living together outside marriage (see *Johnston and Others v Ireland*[13] and *Berrehab v the Netherlands*[14]). The court said that "from the moment of the child's birth, there existed between the applicant and his daughter a bond amounting to family life".

The judges said that Irish law ought to have given Keegan

> a defeasible right to guardianship and, in any competition for custody with strangers, there ought to have existed a rebuttable legal presumption that the child's welfare was best served by being in his care and custody.

---

[13] 18 December 1986.
[14] 21 June 1988.

But the Irish government said this could "give rise to complications, anguish and hardship in other cases".

The ECHR said that, where a family tie with a child had been established, the state must

> act in a manner calculated to enable that tie to be developed, and legal safeguards must be created that render possible, as from the moment of birth, the child's integration in his family.[15]

It said that the

> mutual enjoyment by parent and child of each other's company constitutes a fundamental element of family life, even when the relationship between the parents has broken down.[16]

The court unanimously held that the Irish government had violated Article 8 and Article 6.1 of the European human rights convention. It awarded Keegan IR£10,000 damages for his "trauma, anxiety and feelings of injustice", IR£42,863 in legal costs and expenses, less 52,000 French francs already paid for fees and expenses, and reimbursed IR£2,000 Keegan had paid towards his legal aid.

Under the Guardianship of Infants Act 1964, the mother of an illegitimate child is its guardian. Before 1987, the natural father only had a right to make an application for custody and access. He had no right to apply to be appointed guardian. Today, if both parents agree, they may swear a statutory declaration father for the father to become a joint guardian. If the mother does not agree to this, the father may apply to the court under the Status of Children Act 1987 to be made a guardian.

In *WO'R v EH and the Adoption Board*,[17] the couple had been involved in a relationship from 1981 to 1992 and had two children. They lived together as a family for the last six years of their relationship and considered getting married.

But 11 months after the birth of their son, they separated permanently. The mother married another man in 1993 and she and her husband applied to the Adoption Board to adopt the two children.

---

[15] *Marckx v Belgium*, 13 June 1979.
[16] *Eriksson v Sweden*, 22 June 1989.
[17] [1996] IESC 4.

The natural father applied to the District Court to be appointed guardian of the children but was refused, though he was granted access to his children. The Adoption Board said it would not make any adoption order until the access order had been removed.

An adoption order may not normally be made without the consent of the child's mother or guardian. Under the Adoption Act 1952, the mother or guardian of a child lose all parental rights and duties if an adoption order is made.

The natural father said he would oppose the adoption order if he were appointed guardian, though he did not intend to seek custody of the children. Section 16 of the Adoption Act 2010 now gives the natural father the right to be consulted in the adoption process.

An unmarried father may also be unable to prevent the adoption of his child by someone else, even when he is living with the child's mother. In *CM v Delegación Provincial de Malaga and AB and CD*,[18] CM had been born in Spain in 1995 and had been adopted there by AB and CD, through the agency of the Delegación Provincial.

C's mother, OM, was an Irish citizen, resident and domiciled in Ireland, and was unmarried. C's father, PH, was three years older and married with one child, but his marriage had broken down.

In 1995, after the mother went to Spain to work, she realised she was pregnant. PH joined her there and the baby girl was born in Malaga. The couple looked after the baby for about seven weeks, but eventually gave her up for adoption.

OM then moved back to Ireland and set up house with PH. In April 1996, she and PH went to the Spanish embassy in Dublin and asked to have C returned to them. In September 1996, OM instructed Spanish lawyers to apply to the courts in Spain for the return of her child.

In 1998, the Malaga court refused the parents' application for access to C and said that the adoption should be dealt with under Spanish law. The court also decided that both parents should be deprived of guardianship of their child, on the grounds that they had abandoned her.

---

[18] [1999] 2 IR 363.

OM appealed and applied to the Irish courts for an order requiring the return of C under the Hague Convention and Child Abduction and Enforcement of Custody Orders Act, 1991.

The High Court accepted that, even when a child was not in Ireland, it still had power to declare that the removal from the state of a child who was an Irish citizen was wrongful, though it could only do this if the child's "habitual residence" was Ireland.

The court said a person, whether a child or an adult, must have been actually present in a country for at least some reasonable period of time before he or she could be habitually resident there. In this case, the child had never even been to Ireland.

The judge said the adoption acts specifically permitted the adoption of a child of unmarried parents and the father had no constitutional rights in regard to the child.

The position of the parents was a "sad one," said the judge, but if they wanted to pursue their claim for the return of the child, they would have to do so in the Spanish courts.

But although the child's welfare must be paramount, that is not the sole consideration, otherwise the Oireachtas would have said so.[19] Sometimes, for example, "the mother's happiness and wellbeing is also of importance for the wellbeing of the children" so the welfare of the children may be best served with them all remaining with the mother as their primary carer.[20]

In *GS v PS*,[21] Abbott J said:

> It has been long the practice of the courts to deal with infants' claims and minor matters with the utmost urgency. While this practice does not have statutory backing as it might have in other jurisdictions and in Scotland, for instance (except abduction cases), it has foundations in statute and, indeed, in the Constitution arising from the obligation of the courts to give paramount consideration to the interests of children in relation to issues where they are concerned.

---

[19] *G v An Bord Uchtála* [1980] IR 32.
[20] *B v O'R* [2009] IEHC 247.
[21] [2011] IEHC 122.

However, the difference in treatment between married and unmarried fathers has been found to be compatible with the European Convention on Human Rights.[22]

Changing Views

The views of judges in Ireland and Europe seem to be changing. In *Johnston and Others v Ireland*,[23] the European Court of Human Rights said that Article 8 of the European Convention on Human Rights applied to the 'family life' of the 'illegitimate' family, as well as to that of the 'legitimate' family. In *Lebbink v The Netherlands*,[24] the court reaffirmed that a 'family' may include a non-marital *de facto* family, though "mere biological kinship without more" should not be regarded as coming within the definition of a 'family'.

As Murphy J said in *WOR v EH*[25]:

> For better or for worse, it is clearly the fact that long-term relationships having many of the characteristics of a family based on marriage have become commonplace. Relationships which would have been the cause of grave embarrassment a generation ago are now widely accepted.

McKechnie J agreed.

> What about a person who fathers a child within an established relationship and who, from the moment of birth, nurtures, protects and safeguards his child—sometimes to a standard which all too frequently married fathers fail to live up to... Should there not be a greater recognition of the type of father whom I mention? At a minimum should there not be a means readily available so that such a father, whose children had been removed without forewarning or knowledge, can assert and vindicate his rights? I strongly believe that there should be.[26]

---

[22] *B v UK* [2000] 1 FLR 1 and *Re W: Re B* [1998] 2 FLR 146.
[23] (1987) 9 EHRR 203.
[24] (2005) 40 EHRR 18.
[25] [1996] 2 IR 248.
[26] *GT v KAO* [2007] IEHC 326.

CHILDREN

Introduction

One of the most heartrending aspects of relationship breakdown can be the effect on children. The parents may hate the sight of one another, but both may love their children and want to have custody—living with the children and having the day-to-day control of them.

As one clinical psychologist said in *I v I*[1]:

> There is empirical evidence that divorce or separation *per se* does not have a negative effect on children, but that most of the negative outcomes can be linked to the level of discord between the parents pre-separation and post-separation.

---

[1] [2011] IEHC 411.

The judge agreed. Abbot J said that parents' "constant dragging up of past wrongdoings in the face of continuing actual access" was often "acquired and learned behaviour" caused by the failure of courts and lawyers to deal with actual or perceived wrongs at an early stage.

One parent may wish to deny any access, or contact with the children, to the other parent, but the courts will seldom agree to this, so it is often best to try and work out matters relating to children without a court hearing.

Of the 168 Circuit Court cases relating to children in 2006, 142 were settled. Of the remainder, sole custody was granted to the mother in nine cases, with the father receiving sole custody in three cases.[2]

In *AB v CD*,[3] for instance, a father was granted custody and primary care of his son in a "fraught and highly contested case" where a mother, with a "grudging and highly litigious attitude" made unsubstantiated allegations of violence against the father.

Article 7 of the United Nations Convention on the Rights of the Child says that a child has, as far as possible, the right to be cared for by his or her parents. Yet often in separation and divorce proceedings, "parents seem locked in a power struggle with the other, using the child as a weapon and trophy while ignoring his or her needs".[4]

If a couple separate, the court will always make orders relating to the children, including orders for custody and access. While young children will often be left with their mother; fathers have a right and duty to see their children regularly and to help with their upbringing.

In *LC v Judge Hugh O'Donnell & anor*,[5] Miss Justice Iseult O'Malley said:

> Family law cases—particularly where the interests of children are concerned—are rarely directly analogous to other forms of litigation. A particular feature is that the case will, in general, take the form of a sequence or process of hearings, adjournments and interim orders, leading to a final order or orders, rather than one unitary hearing.

---

[2] Carol Coulter, *Family Law in Practice: A Study of Cases in the Circuit Court* (Clarus Press, Dublin, 2009).

[3] [2012] IEHC 543.

[4] Remarks by author Geoffrey Shannon at launch of Child Law (1st ed, Round Hall, Dublin, 2005), Dublin Castle, 14 March 2005.

[5] [2013] IEHC 268.

Of course, the children have the right to see both parents, and the parents should keep any promises they make to the children.

In *HP v FP*,[6] MacMenamin J said:

> Commitments made to children should be kept. If a commitment is made to take a child on some particular date or some particular occasion, it should not be varied or altered without very good reason. Alterations of this type undermine the relationship between the parent and the child.

Actions brought by institutions such as the courts and the Health Service Executive are required to have the child's best interests at heart so, in family law proceedings, a judge may appoint a guardian *ad litem* to give the child a voice in court. If the High Court refuses to appoint a guardian *ad litem* on appeal from a Circuit Court decision, either spouse may apply to the Circuit Court to do so.[7]

Section 28 of the Guardianship of Infants Act of 1964 allows the appointment of a guardian *ad litem* in family law cases where necessary in the child's best interests. However, s 11 of the Children's Act 1997, which inserted s 28 into the 1964 Act, will only come into operation by ministerial order, which had not been signed at the time of *JO'N v SMcD & ors*.[8] In that case, issues relating to custody and access had proved particularly difficult in "protracted and acrimonious" family law proceedings which had gone on for 13 years.

After a Circuit Court judge made an order—without jurisdiction—to appoint a guardian *ad litem*, the husband sued nine people, including his former wife, his wife's barrister and solicitor, the county registrar and a GP. But Birmingham J struck out the plaintiff's case as being "in every sense of the word vexatious" and an abuse of process.

In cases involving the welfare of children, a judge is generally bound to hear up-to-date evidence.[9] Sometimes a judge may order a report from a psychiatrist, psychologist or social worker, and reports from teachers, doctors or therapists may be used in the proceedings. But, as the judge

---

[6] [2010] IEHC 423.
[7] *LT v JT* [2012] IEHC 588.
[8] [2013] IEHC 135.
[9] *KA v Health Service Executive* [2012] IEHC 288.

said in *LD v TD*,[10] an expert such as a psychologist or psychiatrist should not act as a judge in resolving conflicts of fact; that was the sole prerogative of the court.

Welfare

The Guardianship of Infants Act 1964 was the first major piece of legislation in modern times to address the question of children's welfare after the breakdown of a relationship. The first principle of the Act was that the child's welfare should be the 'first and paramount' consideration.

In *G v An Bord Uchtála*,[11] the Chief Justice said a child had a right "to be fed and to live, to be reared and educated, to have the opportunity of working and of realising his or her full personality and dignity as a human being".

'Welfare' is defined as the child's "religious, moral, intellectual, physical and social" welfare, but the word must be construed "in its widest sense". In *CC v PC*,[12] the Court said the child's welfare wasn't just a question of "totting up the marks which might be awarded under each of the five headings".

In assessing the welfare of a child, a court should consider factors including:

1) the biological parents;
2) the age of the child;
3) the relationships which the child has formed;
4) the situation in which he or she lives;
5) whether the child is born to a couple who have lived together in a settled relationship for years; and
6) any long-standing relationship with a parent.

Although emotional welfare is not expressly mentioned in the 1964 Act, it was recognised in *DFO'S v CA*.[13] A child's welfare may also be affected by a parent's "risky sexual activity".[14]

---

[10] Unreported, High Court, 9 November 1998.
[11] [1980] IR 32.
[12] [1994] 3 Fam LJ.
[13] Unreported, High Court, 20 April 1999.
[14] *P v Q* [2012] IEHC 531.

Normally, a child's religious welfare would be safeguarded by ensuring that the person who had custody of the child was of the same faith. But in *Cullen v Cullen*,[15] the Court accepted that a woman who had lapsed from the practice of her religion would ensure that her son would be taught religion and say his prayers.

In the past, the moral welfare of a child required that he should not be brought up in an adulterous relationship. In *JW v BW*,[16] the court awarded custody to a father because the mother was living in an adulterous relationship with a man who had deserted his own wife and children. The Chief Justice said a "more unhealthy abode for the three children would be hard to imagine".

Conversely, in *JC v OC*,[17] the President of the High Court refused a father custody because he was in an adulterous relationship and the children were sufficiently well-educated by the mother.

In *MacD v MacD*,[18] the President of the High Court granted custody to the father because he said the wife was an adulteress. The Supreme Court, by a two to one majority, said the children's welfare (rather than the parents' behaviour) was the first concern.

But in *S v S*,[19] the Chief Justice said that the conduct of parents was only relevant insofar as affected the welfare of the child. In the case of *G v An Bord Uchtála*,[20] the judge said that, while the welfare of the child was to be "paramount", it was not the sole consideration.

Chief Justice Tom Finlay in *JK v VW*[21] said that the:

> blood link between the infant and the father, and the possibility for the infant to have the benefit of the guardianship by, and the society of, its father is one of many factors which may be viewed by the Court as relevant to its welfare.

---

[15] [1962] IR 268.
[16] (1971) 110 ILTR 45.
[17] Unreported, High Court, 10 July 1980.
[18] (1979) 114 ILTR 60.
[19] [1992] 12 ILRM 732.
[20] [1980] IR 32.
[21] [1990] 2 IR 437.

Finlay's successor, Chief Justice Liam Hamilton, agreed in *WO'R v EH*[22] that the basic issue for the judge was the welfare of the children. He said the blood link alone, along with negative factors, was "of small weight". But where the children were born in a "stable and established relationship", nurtured by father and mother in a *de facto* family, then the natural father had "extensive rights of interest and concern". But these were subordinate to the paramount concern, which was the welfare of the children.

Non-Marital Children

But what if the father is not just single, but a sperm donor too? In *JMcD v PL & BM*,[23] JMcD, a homosexual, was the father of a boy conceived by artificial insemination with a lesbian in 2006.

The donor agreement specified that the child would know his biological father, but that the child would remain with the lesbian couple, with JMcD acting as his "favourite uncle".

But relations between the couple and JMcD deteriorated after the birth when the father tried to play a bigger role in his son's upbringing. In March 2007, JMcD obtained an interim *ex parte* High Court order preventing the lesbian couple from taking the child to Australia (though they were later allowed to go to Australia for 15 days) and a s 47 report was ordered.

The High Court judge ruled that sperm donor agreements might constitute a valid contract, but were enforceable only as long as the rights of any child born as a result were not prejudiced.

He said that the child's welfare had to be the "first and paramount consideration" in guardianship, access and custody matters. He held that, where a lesbian couple lived together in a long-term, committed relationship which would be regarded as a *de facto* family if they were heterosexuals, they should be regarded as a *de facto* family.

The integrity of this family would be "seriously, and even possibly fatally, broken by any order of guardianship or access to the father".

---

[22] [1996] 2 IR 248.
[23] [2009] IESC 81.

He refused the application for guardianship, joint custody and access to the child.

However, in the Supreme Court, Denham J granted the father's appeal and gave him access to the child. She did not make an order of guardianship, although that issue might be "re-addressed in changed circumstances".

She said that the High Court judge had erred in deciding that a s 47 report on the child should be given great weight or its conclusions accepted as mandatory. "The Court is the decision-maker," she said, and had to consider what was in the child's best interests.

She also said the High Court judge erred in his analysis of the family under Irish law. "Throughout our case law, the family is defined as the family based on marriage," she said. Under the terms of the Constitution, "family" meant "a family based on marriage, the marriage of a man and a woman".

The same analysis will apply to circumstances where same-sex couples live together. "Circumstances in which a child is living a settled life, and has a relationship with those with whom he lives, are critical factors," said Denham J.

Custody and Access

Custody and access are not the same thing. The parent or parents with whom the children live permanently is said to have custody. If the court does not award both parents joint custody, the other parent will normally have rights to see the children, which is known as access. Normally, where one parent has custody of the children, he or she will have the greater say in the children's upbringing. However, as MacMenamin J said in *V v U*:

> I do not think that the rights of children … can allow for a presumption in favour of a custodial parent, although the views of such parent are entitled to great weight.[24]

Where parents are separated, if custody cannot be agreed, then one parent will have to apply to court for custody. Generally the courts will try and keep brothers and sisters together.[25]

---

[24] [2011] IEHC 519.
[25] *FN v CO* [2004] 4 IR 311.

Any custody order will necessarily only be for the time being,

> because circumstances may change from time to time. The change
> of circumstances may be due to the current position of the parent
> or parents or the growing up of the child and the changes with the
> passage of time may bring about.[26]

Access involves the right of the child to see the non-custodial parent. Supervised access may be ordered if there are doubts about a parent's ability to care for the children, or if there are allegations of sexual abuse, drug addiction or alcoholism.

Grandparents may also apply to the District Court for access to their grandchildren. If they are the main carers for the children, they may apply to court for maintenance from the children's parents, may have child benefit and other social welfare benefits transferred to them and may also apply to become guardians if both parents die, or adopt the children if appropriate.

Delay

Under the Guardianship of Infants Act 1964, any submission to the court about the custody of a child must be by notice of motion issued "promptly", and anyway within three months of any notification.

In *Minister for Justice & Equality v MP & ors*,[27] a Polish child who had been habitually resident in Ireland moved back to Poland to live with his maternal grandparents. Neither the father nor the mother of the child objected within the required three months. The grandparents wrote to the Irish Court to say that it no longer had jurisdiction to make any decisions about the custody of the child.

A final order of non-return was made by a Polish District Court. On the application of the Minister for Justice as Central Authority, Finlay Geoghegan J closed the case and said the Irish courts would no longer have jurisdiction to decide any matter of parental responsibility about the child.

---

[26] *Per* Walsh J in *B v B* [1975] IR 54.
[27] [2013] IEHC 419.

A court's decision on custody can also be swayed by the age of the child. In *O'D v O'D*,[28] the judge said that children of "tender years" were better in a mother's custody.

Joint Custody

The 1997 Children Act allows a court to award custody jointly to the father and mother,[29] but Mrs Justice Catherine McGuinness said in *EP v CP*[30] that joint custody could not work satisfactorily if there was a high level of conflict between the parents, or where they could not work together sensible and happily in the interests of the children.

As Mr Justice Michael White said in *LD v CD*[31]:

> Joint custody and equal parental rights does not mean that the time with each individual parent is divided equally. Decisions should be made in the best interests of the children to provide a stable and secure environment for them and, because a court may order a particular regime which does not afford equal time, this does not undermine the concept of joint custody or parental equality.

It is possible for the court to grant joint custody to parents living in different countries, in this case, Ireland and Poland.[32]

Where there is joint custody, it is important that both parents observe the other's rights and consult the other parent with regard to any important decisions. In *CF v JDF*[33] a wife unilaterally changed the children's school from Wicklow to Kildare, despite having joint custody with the husband. She was ordered to forfeit €25,000 of a lump sum from her husband for contempt of court.

Sometimes, awarding custody to one parent can worsen the hostility between them. In the case of *DFO'S v CA*,[34] the judge awarded joint custody to two unmarried parents in the hope that caring for their child might help them put their antagonisms behind them.

---

[28] Unreported, High Court, July/August 1979.
[29] s 11(a) of the 1964 Act as inserted by s 9 of the Children Act 1997.
[30] Unreported, High Court, 27 November 1998.
[31] [2012] IEHC 582.
[32] *AOK v MK* [2005] IEHC 360.
[33] [2005] IESC 45.
[34] Unreported, High Court, 20 April 1999.

Where both parents obviously care about the welfare of their children, the views of both must be taken into account. In *BB v AA*,[35] Hogan J said that, where both parents had taken a responsible and conscientious attitude to the welfare of their children, both were entitled to have their views weighed fairly and equally by the court.

Access for Non-Custodians

A parent who is a guardian but does not have custody of a child is entitled to apply for access. Such an order may be varied at any time in the interests of the child. Even where a father might be violent (as in *AMacB v AMacB*[36]) or a potential abuser (as in *O'D v O'D*[37]), a court will try to ensure that children can continue to see that parent, although the access may be supervised.

The 1997 Children Act allows any relative of the child to apply to the court for access. The court will take into account the applicant's connection with the child, the risk of disruption to the child's life and the wishes of the child's guardians.

The court may make whatever order it considers proper in relation to guardianship, custody or maintenance of a child, and may order the father or mother to make 'reasonable payments'. The order can be made when the couple are living together, but then won't take effect unless they separate.

Guardianship

Guardianship gives a parent the right to be involved in the physical, religious, intellectual, social and moral upbringing of a child, including the right to be involved in major issues such as the child's religion, education, country of residence and other major life events, such as medical treatment, passport applications and the right to apply to court for custody or access. A guardian's consent is also required if the mother wants to put the child up for adoption, even by her subsequent husband.

The 1964 Act gave married parents, even if they themselves are under 18, joint guardianship of their children and allowed the court to appoint a

---

[35] [2013] IEHC 394.
[36] Unreported, High Court, 6 June 1984.
[37] [1994] 3 Fam LJ 81.

guardian if necessary. The legislation also provided for court orders on child maintenance, custody and access and for "fit person" orders. A guardian normally has the right to custody, unless a court decides otherwise.

The 1964 Guardianship of Infants Act was updated in 1987 by the Status of Children Act, which equalised the status of legitimate and illegitimate children. It also addressed the question of the rights and duties of single fathers.

The more important effects of the Act were to:

- abolish the concept of illegitimacy;
- allow a child born of a voidable marriage to retain its legitimate status;
- give unmarried fathers legal rights to be appointed guardian or to seek custody and/or access;
- allow payments of birth and funeral expenses to the mother by the father;
- amend the Maintenance Act to allow payments by a father;
- allow a father (or child) to apply for a declaration of paternity;
- provide for blood tests to prove paternity; and
- allow a presumption of paternity where a baby was born in a subsisting marriage within 10 months, or if the father's name was on the birth register.

In the case of unmarried parents, the mother is the guardian of her children, not an unmarried father, civil partner or cohabitant, even if their name is on the child's birth certificate. However, the Law Reform Commission report on family relationships recommends that unmarried fathers should automatically become guardians of their children, unless it is not in the best interests of the child. An unmarried mother already has natural rights to the custody and care of her child under Article 40.3 of the Constitution.[38]

If the mother does not agree to an unmarried father becoming a guardian, he will have to apply to court. In 2010, there was a 12 percent increase in

---

[38] *MOC v Sacred Heart Adoption Society* [1996] 1 ILRM 297.

court applications for guardianship of children. Most of the applications were from unmarried fathers and the figures show that, of the 2,783 applications, only 68 were refused.[39]

An unmarried father can also become a guardian if he marries the mother of the child or the mother agrees and they sign a joint declaration (available at http://irishbarrister.com/guardian.html). The declaration must be signed in front of a peace commissioner or commissioner for oaths. If the couple have more than one child, they should make a separate statutory declaration for each child.

However, this piece of paper is the only evidence of guardianship. In *ERO'B v Minister for Justice*[40] in October 2009, Mr Justice O'Neill said that, while it "may very well be the case that the introduction of a public register for guardianship agreements would be a desirable social reform", the absence of such a register was "a matter solely for the executive and the Oireachtas" and did not breach the child's rights under the Irish Constitution or European Convention.

Of the 9,000 calls received in 2009 by the Treoir National Information Centre, one in five were concerned with guardianship. Yet, by 2014, the government had still not provided for a guardianship register.

Even if parents behave badly towards one another, they still have a natural, statutory and constitutional right to be the guardians of their own children. In *Western Health Board v An Bord Uchtála*,[41] a husband sought custody of his natural child. He had been separated from his wife, who was having an affair with another man. The husband forced his wife to have intercourse in 1988 and she became pregnant. Although she believed her lover was the child's father, she registered her husband as the father on the birth certificate and gave her daughter up for adoption.

The husband refused to consent to the adoption and, two years later, agreed to a blood test which proved he was the child's father. In 1992, when the child had been with its adoptive parents for more than three years, the father brought proceedings for custody of the child.

---

[39] Courts Service Annual Report 2011.
[40] [2009] IEHC 423.
[41] [1995] 3 IR 178.

The Supreme Court refused to confirm the adoption order and said that, just because a parent had failed in his duty to his child and that failure was likely to continue until the child was 18, did not mean that he had abandoned all his parental rights.

But the court said that its refusal to allow the child to be adopted did not affect the issue of custody, where the child's welfare had to be the paramount consideration.

Joint Guardianship

Fathers can be removed as joint guardians of a child if a court believes that is in the child's best interests, whereas a mother can only give up her guardianship rights if the child is adopted.

Where the parents have joint guardianship, any issue affected the children's welfare may be brought to the attention of the court by either parent. In *BB v AA*,[42] the separated parents had joint guardianship of their two children, but could not agree whether their 12-year-old son should go to a state school or a fee-paying private school.

The two children lived with their mother, but had frequent access to their father. The dispute about boy's schooling arose during judicial separation proceedings in the Circuit Court.

The choice was between a State school with a high level of academic achievement, or a private school where the fees were considerable. The judge said the boy was "anxious" to attend the private school and his preference "must carry considerable weight, even if his views could not in the end be in any sense dispositive".

The father said the family could not afford private education. The mother said the family should not pass up the opportunity of the private school, which had agreed to charge only half fees, with the balance being paid by the mother's parents. The father said these commitments were "vague and indefinite" and he objected to his son's school fees being paid by other family members. He was also worried that his son might be "socially isolated" mixing with the children of richer families.

---

[42] [2013] IEHC 394.

On appeal to the High Court, Hogan J said this was a "difficult and troubling question on which there is little, if any, contemporary judicial authority".

Citing *The State (Doyle) v Minister for Education*,[43] Hogan J said the Court had no jurisdiction to make a final and indefinite order about a child's education, and any order must allow for a change in circumstances or a change of heart by one or other parent.

The judge said that, given the boy's scholastic aptitude, he should go to a school best suited for his talents. He allowed the appeal on condition that the private school waived half its fees and the balance was paid by the mother's parents.

Guardians, whether married or not, should appoint a 'testamentary guardian' by their will to act if they die suddenly.[44] If a guardian is single, the child's surviving guardian (if there is one) will act jointly with the new guardian.

In the case of same-sex couples, a partner may not apply to become a joint guardian of a child or to adopt a child, even if one of them is the birth parent of the child.

Abduction

Occasionally a parent who loses custody may decide to breach the court order by removing a child from the jurisdiction. In 2012, the Central Authority for International Child Abduction dealt with 276 cases, of which 147 were new cases, five more than in 2011.

Of the new cases involving 192 children, 64 were concerned with children coming into the state from other countries, while 83 concerned applications relating to children being taken out of the state.

Of the new applications received by the Irish Central Authority, 68 (46 percent) involved the United Kingdom, 14 (10 percent) involved Poland, 12 (8 percent) involved Latvia, 36 (24 percent) involved other

---

[43] [1989] ILRM 277.
[44] *FN and EB v CO and Others* [2004] 4 IR 311.

European countries and 17 (12 percent) other contracting States (such as USA, Canada, Australia and South Africa).

The Irish Central Authority was set up following the passing of the Child Abduction and Enforcement of Custody Orders Act 1991. This Act gave the force of law to the 1980 Hague Convention on the Civil Aspects of International Child Abduction (the Hague Convention) which aimed to facilitate the return of children under 16 who had been abducted from one contracting state to another against the wishes of a parent. If a child is over the age of 16, the High Court may not order the child's return.[45]

The Central Authority also operates under Council Regulation (EC) number 2201/2003 concerning Jurisdiction and the Recognition and Enforcement of Judgments in Matrimonial Matters and in Matters of Parental Responsibility (Brussels II *bis*) and the 1996 Hague Convention on Jurisdiction, Applicable Law, Recognition, Enforcement and Co-operation in Respect of Parental Responsibility and Measures for the Protection of Children (the 1996 Hague Convention). This Regulation and the 1996 Hague Convention strengthen the provisions of the 1980 Hague Convention.

The purpose of the convention was spelled out by an English judge in *P v P (Minors) Child Abduction*[46], cited by Keane J in *W v Ireland*[47]:

> The whole jurisdiction under the Convention is, by its nature and purpose, peremptory. Its underlying assumption is that the courts of all its signatory countries are equally capable of ensuring a fair hearing to the parties and a skilled and humane evaluation of the issues of child welfare involved. Its underlying purpose is to ensure stability for children, by putting a brisk end to the efforts of parents to have their children's future decided where they want and when they want, by removing them from their country of residence to another jurisdiction chosen arbitrarily by the absconding parent.

The Child Abduction and Enforcement of Custody Orders Act 1991 allowed courts in other countries to enforce custody orders made here, and vice versa.

---

[45] *Minister for Justice v CD* [2013] IEHC 114.
[46] [1992] 1 FLR 155.
[47] [1994] ILRM 126.

The Act includes two schedules: the Hague Convention, dealing with breach of the custody rights which are currently being exercised, and the Luxembourg Convention, dealing with improper removal of children across an international frontier, including failure to return a child after access. For EU countries (except Denmark), these conventions were replaced by the Brussels II *bis* Regulation, but the Hague and Luxembourg Conventions still apply to cases outside the EU.

The Hague Convention applies to children under 16 outside the EU who normally lived in the contracting state before the breach. The Convention:

- established custody rights;
- set up a central authority in each State;
- required the immediate co-operation of the central authority;
- set a one-year time limit for any initial request (though late applications were not debarred);
- allowed the court to refuse to return children if their human rights or fundamental freedoms would be affected; and
- allowed a derogation if
  1) the applicant was not exercising custody rights;
  2) the applicant had agreed to the removal;
  3) there would be a grave risk of physical or psychological harm to the child;[48] or
  4) the child objected.

'Psychological harm' refers only to serious psychological harm.[49]

'Custody rights' may be the rights of one of the parents or of a court. In *H v MG*,[50] an American father, who was not married to the mother, had no rights of custody under the laws of New York because he had not obtained a declaration of paternity. An order from the New York Court did not require the mother to obtain either the father's consent or the court's approval to remove her child from the jurisdiction.

However, as McKechnie J said in *GT v KAO*, even when a parent has no custody rights but where he has instituted court proceedings, the removal

---

[48] *E (Children)* [2011] UKSC 84.
[49] *AS v EH* [1999] 4 IR 504.
[50] [2000] 1 IR 110.

of the child without lawful excuse while the proceedings are still pending would be wrongful. "[i]n such circumstances the breach would not be that of the father's rights, but rather of the Court's rights."[51]

Denham J said in *AS v PS*[52] that the object of the Hague Convention was not to decide where the child's best interests lay, but to ensure that the child was returned to the country of habitual residence for his future to be decided by the authorities there.

And in *CPC-PL v EC*,[53] Fennelly J said a court was not entitled to refuse to make a return order based on general considerations about the child's welfare. "It is, naturally, implicit in this policy that our courts must place trust in the fairness and justice of the courts of the other country," he said.

The Luxembourg Convention defines 'child' as a person under 16 of any nationality. The main differences between the two Conventions are:

- the Hague Convention does not require a prior court order;
- the Luxembourg Convention covers breach of access;
- the time limits; and
- the reasons for refusal to return a child are discretionary in the Hague Convention, but technical in the Luxembourg Convention.

However, in the English case of *Re B: (Minors: Abduction) (No 2)*,[54] the judge said that, if Hague Convention proceedings were to be dealt with

> fairly and expeditiously, there must be an element of peremptoriness in the Court's approach to their hearing. Time does not allow for more than a quick impression gained on a panoramic view of the evidence.

The Child Abduction and Enforcement of Custody Orders Act 1991:

- set up a Central Authority;
- gave the court interim powers;
- allowed the court to refuse to return a child; and
- increased garda powers.

---

[51] [2007] IEHC 326.
[52] [1998] IR 244.
[53] [2009] 1 IR 18.
[54] [1993] 1 FLR 993.

The Act came into force on 1 October 1991 and deals only with wrongful retention after that date.

In *LR v DR*,[55] an Irish woman had decided not to return to her American husband in the USA with their two children in 1991. The husband was granted custody in the USA the following year. The Irish Department of Justice said the convention dealt with wrongful retention only after October 1991, but the Irish Court said it had jurisdiction, as the children were within the state. Their welfare required that they stay with the mother and that took precedence over the convention.

However, in *FL v CL*,[56] the High Court said that it would not engage in the "type of wider welfare inquiry" in a child abduction case that it would in a dispute between parents about custody or residence.

In *J v R*,[57] the daughter of an unmarried English couple had been made a ward of court in England in 1990. The mother brought the child to Ireland in 1992 and the father applied for her return. The mother claimed that the child was of "tender years" and her religious welfare would be affected by her return, as the father wasn't a Catholic. But the Chief Justice said an unmarried father also had rights under the 1987 Act, and the Luxembourg Convention provided for unqualified enforcement of child custody orders. He ordered the mother to take the child back to England.

But unmarried fathers may not always have the same rights as married fathers under the Hague Convention. In *HI v MG*,[58] the Supreme Court said:

> It is clear...that the rights of unmarried fathers under the [Hague] Convention present particular difficulties, given the unique relationship of the natural father to his children and the fact that, in a number of jurisdictions, including our own, they do not have any automatic rights to custody equivalent to those of married parents.
>
> However, the appropriate method of addressing difficulties of that nature which may arise in the operation of conventions on private international law is through the machinery of special commissions in The Hague which regularly monitor and review the operation

---

[55] [1993] 2 Fam LJ 41.
[56] [2006] IEHC 66.
[57] Unreported, Supreme Court, 1993.
[58] [2000] 1 IR 110.

of conventions in the contracting states, rather than by innovative judicial responses to admittedly difficult cases in which upholding the convention as enacted may give rise to what seems a harsh or inequitable result.

Habitual Residence

Article 3 of the Hague Convention provides that the removal or the retention of a child is wrongful where:

a) it is in breach of custody rights under the law of the state of the child's habitual residence; and

b) at the time of removal or retention, those rights were actually being exercised.

In *AS v CS*,[59] the Supreme Court rejected an appeal by the Irish mother of an 18-month-old girl against a High Court ruling that she had to return the child to the country of the Australian father.

In the High Court, MacMenamin J had found that the child's habitual residence was New South Wales, and the mother had unlawfully retained the child in breach of the father's custody rights.

The child was born in Australia, and the couple were entitled to joint custody under Australian law. They later came on holiday to Ireland and lived under the same roof for no more than three weeks before separating, with the father going back to Australia. The mother argued that she and the child were 'habitually resident' in Ireland.

The High Court judge referred to *AS v MS*[60] which cited *CM v Delegación de Malaga*[61] in which McGuinness J had stated that 'habitual residence' was not a "term of art", but a matter of fact, to be decided on the evidence.

The habitual residence of the child was not governed by the same "rigid rules of dependency as apply under the law of domicile" and a person must be actually present in a country for some reasonable period before becoming habitually resident there.

---

[59] [2009] IESC 77.
[60] [2008] 2 IR 341.
[61] [1999] 2 IR 363.

The judge found that the father was prepared to "give it a go" in Ireland, but never abandoned his long-term intention to reside in Australia, so the child was not habitually resident in Ireland.

In the Supreme Court, Macken J said there was a

> difference between acquiring habitual or ordinary residence, which permits a stay of comparatively short time, and domicile, which requires an intention to remain there indefinitely.

She said the absence of a settled purpose "may lead to a child being left with no clear habitual residence". The requirement to establish a settled intention by the parents to acquire a habitual residence was essential to guard against such uncertainty.

She cited with approval the English judgment in *Re B: (Minors: Abduction) (No 2)*,[62] in which the judge had said:

> Domicile and habitual residence are essentially different concepts. The acquisition of a domicile of choice requires a combination of residence and intention of permanent or indefinite residence...

> A far more wide-ranging inquiry is needed to establish those elements than is appropriate or necessary when the Court is dealing with a much simpler concept of habitual residence. That is a concept which depends solely upon showing a settled purpose continued for an appreciable time...A settled purpose is not something to be searched for under a microscope. If it is there at all, it will stand out clearly as a matter of general impression.

In *PAS v AFS*,[63] Fennelly J agreed that habitual residence was

> perfectly obvious in the great majority of cases. It is an obvious fact that a new-born child is incapable of making its own choices as to residence or anything else. What the courts have to look at is the situation of the parents and their choices. Where the child has, for a substantial period, been resident in one country with both its parents, while they are in a stable relationship, particularly if they are of the same nationality, the answer will usually be fairly obvious.

The judgment in *Re B: (Minors: Abduction) (No 2)*[64] established that:

---

[62] [1993] 1 FLR 993.
[63] [2005] I ILRM 306.
[64] *ibid.*

1) The habitual residence of young children of parents who are living together is the same as the habitual residence of the parents themselves, and neither parent can change it without the express or tacit consent of the other or a court order.

2) Habitual residence, in the context of married parents living together, refers to the abode in a particular country which they have adopted voluntarily and for settled purposes as part of the regular order of their life for the time being, whether of short or long duration.

3) A 'settled purpose' means that the parents' shared intentions in living where they do should have sufficient continuity.

4) Although habitual residence can be lost in a single day, the assumption of habitual residence requires an appreciable period of time and a settled intention, though the period of habitation need not be long, provided the purpose is settled.

As the Irish courts confirmed, a person cannot become habitually resident in another country in a single day. "An appreciable period of time and a settled intention will be necessary to enable him or her to do so."[65]

In *Mark v Mark*,[66] the judge stated that habitual residence and ordinary residence were interchangeable concepts and in *Re P-J (Children)*,[67] the English Court of Appeal accepted that there was "no difference in the core meaning to be given to the two phrases".

Best Interests of the Child

Even when the child's best interests may be served by remaining in Ireland, the courts here may order the child's return to another jurisdiction. In *PSS v JAS*,[68] an Irish woman, who was divorcing her American husband, brought their young daughter to Ireland in breach of a ruling by the Los Angeles Superior Court. The husband asked the Irish High Court to order the return of the child.

In the High Court, Budd J said that, although he believed it would be in the child's best interests to stay with her mother and grandparents in Ireland, the Hague Convention required that the girl be returned to California. The judge didn't believe this would expose the child to physical

---

[65] See *ZSA v ST*, unreported, High Court, August 1996.
[66] [2006] 1 AC 98.
[67] [2009] EWCA 588.
[68] [1992] 1 ILRM 732.

or psychological harm and he ordered that the husband should pay for his wife to take the child back to America, where she would remain in the mother's custody pending the outcome of the Californian court case.

The following day, the mother handed the child over to the father, in defiance of the High Court order. The judge then ordered that the child should stay with her paternal grandmother in America pending the order of the Californian Court.

While the best interests of the child are also the 'primary consideration' in English law, in the case of *W v W*,[69] Singer J refused to accept that an Irish court order to return three children to Ireland could be disobeyed by a father on welfare grounds.

> There is no basis upon which recognition of this order made after consideration of detailed evidence on express welfare principles, and after a lengthy hearing, could possibly be considered to be contrary to public policy. On the contrary, its non-recognition would be contrary to public policy,

He said.

If there are disputed and unverifiable allegations of violence or abuse, the UK Supreme Court has said the authorities should focus on protective measures to reduce the risk, rather than refuse to return the child.[70] The court said that the best interests of children consisted of being reunited with their parent as soon as possible so that the other parent did not gain an unfair advantage due to the passage of time, and being brought up in a sound environment where they were not at risk of harm.

A court may also make an order for a child's return, but put a stay on the order pending an application to the courts of the other country by the abducting parent or arrangements have been made for the children.[71] A judge may also order the return of children subject to undertakings about conduct, welfare and support.[72]

---

[69] [2005] EWHC 1811 (Fam).
[70] *E (Children)* [2011] UKSC 84.
[71] *SR v SR* [2008] IEHC 162; *MN v RN* [2009] IEHC 213; *CA v CA (orse CMcC)* [2010] 2 IR 162; and *MM v RR* [2012] IEHC 450.
[72] *RT v SM* [2008] IEHC 212.

The constitutionality of the 1991 Act was challenged in *Wadda v Ireland*.[73] In that case, the wife, who was an Irish citizen, married a Moroccan. They lived in the UK and had one daughter. When the marriage broke down, the wife returned to Ireland with her daughter and began proceedings to be appointed sole guardian of the child. The husband asked the Irish courts to order the return of the girl to the UK.

The Irish judge agreed that the husband was entitled to an order returning the child, but he deferred the implementation of the decision while the mother challenged the constitutionality of the Act.

The wife said the Act unconstitutionally deprived her of the right of custody and access, displaced the jurisdiction of the Irish courts and failed to protect the rights of the family.

The judge said Article 20 of the Hague Convention gave the Irish courts jurisdiction to refuse to return the child unless her human rights and fundamental freedoms were protected, and this included the rights in Articles 40 to 44 of the Irish Constitution.

But the judge said that, where the courts were asked to return a child to a country which was not a signatory to the Convention, such as in the case of *LR v DR*,[74] it *could* first inquire into the welfare of the children.

If a court makes a custody order for a child, any application relating to the abduction of that child must be made to the same court. In *C v B*,[75] an unmarried couple living in Ireland had a baby girl. Two months later, the mother took the child to live in England. The father applied for and was granted custody of the child by Castlebar District Court.

The High Court ordered the return of the child under the Luxembourg Convention and the mother appealed. The Supreme Court said that, since the District Court had made the custody order, it should also have made the order under the 1991 Act. The High Court had no jurisdiction to do so.

Even where one parent is awarded custody, both parents remain joint guardians and are entitled to a say in the upbringing of the children.

---

[73] [1994] 1 ILRM 126.
[74] *ibid.*
[75] Unreported, Supreme Court, 1995.

Unsatisfactory access arrangements may be improved by further application to the court, but judges will look very disapprovingly on a parent who takes the law into his own hands by breaching a custody order. Almost invariably, the children will be traced and returned to the original parent, and the offending spouse may find himself further restricted in his access to the children.

Removal of Marital Children

The child of married parents may not be removed from Ireland by one parent, as both parents are entitled to custody under Irish law, unless a court makes an order to the contrary.

The factors which a court should consider where one parent applies to the court for permission to remove a child from the jurisdiction were set out by Flood J in *EM v AM*.[76] The court must consider:

- which outcome will provide the more stable lifestyle for the child;
- the stability of the child's future environment, particularly the influence of his extended family;
- professional advice;
- whether the non-custodial parent can have access, and how often;
- the record of each parent's relationship with the child as it affects the child's welfare; and
- the parties' likely future obedience to court orders.

In *HI v MG*,[77] the Supreme Court said:

Married parents are entitled to the custody of the children without any court order or formal legal agreement to that effect, and the removal by one parent of the child or children to another jurisdiction without the consent of the other will clearly constitute a wrongful removal... unless the rights were not being actually exercised at the time of the removal.

Even where the parent, or some other person or body concerned with the care of the child, is not entitled to custody, whether by operation of law, judicial or administrative decision or an agreement having legal effect, but there are proceedings in being to which he or it is a

[76] Unreported, High Court, 16 June 1992.
[77] [2000] 1 IR 110, cited by Keane CJ in *WPP v SRW* [2000] IESC 11.

party and he or it has sought the custody of the child, the removal of the child to another jurisdiction while the proceedings are pending would, absent any legally excusing circumstances, be wrongful in terms of the convention.

If children are taken without a guardian's permission to one of the 90 countries which are signatories of the 1980 Hague Convention or the 1996 Hague Convention, the guardian can seek their immediate return under Irish law.

The Supreme Court has ruled that the onus of proving consent to the removal rests on the person asserting such consent, and has to be proved according to the civil standard of 'the balance of probabilities'. The evidence in support of consent has to be clear and cogent, and the consent must be real, positive and unequivocal, but there is no need for the agreement to be in writing or that the child expressly stated 'I consent'.[78]

'Grave Risk'

The child won't be returned if the courts decide that he would be at grave risk of harm, that he would be exposed to physical or psychological harm or otherwise placed in an intolerable situation,[79] or if the child objects to being returned and is old and mature enough for the court to take account of his views.

According to Barron J in *RK v JK*,[80] a "grave risk of harm" exists only when the return of the child puts him in immediate imminent danger, such as returning him to a zone of war, famine or disease, or in cases of serious abuse or neglect or extraordinary emotional dependence, when the court in the other country might be incapable or unwilling to give the child adequate protection.

In *RP v SD*,[81] the unmarried mother of a five-year-old girl who was in breach of English High Court order, said there was a 'grave risk' if the child was returned because the child's father was a drug dealer and he would seriously harm or try to kill her. But White J said the fitness of

---

[78] *SR v MMR* [2006] IESC 7.
[79] *AS v PS* [1998] 2 IR 244; *RK v JK* [2000] 2 IR 416; and *SR v MMR* [2006] IESC 7.
[80] [2000] 2 IR 416.
[81] [2012] IEHC 579.

either parent to have custody and access was a matter for the English courts.

Finlay Geoghegan J said in *IP v TP*[82] that any claim of grave risk must be proved on the balance of probabilities, and the burden of proof normally lay with the person who oppose the child's return.

She said that 'intolerable' meant a situation which a particular child in particular circumstances should not be expected to tolerate, such as physical or psychological abuse or neglect. But discomfort and distress were almost inevitable for a child whose parents were in dispute.

In *G v R*,[83] Peart J said 'intolerable' meant 'unbearable' or "other than what the child should reasonably be expected to endure".

The Child's Opinion

In *SJO'D v PCO'D*,[84] Abbott J set out the considerations a court might take into account when deciding whether to talk to children informally in chambers:

1) The judge must be clear about the legislative or forensic frame-work in which he is talking to the children, as different codes may require (or only permit) different approaches.
2) The judge should never seek to act as an expert and should only reach conclusions which are justified by common sense or the judge's own experience.
3) To ensure a fair trial and natural justice, the terms of reference should be agreed with the parties before relying on the record of the meeting.
4) The judge should explain that *he* has to resolve issues between the parents, and should reassure the children that they are not taking on the task of judging the case.
5) He should assure the children that, while their wishes may be taken into account, the court's ultimate decision will not solely (or even necessarily) depend on those wishes.

---

[82] [2012] IEHC 31.
[83] [2012] IEHC 16.
[84] Unreported, High Court, 26 May 2008.

6) The judge should explain in simple terms how the practice of asking children for their opinion has developed in recent times.

7) At an early stage, the judge should decide whether the children are old enough and mature enough to be heard. If the parents don't agree about this, the judge may ask for a s 47 report.

8) The judge should avoid a situation where the children speak in confidence, unless the parents agree.

In *MN v RN*,[85] Mrs Justice Mary Finlay Geoghegan held that a court had a "mandatory positive obligation" to give a child a chance to be heard, except where this appears "inappropriate having regard to his or her age or degree of maturity".[86]

"The starting point is that the child should be heard," she said. "The court is only relieved of the obligation where it is established that it would be inappropriate for the reasons stated."

The views of a six-year-old child may be heard,[87] though it may be inappropriate to inquire into the views of a child under the age of six, depending on the circumstances.[88] In *RP v SD*,[89] the mother sought an order under Article 11(2) of Council Regulation (EC) 2201/2003 seeking to have a five-year-old child interviewed by a child psychologist. But Finlay Geoghegan J said that the child was

> not of an age where, as a matter of probability, she is capable of forming her own views in relation to everyday matters of potential relevance to the issues.

Even where boys aged eight and nine—who had lived with their mother in Ireland for two years—said they wanted to stay with their mother, the court made an order for their return to England.[90]

In *AS v CS*,[91] Macken J said:

---

[85] [2008] IEHC 382.
[86] *R v R* [2007] IEHC 423.
[87] *MN v RN* [2009] IEHC 213.
[88] *ABu v JBe* (Child Abduction) [2010] 3 IR 740.
[89] [2012] IEHC 579.
[90] *MM v RR* [2012] IEHC 450.
[91] [2009] IESC 77.

It is not possible for very small children to explain or give any indication of their views as to where they may wish to reside, or with whom. The older a child grows, the more facility there is to take into account the views of such a child.

In *MKD v KWD*,[92] a "highly intelligent and academically bright" 12-year-old boy objected to returning to his father in Poland, but Finlay Geoghegan J said the court must exercise its discretion

in accordance with the policy and principles of the Convention and having regard to the overall facts of the case, in the best interests of the children.

In *GW v EB*,[93] Miss Justice Elizabeth Dunne said that the views of a 14-year-old boy were "independently informed" and the Court could take into account his objection to returning to his live with his father, despite the mother's "clear breach" of a US court order.

And in *P v P*,[94] the Court was told that a 15-year-old girl was capable of forming and articulating her own views. Mrs Justice Mary Finlay Geoghegan said it was appropriate to take account of her objection to returning to Poland, though "the weight to be attached to those objections in the exercise of the Court's discretion is a separate matter".

In *HP v FP*,[95] MacMenamin J interviewed the daughter of the couple concerned in the presence of the registrar and counsel on both sides. He ordered that she should see her father, but not while his partner was present.

In *FN v EB*,[96] Finlay Geogheghan J said it was "well established" that individuals had a right to constitutional justice when any important decision was to be taken about them. She said that s 25 of the 1964 Act gave children of a certain age and understanding the right to have their wishes taken into account when a court made a decision about their guardianship, custody or upbringing.

---

[92] [2012] IEHC 378.
[93] [2012] IEHC 213.
[94] [2012] IEHC 31.
[95] [2010] IEHC 423.
[96] [2004] 4 IR 311.

In *JE v DE*,[97] where a husband sought unsupervised access to his two children, counsel for the wife was asked to ascertain the views of the children, aged 13 and nine. He said that the most recent views of the children, in the last year, were that neither child wanted unsupervised access with their father. Sheehan J held that the children had been "adequately heard".

Neither parent can exercise a veto on a child's right to be heard and, where one parent objects to a judge interviewing a child, as in *V v U*,[98] "a judge could not and must not be precluded from interviewing children when they are of an appropriate age".

However, the child's views do not mean that the court has to abide by his wishes. In *ZD v KD*,[99] MacMenamin J stated that "the views of the child are not synonymous with an obligation to bow to the child's wishes". In *LJ v VN*,[100] the High Court ordered the return of a nine-year-old boy to the Czech Republic, even though he said he would prefer to stay with his father in Ireland.

In *AU v TNU*,[101] Denham CJ cited the decision of Baroness Hale in *Re M (Abduction: Zimbabwe)*[102] that,

> the older the child, the greater the weight that her objections are likely to carry. But that is far from saying that the child's objections should only prevail in the most exceptional circumstances.

The Supreme Court dismissed an appeal against a High Court ruling that two children should not be returned to their habitual residence in New York. Although the High Court judge ruled that their removal was wrongful and there was no defence of grave risk, the children had reached an age and degree of maturity where their views could be taken into account, and they objected to being returned.

Where a child objects to being returned, Finlay Geoghegan J said the court should conduct a threefold test:

---

[97] [2013] IEHC 379.
[98] [2011] IEHC 519.
[99] [2008] 4 IR 751.
[100] [2012] IEHC 307.
[101] [2011] IESC 39.
[102] [2008] 1 AC 1288.

- whether the child's objections had been made out;
- whether the child is old enough and mature enough for the court to take account of his objections; and
- whether the court should exercise its discretion in favour of retention or return.[103]

In *V v U*,[104] the judge said the relationship of two boys with both parents was "a very strong consideration" in his decision not to allow their Spanish mother take them back to Spain to live.

Although the courts do their best to uphold children's rights, in the final analysis legislation is a matter for government, not the courts. The Supreme Court has regularly held that the state is responsible for upholding and ensuring children's rights, including health, education, welfare and citizenship.[105]

Adoption

A number of people are entitled to be consulted about any prospective adoption, or the adoption order may be set aside by the courts. Section 43 of the Adoption Act 2010 lists the people who are entitled to be heard by the Adoption Authority:

- the applicant;
- the child;
- the child's mother;
- the child's father (or person who believes himself to be the father);
- the child's guardian;
- the person who had control of the child immediately before the adoption;
- the child's relatives;
- a representative of an accredited body or the HSE which has been concerned with the child;

---

[103] *CA v CA (orse CMcC)* [2010] 2 IR 162.
[104] [2011] IEHC 519.
[105] See *North Western Health Board v HW & CW* (the PKU case) [2001] 3 IR 635; *Sinnott v Minister for Education and others* (free education for mentally-disabled man) [2001] IESC 63; *TD v Minister for Education and others* (education for troubled youngsters, in which Murray J said judges could not substitute a "judicial imperative" for executive policy) [2001] IESC 101 and *Lobe and Osayande v Minister for Justice* (residency rights) [2002] IESC 109/02.

- an employee of the authority; and
- anyone else the authority decides to hear.

In *S v The Adoption Board*,[106] the natural father of S sought an order quashing the adoption of his daughter, born in January 2001. He said the Adoption Board should have notified him about the application to have his child adopted by the child's mother and her husband.

The father had been charged with assault after trying to strangle the mother during an argument. He agreed to leave the family home, but later set it on fire. After being charged with arson, he absconded to England in May 2004.

The mother married another man in October 2005, and they applied to adopt S the following month. She said she and the child would be placed in great danger if the father was contacted about the application to adopt the child.

The father said he only learned of the adoption order when he made an access application to the District Court in November 2007. He said the mother was "well aware" that he had returned to Ireland before the adoption was finalised, but never told the social worker or the Adoption Board.

The registrar of the Adoption Board said the father was not consulted because the board did not know his exact address, and he had behaved in such a way towards the natural mother that it would be "inappropriate for the board to consult with him".

Mr Justice Iarfhlaith O'Neill, in his 21,000-word judgment, said the child's welfare must be "the first and paramount consideration". The Adoption Board could make an adoption order without consulting the father if,

> having regard to the nature of the relationship between the father and the mother or the circumstances of the conception of the child, it would be inappropriate for the Board to consult the father.

---

[106] [2009] IEHC 429.

He cited a number of judgments of the European Court of Human Rights. In the case of *Eski v Austria*,[107] a natural father challenged the decision of the Austrian courts to allow his former partner's husband to adopt his daughter without his consent. However, as the father was aware of the application and had been invited to take part in the proceedings, the court held that the interference with his Article 8 rights was proportionate.

In the cases of *Soderback v Sweden*[108] and *Kuijper v The Netherlands*,[109] the court noted that the natural parent did not have custody of the child, and contacts were very limited.

O'Neill J said that, according to the ECHR, there was an obligation to inform the natural father of a child about a proposed adoption unless the circumstances of the conception or the nature of the relationship between the child's father and mother

> were of such extreme or exceptional kind as to have either severed the Article 8 [ECHR] family tie or to have been a proportionate response in the light of the circumstances.

He added:

> When considering the circumstances of conception, clearly what the Oireachteas had in mind was a distinction between conception as a result of rape, or an isolated casual encounter or some other incident of sexual contact which right-thinking people would readily recognise as failing to confer on the natural father any of the normal rights of paternity. In clear contradistinction is the conception of a child out of a normal relationship between the father and the mother.

He said a short relationship between the father and child would be good grounds for withholding notification to the natural father. But where there had been a relationship of significant duration between the mother and the father, the Adoption Board must be careful not to punish the father for what may have been his ill-treatment of the mother.

The board must also use great care to ensure its decision was not driven solely by the threat of violence. "The making of an adoption order without

---

[107] [2007] 1 FLR 1650.
[108] (2000) 29 EHRR 95.
[109] (2005) 41 EHRR SE 16.

consulting a natural father would, in all probability, be more likely to exacerbate a potentially violent situation," said the judge.

If the board did not have the father's address, it had a "mandatory duty" to take reasonably practicable steps to find out where he was living.

O'Neill J said excluding the natural father from the adoption process on the basis of information supplied by the mother could result in a "very serious injustice being done to the natural father and, by extension, the child".

In this case, he said the natural father was entitled to be consulted. He declared the adoption order invalid and remitted the application to the Adoption Board to consult the father.

An Bord Uchtála was replaced by the Adoption Authority of Ireland as the central authority for adoptions by the Adoption Act 2010. The Act, which repealed the Adoption Acts 1952-1998, also gave the force of law to the 1993 Hague Convention on Protection of Children and Co-operation in Intercountry Adoption, and provided for the making and recognition of intercountry adoptions and certain adoptions outside the state. The Act was passed followed the decision in *EL & anor v An Bord Uchtála*[110] in which Sheehan J awarded damages against the board for its failure to explain to a Sligo couple why the board was warning against adoptions from Ethiopia or Rwanda.

Referendum on Children's Rights

A constitutional referendum on children's rights was held in November 2012. Although voters approved the proposal by 615,731 votes to 445,863, the amendment had not been signed into law at the time of writing because of a High Court challenge. If the court rejects the challenge, the Constitution will be amended by repealing Article 42.5 and inserting a new Article 42A.

The Thirty-First Amendment of the Constitution (Children) Bill 2012 proposes that Article 42A should say:

---

[110] [2007] IEHC 402.

a) in exceptional cases, where the safety or welfare of children is likely to be 'prejudicially affected', the State will try and replace the parents 'by proportionate means as provided by law';

b) children may be adopted where their parents have failed in their duty towards them and the best interests of the children require it;

c) children can be voluntarily placed for adoption;

d) in all proceedings concerning children, their best interests will be 'the paramount consideration';

e) in all proceedings concerning children, as far as practicable, any child who is capable of forming his own views shall have his views 'ascertained and given due weight, having regard to the age and maturity of the child'.

Maintenance

Introduction

Both parents have a legal responsibility to maintain their children. Where parents are separated, maintenance is usually paid either by a lump sum or a regular weekly or monthly payment.

Maintenance is not calculated according to a precise formula. In *PH v FD*,[1] Irvine J said: "The issue of maintenance is not a mathematical exercise." The cost of feeding and clothing children and catering to their needs obviously grows as they get older.

Under the 1976 Family Law (Maintenance of Spouses and Children) Act, maintenance—or 'periodic payments'—can be reviewed in accordance with needs and other changes of circumstance. In *HP v FP*,[2] the husband had just lost his job when the case was heard by the Circuit Court. In the High Court, MacMenamin J ordered the husband to pay maintenance of €30 a week from his €196 social welfare, plus half his redundancy payment. The judge also ordered the husband to transfer his interest in the family home to the wife.

In *ES v DS*,[3] White J said there was "no reality" in another judge's order of €50,000 a year maintenance for a wife and €800 a month for the children. He varied the maintenance to a total of €2,400 a month.

---

[1] [2011] IEHC 233.
[2] [2010] IEHC 423.
[3] [2012] IEHC 589, and earlier [2010] IEHC 474.

In *LC v Judge Hugh O'Donnell & anor*,[4] the father of two children who had not paid maintenance sought judicial review of a District Court order reducing the amount of maintenance payable for the children and refusing to vary an access order or deal with an alleged breach of access. The father complained that he was not allowed to give sworn testimony, despite his wish to be heard.

District Judge Hugh O'Donnell had ordered the father to pay €100 a week for each child or a lump sum of €10,000, as the father's solicitor had said the father had €30,000 available from the sale of a property. However, the father said that his solicitor had misunderstood him and he had no money.

When told that the father's only income was the Jobseeker's Allowance, the judge is alleged to have said: "[w]e all know he is working." He then allegedly said he would give the father five minutes and, if he did not make a proper proposal, he would be going straight to Mountjoy.

Miss Justice Iseult O'Malley said the proceedings had been before the District Court for eight years. The parents had joint custody of the two children, who lived with their mother. Maintenance for the children was an "ongoing source of contention". In 2011, the father was committed to prison for three days for contempt due to the build-up of maintenance arrears.

He claimed he had been unemployed since his business failed in 2007, but various District and Circuit Court judges who had dealt with the matter believed that he had a source of income which he was concealing from the court. He admitted that he had access to funds in an account in the name of an adult son. The mother claimed that he had spent money on foreign travel, living in a hotel and buying a car while he was not paying maintenance. The judge refused the reliefs sought.

Lump Sums

A lump sum payment order may not be varied. In *MD v EHD*,[5] a husband sought a review of part of a High Court order for payment of a lump sum of €75,000.

---

[4] [2013] IEHC 268.
[5] [2012] IEHC 580.

Under s 18 of the Family Law Act 1995 and s 22 of the Family Law (Divorce) Act, some orders can be reviewed if there is a change in circumstances or new evidence. But for a lump sum to be reviewed, it has to be an instalment order.

This interpretation of the law was approved by the Supreme Court in *DT v CT*.[6] Keane CJ said there could be no variation of the lump sum, even if circumstances changed, but the court could vary the payment of the sum by instalments. It was also not possible to order periodic maintenance, since the power of the court was confined to varying or discharging an order for periodic payments already made.

Applicants for the one-parent family payment have to seek maintenance from the other parent, if necessary by applying to court. But sometimes maintenance applications can take more than a year to be resolved by the court. One TD said that the system was now "in complete disarray, with many women and children living on the edge".[7] She said 175 cases had been adjourned by the family courts on just one day.

Generally, one parent (most frequently the mother) will have primary custody of the children and the other parent (generally the father) will pay maintenance and have regular access arrangements. Occasionally, parents may agree to joint custody, where the children spend equal time with each parent and this will affect the amount of maintenance payable, if any.

It is possible—especially in the case of a wife who earns more than her husband, or of joint custody of children—that a husband will seek maintenance from his wife. But the courts often maintain a traditional attitude to such applications.

In *LD v MA*,[8] the Circuit Court had granted a decree of judicial separation to two medical consultants. The wife had had an affair—though, on appeal to the High Court, White J said he would not take conduct into account.

The husband sought maintenance and a lump sum from the wife under the Family Law Act 1995. He said that he'd supported his wife in her career, so his earning capacity had been reduced. But the judge said the

[6] [2002] 3 IR 334.
[7] Mary Mitchell O'Connor in the Dáil, July 2012.
[8] [2012] IEHC 584.

wife was "generous to a fault" and the husband's maintenance application was "without merit".

The issue of maintenance is a separate matter from custody and access, so a person paying maintenance does not have an automatic right to custody, access or guardianship.

Maintenance may be awarded to a dependent spouse and to children under the age of 18, or up to the age of 23 if in full-time education. There is no age limit for maintenance for physically or mentally disabled dependants.

Awareness of Order

If maintenance is awarded for children—particularly if there is an attachment of earnings order—it is vital that the maintenance debtor ensures that the payments do not continue for longer than ordered.

In *McGrath v District Court Clerk & Anor*,[9] the applicant's employer wrongly deducted more than €40,000 from his salary in maintenance payments for his children. Galway District Court had ordered McGrath to pay IR£80 a week maintenance to his wife and IR£40 a week for their three children until they reached the age of 18 (which, for the eldest child, was six months after the order.) An attachment of earnings order was subsequently made because McGrath was not complying with the maintenance order.

The attachment of earnings order was sent to McGrath's employer, Telecom Eircom, but did not mention that the payments were to stop when the children reached the age of 18. Under s 18(2) of the Family Law (Maintenance of Spouses and Children) Act 1976, the clerk of the court should have informed the employer that the attachment of earnings notice had ceased as each child turned 18.

McGrath said he was unaware of the maintenance order, as he was working in the United Kingdom at the time and was not served with a summons. He said he had been paying his wife cash but, on finding out about the court orders, stopped doing so.

---

[9] [2008] IEHC 116.

By 2004, Eircom had wrongly paid out €40,022 for the children, but the company said it would continue to abide by the maintenance order, as it did not know when each child would turn 18.

In the District Court, the judge said she had no jurisdiction to vary a maintenance order which had expired. Subsequently, the District Court clerk successfully applied to have the attachment of earnings order varied.

But in the High Court, Peart J said that McGrath's lack of awareness of the details of the maintenance order was "irrelevant" to the issue of whether the District Court clerk should have notified Eircom as the three children reached the age of 18.

Although McGrath might have a potential claim against his wife for accepting money to which she was not entitled, the judge said it was not for the Court to decide whether such a claim existed.

He said McGrath "could have taken the reasonable step of making his own application to the District Court" to vary the attachment of earnings order. He was not entitled to damages as the District Court clerk had not acted in bad faith.

The upper limit for maintenance for a child in the District Court in 2014 was €150 a week, or €500 a week for a spouse or civil partner, with a maximum lump sum payment of €6,350. In the Circuit Court, the amount of maintenance is unlimited.

Maintenance may be paid by agreement, in which case there is no upper limit, or by court order. In *SD v ML*,[10] the judge said that an unmarried father had "always acted responsibly" by paying maintenance for his child, but payments should be made "in a more structured manner". He ordered the father to pay €450 a week maintenance for the child, rather than a wage from the father's company.

Remedies for Non-Payment

If there is a court order and maintenance is not paid, a spouse, parent or partner may go back to court and seek a remedy, including the jailing of

---

[10] [2012] IEHC 583.

the maintenance debtor. But under s 6(2)(b) of the Enforcement of Court Orders Act 1940, a summons for arrears of maintenance must include details of the consequences of failing to comply with an instalment order, particularly the possibility of imprisonment.

In *H v Governor of Wheatfield Prison & Anor*,[11] H was jailed for seven days for contempt after his wife claimed that he was €3,600 in arrears with his maintenance. The judge did not warn H that he was liable to be found in contempt or give him any real opportunity to pay the arrears.

The District Judge's "manifest non-compliance with the notice requirements" meant that he had no jurisdiction to impose a custodial sentence, said Hogan J in the High Court. However, s 31 of the Civil Law (Miscellaneous Provisions) Act 2011 amends the Family Law (Maintenance of Spouses and Children) Act 1976 by inserting a section which makes it contempt of court for a maintenance debtor to fail to make a payment under a court order. The legislation gives a District Judge the same powers as a High Court judge in contempt proceedings.

There may be a temptation to prevent children from having access to the defaulting parent, but the courts will not approve of this. It is the child's right to see the parent which is at stake, rather than the parent's right to see the child.

Evidence of Income

A judge will take into account the income of each parent and the needs of the children. Both parents should produce evidence of their income, assets, savings and expenditure.

The court may take account of capital assets when ordering payment of maintenance.[12] In a 2010 case stated from the Circuit Court in Roscommon, the Supreme Court ruled that a father-of-two was entitled to obtain details of a €200 a month award from the Residential Institutions Redress Board to the children's mother in a District Court maintenance appeal.[13]

---

[11] [2011] IEHC 492.
[12] *CP v DP* [1983] 3 ILRM 380; *RK v MK*, unreported, High Court, 24 October 1978; and *JD v DD* [1997] 3 IR 64.
[13] *FMcK v OL* [2010] IESC 51.

In *S v F*,[14] the court could not make a maintenance order as the husband was unemployed, so McGuinness J ordered that investment income from a trust should be paid to the wife as maintenance for the children.

As evidence of assets, bank statements, pay slips, credit card records, tax returns and expenses should be stapled together, summarised and vouched in date order. Maintenance payments may be linked to the consumer price index so that they increase each year in line with inflation.

In *BC v MC*,[15] Peart J said that, where a wife's earnings had been reduced through no fault of her own, she had tried unsuccessfully to get work and her husband could increase her maintenance "without any great difficulty", he should be required to do so. He ordered the husband to increase his ex-wife's maintenance by 50 percent to an index-linked €300 a week, plus pay her a lump sum of €35,000.

In *McE v O'S*,[16] the judge ruled that a mother was not entitled to a carer's allowance in addition to maintenance for her non-marital child, and that the Circuit Court had no jurisdiction under the Guardianship of Infants Act 1964 to order the father to pay a lump sum to provide a home for the mother and their child. The father was ordered to pay €1,200 a month maintenance plus half the expenses for the child's speech therapy.

Don't be tempted to try and hide assets. In *ES v DS*,[17] because the husband withheld information about his financial affairs from the High Court and Supreme Court, White J transferred the family home and three rental properties into the wife's sole name.

If there is an informal agreement for maintenance, evidence of past payments should be brought to court. If there is a change in financial circumstances for the parent who pays maintenance, that parent may seek a variation order and should produce evidence of the change, such as unemployment or sickness.

In family law matters, a judge can order payment of maintenance (or a lump sum) in the currency of the residence of either party.[18]

---

[14] Unreported, Circuit Court, 1995.
[15] [2012] IEHC 602.
[16] [2009] IEHC 52.
[17] [2012] IEHC 589.
[18] *GW v RW* [2003] 2 FLR 197 and *MK v JPK* [2006] IESC 4.

Tax relief is not available on maintenance paid for children, but is available to the payer on maintenance paid for a spouse or civil partner. The person receiving maintenance may be liable to pay tax on it.[19]

Enforcement of Maintenance

An employer may be ordered to deduct maintenance from a person's earnings or pension. An Irish court's maintenance order can be enforced in all countries that are signatories to the UN Convention on the Recovery Abroad of Maintenance Payments.

The recognition and enforcement of maintenance orders in EU member states is governed by Regulation 4/2009 of December 2008. The 'maintenance regulation', as it's called, allows anyone owed money under a maintenance order to obtain an order which can be enforced throughout the European Union easily, quickly and generally free of charge.

The court may also enforce non-EU foreign maintenance orders. In the case of *McC v McC*,[20] the respondent—an Irish citizen—married his wife in England in 1961 and divorced her in Hong Kong in 1986. The Hong Kong court had ordered him to pay maintenance but, in 1989, the respondent returned to Ireland, remarried and stopped the payments. The Circuit Court decided that the maintenance order could be enforced in Ireland. On appeal, the High Court agreed, but said that, in enforcing foreign maintenance orders, the Irish courts had ample powers to ensure that no injustice resulted.

The Jurisdiction of Courts and Enforcement of Judgments (Amendment) Act 2012 amended the Maintenance Act 1994 to give effect to the Lugano Convention 2007 on the enforcement of foreign maintenance orders.

Maintenance may also be claimed by same-sex couples under Part 5 of the Civil Partnership and Certain Rights and Obligations of Cohabitants Act 2010. Technical changes in the 2012 Finance Bill also resulted in greater tax equality for same-sex couples and their families. Amendments provided for the legal recognition of maintenance agreements made on the break-up of a civil partnership.

---

[19] *FF v PF* [2012] IEHC 581.
[20] [1994] IR 293.

DOMESTIC VIOLENCE

Introduction

The breakdown of a relationship is not infrequently accompanied by ill-feeling to the point of mental cruelty, threats or even violence.

Domestic violence is defined as

> the use of physical or emotional force or threat of physical force, including sexual violence, in close adult relationships. This includes violence perpetrated by spouse, partner, son, daughter or any other person who is a close blood relation of the victim.[1]

Historically, a spouse (usually a wife) whose husband owned the family home had to put up with his behaviour, or else leave home. Changing attitudes in society led to amendment of the law to protect spouses, partners, parents and children.

Since 1976, the courts have been able to grant a barring order if required for the "safety or welfare" of either spouse or any dependent child under s 22 of the Family Law (Maintenance of Spouses and Children) Act. The term 'welfare' includes physical and psychological welfare.

---

[1] *Med Report of the Task Force on Violence against Women, Office of the Tánaiste,* April 1997; available from http://www.justice.ie/en/JELR/dvreport.pdf/Files/dvreport.pdf; accessed 7 January 2014.

The 1976 Act was updated and extended by the 1981 Family Law (Protection of Spouses and Children) Act. That Act applied only to spouses and children, not to other family members or non-marital couples, such as civil partners or cohabitants or so-called 'common-law spouses'.

The 1981 Act was replaced by the 1996 Domestic Violence Act, which also allows health boards (later the Health Service Executive) to apply for orders. The Health Act 2004, which established the Health Service Executive, said at s 66 that references to a health board or "specified body" were henceforth to be read as references to the HSE.

The 1996 Act extended the availability of safety, protection, interim barring and barring orders beyond spouses and children under 18 to "persons in other domestic relationships".

Statistics

The District Court can grant a variety of orders to those who are assaulted or put in fear by another person, and is increasingly doing so. Applications under the domestic violence legislation rose by almost 20 percent between 2011 and 2012, from 10,652 to 12,655.

However, the number of barring orders granted by the District Court has dropped since the enactment of the Domestic Violence Acts. In 1996, 2,059 barring orders were granted. Although there were 2,789 applications in 2012, the number of barring orders granted was just 1,165. The number of protection orders granted rose from 3,521 in 1996 to 3,849 in 2012.

Most barring orders in 2012 were granted against spouses, rather than cohabitants or common-law spouses (1,427 against 844), although 511 barring orders were granted to parents against their children. The number of safety and protection orders granted against spouses was about the same as the number of those granted against cohabitants and common-law spouses—around 2,000 and 1,700 respectively.

The two areas which showed huge increases were safety orders and interim barring orders. The number of safety orders granted by the District Court rose from 188 in 1996 to 2,255 in 2012. Interim barring orders showed a similar increase, with the number granted trebling from 170 in 1996 to 520 in 2012.

It's not just women who are affected. A study of more than 3,000 adults published by the National Crime Council in association with the Economic and Social Research Institute (ESRI) in 2005 reported that:

- 15 percent of women and 6 percent of men suffered severe domestic abuse;
- 13 percent of women and 13 percent of men suffered physical abuse; and
- 29 percent of women and 5 percent of men reported the abuse to the gardaí.

Evidence of domestic violence may include the victim's own statement, the evidence of a witness or medical or other reports. Breach of a court order is a criminal offence and the perpetrator can be arrested without a warrant and prosecuted.

A barring, interim barring, protection or safety order may also be sought against adult non-dependent children or any violent adult in the same house. Applicants who are under 18 can ask an adult or organisation such as the Health Service Executive to apply on their behalf for an order.

Anyone over 18 can seek a protection or safety order against their parents, and people living with someone such as a relative in a 'non-contractual relationship' can also apply for protection and safety orders.

While you cannot seek a barring order against the spouse of an adult child living with you, you can apply for a protection or safety order.

Types of Court Order

Four types of court order may now be obtained to protect a spouse, dependent child or 'persons in other domestic relationships':

1) a protection order;
2) a safety order;
3) an interim barring order; or
4) a barring order.

A 'protection order' is an interim (temporary) order which has the same effect as a safety order. It may be made *ex parte*, that is without both parties being represented, but an *ex parte* order should not be considered an indictment of anyone's behaviour.

Charleton J said:

> The making of a protection order is not a stain against someone's character. No right-thinking person would consider it to be the case that, because a protection order has been made on an *ex parte* basis against a respondent, he or she is guilty of contumelious conduct.[2]

A protection order may be granted only where an application has also been made for a safety order or barring order.

A 'safety order' prevents the respondent using (or threatening to use) violence against the applicant, or molesting or frightening that person. It may only be granted where required for the safety or welfare of the applicant or a dependant. If the applicant and respondent do not live in the same house, the safety order also prevents the respondent from "watching or besetting"[3] the place where the applicant lives. If they do live in the same house, the respondent does not have to leave.

A District Court safety order lasts for up to five years and is renewable. The Circuit Court can make a safety order for an unlimited period. The order may be varied on application by the respondent or the Health Service Executive.

A safety order may be granted to:

1)   the spouse of the respondent;
2)   a person who has lived with the respondent as husband or wife for six of the previous 12 months;
3)   the parent of a non-dependent adult;
4)   an adult who lives with the respondent in a mostly non-contractual relationship; or
5)   the civil partner or former civil partner of the respondent.

A "much more drastic"[4] interim barring order may be made where there is an immediate risk of significant harm to the applicant or a dependent

---

[2] *L v Ireland & Ors* [2008] IEHC 241.
[3] s 2(2)(b) Domestic Violence Act, 1996.
[4] *Per* Hardiman J in *Collins & Ors* [2004] IESC 38.

person, and a protection order would be insufficient. It has the same effect as a barring order and ceases to have effect when the court decides the barring order application. An interim barring order is typically granted where

> the relationship between the parties has effectively broken down and disputes have arisen, or will arise, in relation to matters such as custody of children, the payment of maintenance and adjustment of property rights.[5]

Interim barring orders should only be granted in very limited circumstances, yet the statistics show that, of the 648 applications in 2012, more than 80 percent (520) were granted.

A barring order has a similar effect to a safety order, except that it requires the respondent to leave home and not to re-enter the property for three years, or less if specified by the court. The order may also bar the respondent from using or threatening violence, molesting or frightening the applicant or any child or going anywhere near the applicant's home.

A barring order may be granted to:

1) the spouse of the respondent;
2) a person who has lived with the respondent as husband or wife for six of the nine months before the application;
3) the parent of an adult non-dependent respondent; or
4) the civil partner or former civil partner of the respondent.

As one High Court judge pointed out:

> A person has a right to reside in their own home. This right must include the right to come and go as they please. A person has a right to see their spouse and to see their children and to enjoy their company, engaging in the responsibilities of family life. These rights are entirely removed, as regards access to the home, by a barring order.[6]

---

[5] *Per* Charleton J in *L v Ireland & ors, ibid.*
[6] *Per* Charleton J in *L v Ireland & ors, ibid.*

In *LB v Ireland and the Attorney General and PB*,[7] the plaintiff, against whom a barring order had been made, sought damages for what he said was essentially state expropriation of his family home.

In Circuit Court divorce proceedings, the High Court on appeal ordered that the family home be sold, with the husband getting 40 percent and the wife 60 percent. She also got a quarter of his pension.

He had unsuccessfully challenged the constitutionality of parts of the Family Law Act 1995, the Family Law (Maintenance of Spouses and Children) Act 1976, the Judicial Separation and Family Law Reform Act 1989 and the Family Law (Divorce) Act 1996 in *LB v Ireland*.[8] That decision was affirmed on appeal to the Supreme Court in 2009.

In the judicial review proceedings, Hogan J said:

> Neither the 1989 Act nor the 1996 Act should be seen as involving the taking of any property of a spouse by the state, inasmuch as the legislation provides for the intra-spousal transfer of capital assets.

The court has to take into consideration the safety and welfare of any of the respondent's children who live in the family home. But the court will not make an order barring a person from his own home where a cohabitant or parent has a lesser interest in the property.

The District Court may renew the order for up to three years at a time if the applicant's welfare or safety requires. A Circuit Court barring order may have no time limit. Other conditions may also be attached to the order.

Challenge to *Ex Parte* Interim Barring Orders

Because domestic violence applications are heard *in camera*, details of applications are generally not available to the public or to the legal profession. However, the background to one application came out in a judicial review application which reached the Supreme Court in 2002.

---

[7] [2012] IEHC 461.
[8] [2006] IEHC 275.

In *DK v Judge Timothy Crowley, Ireland and the Attorney General and Ors*,[9] the Supreme Court declared that s 4(3) of the Domestic Violence Act 1996 was unconstitutional because a person could be ordered to leave his home without having an opportunity to respond to allegations against him.

In November 1998, Judge Timothy Crowley granted LK an interim barring order *ex parte* against her husband, DK. In her application, the wife said her husband had been "physically and verbally abusive", had hit her, pulled her around by the hair and smashed ornaments. "I am under stress and in fear," she said.

In his own affidavit, the husband said he was "most distressed" at the contents of his wife's affidavit which, he said, were "largely untrue". He sought a declaration that the 1996 Act was unconstitutional.

In 2000, Mr Justice Peter Kelly in the High Court refused to declare the legislation unconstitutional because DK had not gone ahead with a District Court application to discharge the interim barring order.

In the Supreme Court, counsel for the husband said the 1996 Act deprived him of his right to be present in court to hear the allegations made against him and to cross-examine his wife about her accusations.

He said an interim barring order could last for an unspecified period, in contrast to the provisions of the 1991 Child Care Act, under which a "fit person" order depriving a parent of the custody of a child could last for no more than eight days.[10]

Counsel for the state said the 1996 Act was a necessary and reasonable legislative response to a pressing social need.

Former Chief Justice Ronan Keane said the mandatory nature of the interim barring order, even when granted on an *ex parte* application, was in sharp contrast to the interim or interlocutory injunctions typically granted in civil proceedings. Injunctions were normally intended to preserve the *status quo*, were rarely mandatory and were as limited as practicable in duration.

---

[9] [2002] 2 IR 744.
[10] Increased to 28 days by s 267(1)(a) of the Children Act 2001.

An interim barring order, on the other hand, had "draconian consequences which are wholly foreign to the concept of the injunction as traditionally understood", including the possibility of being arrested without warrant. Even where an interim order should never have been granted, the applicant could not be required to compensate the respondent.

Keane CJ said the Oireachtas could limit the constitutional right to due process in order to uphold other constitutional rights, but the extent of that restriction must be no more than was reasonably required to secure protection of the right in question:

> In the present case, it results in the forcible removal of the applicant from the family home and the society of his child, on the basis of allegations in respect of which he has no opportunity of being heard, treats him as having committed a criminal offence resulting in a possible custodial sentence in the event of his non-compliance with the order and makes him liable to arrest by a garda without a warrant if the latter entertains a reasonable suspicion that he has failed to comply with the order.
>
> That the legislature were entitled to effect such an abridgement of the rights of individual citizens in order to deal with the social evil of domestic violence is beyond dispute. The question for resolution in this case is as to whether the manner in which the abridgement of the right to be heard has been effected is proportionate.
>
> The failure of the legislation to impose any time limit on the operation of an interim barring order...is inexplicable.

The court declared the section of the 1996 Act unconstitutional and quashed the interim barring order. As a result, the Domestic Violence Act 1996 was amended by the Domestic Violence (Amendment) Act 2002.

An interim barring order made *ex parte* now only lasts for up to eight working days (excluding Saturdays, Sundays and public holidays). An *ex parte* application for an interim barring order is grounded on an affidavit sworn by the applicant. A note of the evidence given by the applicant must be prepared 'forthwith' by the judge or by the applicant or her solicitor, and then approved by the judge. A copy of the order, affidavit and note must be served on the respondent 'as soon as practicable'.

Civil Partners and Other Applicants

Part 9 of the Civil Partnership and Certain Rights and Obligations of Cohabitants Act 2010 extends to civil partners the same protections that spouses have under the Domestic Violence Acts 1996 and 2002. It allows civil partners to apply for a safety order or a barring order subject to the same rules as a spouse.

The Civil Law (Miscellaneous Provisions) Act 2011 also extended the powers of the courts under the 1996 and 2002 acts. Under s 60 of the 2011 Act:

i) A parent may apply for a safety order against the other parent of their child, even where the parents have never lived together. This prevents access becoming a cause of intimidation—or even violence—between disputing parents;

ii) Unmarried opposite-sex couples and same-sex couples who have not registered a civil partnership but are in an 'intimate and committed relationship' can obtain a safety order (as well as those 'living together as husband and wife');

iii) Couples who are not married or are not in a registered civil partnership do not have to have lived together for a minimum period before one of them can obtain a safety order against the other. Previously, the applicant had to have lived with the respondent for at least six of the previous 12 months.

A cohabitant who has been living with a partner for six of the previous nine months may apply for a barring or safety order, but will not get a barring order if the other cohabitant owns the home where they live together, or has greater ownership rights in the property.

Challenge to *Ex Parte* Protection Orders

Applications may be made to the District or Circuit Court and will be heard informally in private. If necessary, an applicant may ask the District Court for a protection order *ex parte*, that is without notifying the other spouse. The constitutionality of the power to grant a protection order *ex parte* was challenged in *Goold v Collins*,[11] but the Supreme Court decided that any decision it might make was moot.

The challenge was subsequently unsuccessful in *L v Ireland & ors*.[12] The applicant and his wife disagreed about home-schooling for their five children. The day after husband went to Australia, his wife applied *ex parte* for a protection order. The wife claimed L had a history of mental illness and held "unorthodox views" about his role in his children's lives. A safety order was made later with the husband present in court.

Rejecting the husband's challenge, Charleton J said:

> A protection order is, in effect, no more than a warning...It is never lawful to threaten to use violence against a person, unless one is oneself under attack or one is effecting a lawful arrest. It is not lawful to molest a person or make a person fear for dire consequences. These are all already criminal offences of long standing at common law.

> It is not lawful to watch a person's premises, other than by passing and re-passing on the highway for lawful and reasonable purposes, and no one has a right to sit outside another person's home staring in...Nor is it lawful to beset a premises, meaning to surround the persons residing there with a feeling of hostile intent.

The judge said the Oireachtas could decide what activity should be made criminal,

> provided the definition is precise and the wrong that is characterised as a crime is truly an attack on the good order of society. A protection order breach fits comfortably within that competence.

The effects of an *ex parte* order were set out in *Adam v Minister for Justice*. Hardiman J said that, while an *ex parte* order was only provisional, it may "constitute a grave injustice to the defendant or respondent".[13]

The same judge said the domestic violence legislation served a "vital social purpose" by protecting applicants against "assault and, on occasion,

---

[11] [2004] IESC 38.
[12] [2008] IEHC 241.
[13] [2001] 3 IR 53.

terrorisation" and sometimes such protection had to be "provided immediately in an acute situation".[14]

However, he said that the courts were "fully aware that *ex parte* procedures may be abused out of spite or for tactical purposes"—though he added that:

> no court would be justified in allowing the mere fact that *ex parte* relief had been granted against a party to litigation to tilt the balance of that litigation in any way.

If a protection order is granted, the judge will set a date for the hearing of a barring or safety order application, when the other spouse may be represented. The protection order is sent to the local garda station and, if any further incidents occur, the gardaí may take action.

Until a court finally decides whether or not to grant a barring or safety order, a spouse or civil partner is not permitted to remove or dispose of any household goods.

HSE Application

If someone is too frightened to apply for a safety or barring order, the HSE may do it on his or her behalf, but only if the executive becomes aware of an incident which threatens a person's safety or welfare. The HSE must have reason to believe the 'aggrieved person' is frightened for his or her safety or has been molested or subjected to threats or violence.

The HSE has to take into account the wishes of the aggrieved person 'as far as is reasonably practicable'. Clearly this section could give the HSE power to interfere in a family relationship where neither partner wished it to do so. Whether such a bystanders' charter would withstand a constitutional challenge is open to question.

An order is effective once the respondent has been told about it and shown a copy. Anyone who breaks a safety, barring, interim or protection order may be arrested without warrant.

---

[14] *Collins & Ors* [2004] IESC 38.

If the respondent appeals against the order, the court can suspend the operation of a barring or safety order, but not a protection or interim barring order.

Where anyone (except the HSE) applies for an order and it appears that a child care or supervision order might be necessary, the court may adjourn the proceedings and order the HSE to investigate and report back to the court. In the meantime, the court may make whatever order as it sees fit under the Child Care Act 1991 for the care and custody of the child.

The court may also make orders relating to maintenance of a spouse and children, custody and access, child care, a child's birth or funeral expenses, protection of the family home and compensation for the loss of the home, even if proceedings have not been instituted under these headings.

THE FAMILY HOME

Introduction

One of the biggest problems facing couples whose relationships break down is what happens to the family home.

The issue of the family home—and, in Ireland, of the family farm—is at the centre of many of the legal disputes which follow a marriage breakdown. In 2006, for instance, there were 339 Circuit Court cases involving the family home. The property was transferred to the wife in 107 instances, to the husband in 41 cases and was sold in 49 cases, with the proceeds divided between the spouses.[1]

The issue really came to the fore in 1986 when the electorate rejected the introduction of divorce, largely because of husbands' fears about the family farm being taken over by their former wives.

Matrimonial Home Bill Challenge

The government attempted to reassure voters by introducing new laws and, in 1993, produced draft legislation to deal with the issue. The

---

[1] Carol Coulter, *Family Law in Practice: A Study in the Cases of the Circuit Court* (Clarus Press, Dublin, 2009).

controversial Matrimonial Home Bill was referred to the Supreme Court by former President Mary Robinson to test its constitutionality, but the court ruled that the bill was unconstitutional.

It agreed that the institutions of marriage and the family would be strengthened if joint ownership of the family home could be encouraged by appropriate means, but it said a couple had the right under Article 41.1.1° of the Constitution to make their own decision about the family home, without the interference of the Oireachtas. The Bill interfered with that right, whether or not the joint decision was oppressive or unfair to either of them.

The Supreme Court said it was not satisfied that

> the potentially indiscriminate alteration of what must be many joint decisions validly made within the authority of the family concerning the question of the ownership of the family home could reasonably be justified, even by such an important aspect of the common good.

The judges said it was not their job to decide which sections of the bill were unconstitutional, so the Court ruled that the entire Bill was unconstitutional.

Family Home Protection Act 1976

The common law concept of marriage involved a duty by the husband to provide accommodation for his wife, even if she was separated from him. A wife might have had a right to prevent her husband mortgaging or selling the home in which she lived, even if he owned it. But those rights did not bind a third party who bought a family home in good faith, even without the wife's consent. In other words, if a husband sold the family home and the purchaser bought it in good faith, the sale would be valid, even if the wife had not consented beforehand.

Where homes are owned by one spouse alone, it is often the man. In the case of marital disputes, the husband could sell his house and disappear with the proceeds. The 1976 Family Home Protection Act was the first major piece of legislation to deal with this problem.

The Dáil was told that the main purpose of the 1976 Act was to prevent a vindictive spouse selling the family home over the heads of other family members. It also gave the courts power to prevent a spouse removing and selling furniture or other belongings.

Mr Justice Richard Johnson, in the case of *Bank of Ireland v Slevin*,[2] said the purpose of the Act was to protect the family home and

> to prevent families being evicted when a spouse, through either stupidity or greed or whatever else—or bad business or bad luck—lost the family home.

In a strictly legal sense, the person whose name is on the title deeds of a property has legal ownership, while a spouse whose name is not on the title deeds may have only an equitable interest.

Traditionally, a husband—as the main wage-earner—may have bought a property in his sole name and paid the mortgage himself. Even if his wife contributed to the running costs of the home, or paid for the improvement of the house or building of an extension, she would not have a legal right to the property.

Wives who stay at home, giving their husbands the opportunity to go out and earn money, undoubtedly make a contribution towards the home, but that contribution was not recognised in terms of ownership until the case of *L v L*.[3] In that case, Mr Justice Robert Barr said that Article 41 of the Constitution enabled the court to take into account the 'money's-worth' contribution of mothers who stayed at home to rear the family. But the Supreme Court unanimously overturned that judgment on the grounds that this was a new legal right which could only be created by legislation.

The Oireachtas obliged with the 1989 Judicial Separation and Family Law Reform Act which allows a court, when making a property adjustment order, to take into account the contribution made by a spouse who looks after the home or cares for the family. That provision is mirrored in the 1995 Family Law Act and the 1996 Divorce Act.

Prior Written Consent and Legal Advice

Under the Family Home Protection Act, if the family home is sold by one spouse—who may be the legal owner of the property—without the written consent of the other spouse, the transaction is void.

---

[2] [1995] 2 ILRM 454.
[3] [1992] 2 IR 77.

During the recession, when banks were often seeking to repossess family homes, many spouses, particularly wives, claimed they had either not given prior written consent to the sale of the family home or had not received independent legal advice. Generally the claims were not successful.

In *Irish Nationwide Building Society v Patrick and Patricia Raftery*,[4] the Irish Bank Resolution Corporation sought possession of a family home in Roscommon after the defendants failed to repay a IR£69,000 mortgage.

Patricia Raftery argued that she did not have independent legal advice when she signed the mortgage as co-owner. The Rafterys also argued that the mortgage did not specify the payments to be made. "This argument lies uneasily in the hand of those who made no repayments whatever," said Hedigan J.

The bank relied on the unanimous decision of the Supreme Court in *Nestor v Murphy*,[5] where the court held that s 3(1) of the Family Home Protection Act 1976 was

> directed against unilateral alienation by one spouse. When both spouses join in the 'conveyance', the evil at which the sub-section is directed does not exist". Otherwise mortgages could be "unfairly or dishonestly repudiated by parties who entered into them freely, willingly and with full knowledge.

In *GE Capital Woodchester Home Loans Ltd v Reade & Anor*,[6] the wife unsuccessfully claimed that she had no choice but to sign a second mortgage because of the "menacing and oppressive situation" created by the bank, and claimed she was not advised of her right to seek independent legal advice.

In England, the House of Lords ruled in *Barclay's Bank v O'Brien*[7] that a transaction was not invalidated just because a wife did not fully understand it—although, where a person signed a document under duress or through misrepresentation, the transaction would not be valid.

---

[4] [2012] IEHC 352.
[5] [1979] IR 326.
[6] [2012] IEHC 363.
[7] [1994] 1 AC 180.

In the case of *Bank of Ireland v Michael and Una Smyth*,[8] the Supreme Court ruled that a person had to be properly informed in order to consent to a charge over the family home.

In 1978, Mrs Smyth had agreed to mortgage the 124-acre family farm in Co Tipperary and signed a form under the 1976 Act consenting to the mortgage. Ten years later the couple owed IR£180,000 and in 1993 the bank asked the High Court for an order of possession, which was refused. Mrs Smyth said the bank never explained to her that she would lose her home if the mortgage payments were not made.

The Supreme Court said the bank did not have a duty to explain the mortgage fully to Mrs Smyth or to advise her to take independent legal advice. But it should have done so, to obtain good title to the land. In the circumstances, Mrs Smyth's uninformed consent was invalid and the mortgage agreement was void.

Bank of Ireland v Smyth was mentioned in the explanatory memorandum to a private member's Bill introduced in the Dáil by Independent TD Stephen Donnelly in 2012. But justice minister Alan Shatter said the case was "of no real relevance" to the bill which he said was "poorly drafted" and "somewhat confused in its approach".[9]

In *Bank of Ireland v Hanrahan*,[10] a couple claimed that a mortgage was void because the wife had not given her consent until two hours *after* her husband deposited the title deeds with the bank. The judge said the mortgage was valid because there had been an implied agreement that the bank would only hold the deeds as custodian until the wife gave her consent.

Family Law Act 1995

Anyone buying unregistered property formerly had to check every conveyance of the land after 1976, as a transaction which failed to comply with the law might have meant the property did not belong to its apparent owner.

---

[8] [1995] 2 IR 459.
[9] Dáil Éireann, Family Home Protection (Miscellaneous Provisions) Bill 2011: Second Stage Friday, 3 February 2012.
[10] [1987] IEHC 24.

But the 1995 Family Law Act says a conveyance will be valid unless declared void by a court. Any proceedings to declare a conveyance void must be instituted within six years of the transaction. This procedure is not necessary with registered land, as an entry in the register is regarded as proof of the title of the registered owner.

Sometimes couples agree to sell their home and then want to back out of the sale for some reason. But in *Nestor v Murphy*[11] the court decided that, where spouses were co-owners of the home and they both agreed to sell it, they couldn't wriggle out of the deal just because the wife did not give her prior consent in writing.

General written consent to all future loans is now covered by an amendment to the 1976 Act by the 1995 Family Law Act. This may mean that, once a general written consent is given by one spouse, the other spouse may thereafter secure any future borrowings against the family home, effectively contracting out of the safeguards of the original legislation.

In *Mary O'Keeffe v Brian Russell and AIB*,[12] Mr and Mrs O'Keeffe sold their 111-acre farm in Cork in 1978 and bought a 206-acre farm in Limerick for IR£700,000. They borrowed the deposit from the AIB and the couple's solicitor promised to lodge the land certificate of the new farm with the bank. He also promised to lodge the proceeds of sale of the Cork farm in a joint account.

But the money from the Cork farm was lodged in the sole name of Mr O'Keeffe and the bank made the loan for the new farm to him alone. Mrs O'Keeffe refused to accept joint responsibility for her husband's debt. In 1980, she left him and told the solicitor not to lodge the land certificate with the bank. He said he was bound to do so, and lodged the certificate.

Eventually Mr O'Keeffe fell behind in his loan payments and in 1982 the bank obtained a judgment against him. The farm was sold and most of the proceeds used to pay off Mr O'Keeffe's debt. The High Court ruled that the bank had no charge over Mrs O'Keeffe's share of the farm and the bank appealed.

---

[11] [1979] IR 326.
[12] Unreported, High Court/Supreme Court, 1994.

The Supreme Court rejected the appeal and said Mrs O'Keeffe had not been party to the loan contract because it was not a joint loan, so there was no mortgage on her half of the farm.

A more straightforward case was *Bank of Ireland v Slevin*[13] where the bank claimed quarter of a million pounds from farmer Harry Slevin. The deeds of Mr Slevin's farm were deposited with the bank in 1977 as security for a loan, but Mrs Slevin had not consented in writing to the deposit. Mr Slevin claimed the whole mortgage was void for lack of consent, but the judge ruled that the mortgage was only void in relation to the family home, and he granted a charge over the rest of the farm.

However, the 1976 Act does not confer any right of ownership on the spouse whose consent is required.

Definition of 'Family Home'

The term "family home" was defined in the case of *National Irish Bank v Graham*,[14] where the Supreme Court said that the definition was restricted to the precise terms of the Family Home Protection Act 1976, that is "primarily a dwelling in which a married couple ordinarily reside". It also means "a dwelling in which a spouse whose protection is in issue ordinarily resides" or, if that spouse has left the other spouse, where he or she ordinarily used to reside. It may not include a holiday home or a house into which a couple have not yet moved. The Court said judges could not extend that definition.

In the case of *BMC v PJC*,[15] the judge said the court would not allow the owner of a family home to evade the law by transferring it into the name of a company controlled by one of the spouses, and then occupying the home under licence from the company.

In an effort to tie down the meaning of a family home, the 1995 Family Law Act said a dwelling was

> any building or part of a building occupied as a separate dwelling and includes any garden or other land usually occupied with the dwelling, being land that is subsidiary and ancillary to it, is required for amenity

---

[13] [1995] 2 ILRM 454.
[14] [1995] 2 IR 244.
[15] Unreported, High Court, 12 May 1983.

or convenience and is not being used or developed primarily for commercial purposes, and includes a structure that is not permanently attached to the ground and a vehicle, or vessel, whether mobile or not, occupied as a separate dwelling.[16]

That definition suggests that a farmhouse could be a family home, but the farmlands would not. Such clarification was needed because of the contentious issue, in the Irish context, as to whether the family farm constitutes a family home under the Act.

In *AIB v Austin and Susan O'Neill*,[17] Mrs O'Neill deposited the land certificate for a 63-acre farm in Co Carlow as an equitable mortgage against a loan of IR£50,000, without the prior written consent of Mr O'Neill. The bank obtained a court judgment for IR£48,000 and—while it accepted that it could not seize the couple's house and gardens—claimed it had an equitable mortgage over the rest of the land.

The High Court said the legislature clearly intended that the family home might form only part of a larger holding and the Act only required the prior written consent of the other spouse in relation to the home, not to the rest of the land. The judge ruled that the mortgage was valid against the farmlands, but not against the house and gardens.

Court Applications

If a spouse deserts the family home or refuses to agree to its sale for reasons of malevolence, stubbornness or mental illness, the other spouse may apply to the court for an order dispensing with the need for that spouse's consent. But a dispensation is not retrospective and must be obtained before any sale.

A co-owning spouse who wants to separate, sell the home and divide the proceeds with the other spouse, may apply to the court for an order for sale in lieu of partition, as no purchaser is likely to want to buy a half share of the house and become a co-owner with the remaining spouse. The Partition Act 1868 says the court must order the sale, unless there is good reason to the contrary.

---

[16] s 54(1)(a) Family Law Act, 1995.
[17] [1995] 2 IR 473.

In *Sheehy v Talbot*,[18] the defendant claimed that the Partition Acts were solely designed for married couples and could not be used to decide property disputes between an unmarried couple. "He is quite simply wrong about this," said Edwards J.

The judge ruled that the disputed property was owned in equal shares, and he ordered its sale under the Partition Acts and the equal division of the proceeds.

If a spouse deliberately engages in conduct which may lead to the loss of the home or make it unsuitable to live in, with the intention of depriving the dependent spouse or children of their home, the court may make "such order as it considers proper".[19] If the home has already been lost or rendered uninhabitable, the court may order the spouse to pay compensation. But this section does not apply to a spouse whose behaviour, although immature or foolish, is not intended to deprive the other spouse of the family home.

Ownership

Occasionally the family home is apparently owned by third parties through offshore trusts. The rules of natural justice and the statutory requirements mean that these 'owners' must be put on notice of any claims for property transfers or declarations of beneficial interest. Since they are outside the jurisdiction, it is not easy to compel them to obey Irish court orders. Without their co-operation, it may be impossible to achieve discovery of documents, and lawyers may be left relying on limited public records.

Sometimes in family law matters, the courts have to decide the ownership of the family home. In *CF v CF*,[20] the applicant wife claimed ownership of the family home. Her husband had paid her father IR£100,000 for the property, but it had been registered in the wife's name. The husband said he ran his practice from the home. He claimed that he was the beneficial owner and sought a transfer order giving him legal title.

---

[18] [2008] IEHC 207.
[19] s 5, Family Home Protection Act 1976.
[20] Unreported, High Court, 11 June 2002.

Mr Justice Philip O'Sullivan held that, in the absence of any explicit agreement, the family home should be shared equally between the husband and wife. He said the balance of fairness required him to make a property adjustment order vesting the legal and beneficial title of the family home in the husband, subject to his payment to the wife of a lump sum representing her half share in the home.

Judgment Mortgage

No written consent is needed for a court to grant a judgment mortgage. In the case of *Containercare v Wycherley*,[21] a husband and wife were joint owners of the family home. A creditor obtained a judgment mortgage against the husband for outstanding debts, and the mortgage was registered against the husband's share of the home. In this case, the wife and the creditor effectively became joint owners of the property.

Even if one spouse is not on the deeds, she (or he) may register an interest in the property to take precedence over any judgment mortgage registered against it. A judgment mortgage does not rank in priority to a claim by a dependent spouse in judicial separation proceedings, even where the proceedings are not registered as a *lis pendens*.[22]

In *ACC Bank plc v Vincent Markham and Mary Casey*,[23] the bank obtained a judgment which it registered against the interest of Vincent Markham in a family home.

Markham and Casey were married but had separated in 2001, when both had left the family home. In 2003, Casey instituted proceedings against Markham for judicial separation and an order under s 9 of the Family Law Act 1995. The bank registered a judgment mortgage the following year.

The issue was whether any interest which Casey might be granted in the property, which was then owned by Markham, would rank in priority to the bank's judgment mortgage.

---

[21] [1982] IR 143.

[22] See *Dovebid Netherlands BV v William Phelan trading as the Phelan Partnership and Denise O'Byrne* [2007] IEHC 239.

[23] [2005] IEHC 437.

Following the decision in *S v S*,[24] Clarke J said that a party in family law proceedings who claimed an interest in property owned by the other party was entitled to register a *lis pendens* which would bind a purchaser or mortgagee for value. Any direction to transfer the property which might later be made would rank in priority to the interests of any purchasers or mortgagees for value who acquired their interest subsequent to the registration of the *lis pendens*. Even without actual notice or the registration of a *lis pendens*, a judgment mortgagee would rank behind the interest of a spouse to whom a transfer order was made, provided the family law proceedings had been begun before the registration of the judgment mortgage.

Value of Home

If a spouse is responsible for a drop in the value of the family home, that may be reflected in the court's order. In *BH v PH*,[25] MacMenamin J cut a lump sum payment by a husband to his ex-wife from €500,000 to €330,000 because of the wife's "misguided and misconceived" actions.

A buyer had offered €620,000 for the family home in 2007, but ultimately withdrew the offer because of the wife's repeated court applications. The matter was in court up to 40 times, and the wife had to pay substantial legal bills, including at least one bill of €30,000.

The house was eventually sold in 2010 for €355,000. "The consequence of the respondent's own conduct has been to diminish the assets which are available to her and to the children," said the judge.

But assets such as property can be subject to differing valuations. As de Valera J said in *CED v AD*[26]:

> Valuation is not an exact science, and the value of any property on a given day depends largely on who might want it and how much they are prepared to pay.

---

[24] Unreported, High Court, 2 February 1994.
[25] [2010] IEHC 425.
[26] [2005] IEHC 412.

PRE-NUPTIAL AGREEMENTS

Introduction

Pre-nuptial agreements are still not formally admissible in family law courts in Ireland, as they are considered contrary to public policy. However, civil partners are permitted to regulate their financial affairs under the 2010 legislation, and courts in other countries, such as those in mainland Europe, the US and Australia, tend to enforce pre-nuptial agreements.

Pre-civil partnership or pre-cohabitation agreements may also set out how assets will be divided if the partnership is dissolved or the cohabitation ends. But traditionally, marriage involved a duty to live together, so an agreement providing for the possibility of separation was void, as it might encourage a couple to separate.[1]

Pre-nuptial agreements were ruled contrary to public policy in the 1929 English case of *Hyman v Hyman*.[2] They remain unenforceable as ordinary contracts in the courts of Ireland and Britain. But in 2004, the Solicitors Family Law Association (SFLA), which represents more than 5,000 solicitors in England and Wales, recommended that pre-nuptial agreements should be made legally binding and enforceable, except where that would cause "significant injustice".

---

[1] *Cocksedge v Cocksedge* (1844) 13 LJ Ch 384 and *H v W* (1857) 3 K & J 382.
[2] [1929] AC 601.

The SFLA said that the demand for pre-marital agreements had increased because of:

- the higher number of second and subsequent marriages;
- the increased awareness of such agreements by a multinational community;
- media publicity;
- a desire by couples to decide their own future; and
- the fear of failing to protect wealth.

Nowadays, judges in both jurisdictions will take note of agreements between spouses, but there is a statutory requirement for the Irish courts to make proper provision for both spouses and any dependants. This takes precedence over any pre-nuptial or post-nuptial agreement, even if that agreement is said to be in 'full and final settlement' of all financial matters.

Post-Nuptial Settlements

The Irish courts have frequently considered post-nuptial settlements, typically separation agreements, when the couple subsequently seek a divorce. In *FJWT v CNRT and, by order, Trust Corps Services Ltd*,[3] McKechnie J said the concept of settlement should be widely construed, suggesting that pre-nuptial and post-nuptial settlements could be varied under the 1995 and 1996 Acts.

Variation of Agreements

Since *Hyman v Hyman*,[4] pre-nuptial agreements have remained unenforceable as ordinary contracts in the courts of Ireland and Britain. But nowadays, the courts in both jurisdictions will take note of agreements between spouses, though judges retain the right to vary their terms.

In the 1980 English case of *Edgar v Edgar*, Lord Ormrod set out the factors which the courts would consider in such agreements:

- undue pressure by one side;
- exploitation of a dominant position to secure an unreasonable advantage;
- inadequate knowledge;

---

[3] [2005] 2 IR 247.
[4] [1929] AC 601.

- possibly bad legal advice; or
- an important change of circumstances, unforeseen or overlooked at the time of the agreement.

The Judge stated:

> Important, too, is the general proposition that, formal agreements—properly and fairly arrived at, with competent legal advice—should not be displaced unless there are good and substantial grounds for concluding that an injustice will be done by holding the parties to the terms of their agreement.

The 'Edgar principles' have also been said to apply to post-nuptial agreements. But in a 2008 case, the Privy Council distinguished between pre-nups and post-nups[5]:

> There is an enormous difference—in principle and in practice—between an agreement providing for a present state of affairs which has developed between a married couple, and an agreement made before the parties have committed themselves to the rights and responsibilities of the married state, purporting to govern what may happen in an uncertain and unhoped for future ... "Hence, where legislation does provide for such agreements to be valid, it gives careful thought to the necessary safeguards.

The Privy Council pointed out that the MacLeods were now married:

> They have undertaken towards one another the obligations and responsibilities of the married state. A pre-nuptial agreement is no longer the price which one party may extract for his or her willingness to marry. There is nothing to stop a couple entering into contractual financial arrangements governing their life together.

Pre-Nups in Ireland

Courts in other European countries are tending to give greater weight to pre-nuptial agreements. Since Irish citizens are now permitted to divorce in almost all EU states, the Irish government has come under increasing pressure to allow couples to regulate their financial affairs before and after marriage, as they do in other EU States.

---

[5] *MacLeod v MacLeod* [2008] WLR (D) 402.

But despite an expert report on pre-nuptial agreements,[6] and reports that the government had drafted the heads of legislation to formalise the recognition of pre-nups, the law has still not been changed.

The expert study group appointed by former Minister for Justice Michael McDowell in 2006 said that a pre-nuptial agreement was no more than a factor to be take into account by an Irish court. While the courts appeared to be able to take a pre-nuptial agreement into account under existing law, ultimately the judge could make whatever financial orders he considered necessary. The expert group's report proposed that the law be clarified to *require* the courts to consider any pre-nuptial agreement, though the court would not be bound by it if that would lead to an unfair outcome.

Pre-nuptial agreements have been upheld by the Irish courts, but only in the most exceptional of cases. For example, the High Court refused to overrule a pre-nuptial agreement in a divorce case involving a French couple who lived in Ireland.[7] The couple had married in France in 1978 and had signed a pre-nuptial contract. In 1988, the couple moved to Cavan to live but, four years later, the marriage broke down and the wife returned to France. The husband, who was a multi-millionaire, remained in Ireland to run his businesses, but filed for divorce in France.

The wife then instituted proceedings in the Irish High Court challenging the right of the French court to hear the case, though she also counter-claimed for divorce in the French courts.

The Irish High Court declared that it had no jurisdiction, as the French court was dealing with the case. Mr Justice Kevin O'Higgins said that, since the couple had lived in Ireland for most of their marriage, the wife might have had a right to challenge the jurisdiction of the French court. But since she had counterclaimed for divorce in the French court, she was precluded from arguing a constitutional case before the High Court.

"It is clear that the Irish courts have no role in the supervision of the French courts in doing their legitimate business," said the judge.

---

[6] Report of the Study Group on Pre-nuptial Agreements, 25 April 2007.
[7] *YNR v MN* [2005] IEHC 335.

Factors in Recognising Pre-Nups

A pre-nuptial agreement is most likely to be recognised and implemented where the couple:

- are childless;
- are middle-aged or elderly and want to preserve assets which have been built up over a long time before the marriage;
- have agreed 'proper provision'; and
- follow practical guidelines and recommendations.

The 1998 British Home Office document 'Supporting Families' suggested that a pre-nup or post-nup should not be enforceable where:

1) there is a child of the family;
2) the contract is unenforceable;
3) both spouses did not receive independent legal advice before signing;
4) the enforcement of the agreement would cause 'significant injustice';
5) there wasn't full disclosure of assets and property before the agreement; or
6) the agreement was made less than 21 days before the marriage.

These are similar to the subsequent recommendations of the Irish Government's working group on pre-nuptial agreements, except that the British proposal of 21 days is 28 days in the Irish report.

The decision of the UK Supreme Court in *Radmacher v Granatino*[8] suggested that the factors likely to be considered when deciding the appropriate weight to give to a pre-nup are:

1) the length of time the parties have lived together;
2) the financial contributions of each party;
3) the dependency of each spouse;
4) the work carried out in the home; and
5) the number of children.

---

[8] [2010] UKSC 42.

As Murray J said in *T v T*[9]:

> The court should, in principle, attribute the same value to the contribution to the spouse who works primarily in the home as it does to a spouse who works primarily outside the home as the principal earner.

To have any chance of being upheld by a court, a pre-nup should comply with general contractual principles. A certificate from both parties' solicitors should confirm that each has received independent legal advice and that there is no duress or undue influence. It's best if a pre-nup is signed at least five or six weeks before marriage, so that there is no appearance of haste.

There should be a full schedule of assets, and any pre-nup should be renewed—or at least reviewed—on the birth of any child. The Law Society of Ireland's Family Law Committee recommended in 2008 that vouched affidavits of means be sworn by both parties to satisfy the requirements of full financial disclosure. The affidavits could be attached to the pre-nup (or to a separation agreement) as a schedule.

Signatories might also consider so-called 'sunset clauses', meaning that the agreement would be reviewed after a specified period, or there would be an agreement to end it after a set time.

Pre-nuptial agreements are also very suitable for the collaborative law method of negotiation. The longer the lead-in time for discussing pre-nuptial agreements before the marriage, the better the atmosphere for the negotiations.

Many pre-nuptial agreements have a clause requiring the parties to refer any dispute to an accredited family law mediator at first instance. Family law mediators can help the parties with this or, if there are significant commercial issues, lawyer-assisted mediation could help.

The courts are least likely to uphold a pre-nuptial agreement where the agreement would lead to "significant injustice" and be manifestly unfair in making proper provision for the dependent party.

---

[9] [2002] 3 IR 334.

It also unlikely that a pre-nup which purports to oust the jurisdiction of the courts to ensure proper provision under Article 41.3.2° of the Constitution or family law legislation will be upheld by the courts.

Effect of Recession

Relationship breakdown jurisprudence in Ireland coincided with the Celtic Tiger boom years where wealthy couples could afford to litigate. Those days are gone. Many partners and spouses—particularly husbands—see acrimonious litigation as a waste of time and money. Having a pre-nuptial agreement provides a road map in the event of marital breakdown.

A rich person may see a pre-nup as a way of avoiding the wasted time and energy in expensive litigation if there is a separation or divorce. The other partner is guaranteed a significant sum whether the marriage is short or long, and the children are provided for.

However, the recession has forced many divorced spouses to seek a variation of previous orders for maintenance and lump-sums, on the grounds that they can no longer afford the payments.

But courts that are willing to vary orders owing to the recession are likely to be even more willing to disregard the terms of a pre-nuptial agreement from the boom years.

Parties to such agreements who want to maintain an element of control of the division of assets in any possible future divorce may consider entering into a post-nuptial agreement after marriage and before separation. Like pre-nups, these are not officially enforceable, but may be taken into account by the Irish courts.

A post-nuptial agreement would aim to keep the terms of any pre-nuptial agreement relevant and effective in light of the economic climate.

The Oireachtas has not expressly dealt with the matter of pre-nuptial and post-nuptial agreements, although the Family Law Act 1995 and the Family Law (Divorce) Act 1996 give the courts power to vary any prenuptial or postnuptial settlement.

PENSIONS AND TAX

Introduction

Tax and pension rights may be a very significant part of the financial considerations in the breakdown of a relationship. Nowadays, pension rights may represent a family's second-biggest asset, after the family home. Pensions can be a complicated area and expert advice is likely to be needed when spouses separate.

Pension adjustment orders (PAOs) were introduced by the Family Law Act 1995 and the Family Law (Divorce) Act 1996. More recently, the Civil Partnership and Certain Rights and Obligations of Cohabitants Act 2010 provided for a PAO to be granted in the case of a same-sex couple or opposite-sex couples separating under certain circumstances.

However, spouses or partners may not arrange a pension adjustment order themselves. Only the court has the power to make such an order-though, with the assistance of both solicitors and possibly actuaries, the court will often make such an order by consent.

A pension adjustment order transfers the ownership of designated and death benefit rights to the non-member spouse or civil partner, qualified cohabitant or other dependant. A PAO overrides the pension scheme rules, trustee discretion and legislative restrictions in relation to pensions.

The trustee of a scheme is not liable for any loss or damage caused by his non-compliance with the rules of a scheme if the non-compliance was caused by obeying a direction or the court under family law legislation.

Only a spouse (or in some cases a person acting on behalf of the dependent member of a family) can apply for a PAO under the:

- Family Law Act 1995, in the context of judicial separation; or
- Family Law (Divorce) Act 1996, in the context of divorce.

Under the Civil Partnership and Certain Rights and Obligations of Cohabitants Act 2010, a PAO can be sought by a:

- civil partner following a decree of dissolution or a registered civil partnership; or
- qualified cohabitant at the end of the relationship, whether by break-up or death.

Under the 2010 Act, a PAO can only be made in favour of a civil partner or qualified cohabitant. There is no provision for making an order for a dependant.

After proceedings have been initiated, a non-member spouse must be provided with certain information, such as the member booklet or annual report. The court may direct the trustees of a pension scheme to provide more specific information about the pension benefits.

Definition of 'Pension Scheme'

For the purposes of these Acts, 'pension scheme' is defined to include occupational pension schemes (whether defined contribution or defined benefit), retirement annuity contracts (personal pensions), personal retirement saving accounts (PRSAs), approved buy-out bonds and annuities in payment. A life office is deemed to be the trustee of buy-out bonds and personal pensions, as these are administered by the life office. For PRSAs, it is the PRSA provider.

Approved Retirement Funds (ARFs) and Approved Minimum Retirement Funds (AMRFs) are not specifically mentioned in the acts and do not fall under the remit of a pension adjustment order. A property adjustment order may be needed in this instance.

Types of PAO

There are two types of pension adjustment order: a retirement benefits order and a contingent benefits order. A retirement benefits order refers to all benefits payable to the pension scheme member, including retirement pension, retirement lump sums and gratuities, benefits payable following the member's death in retirement and periodic increases on pensions in payment (or the fund values in the case of a defined contribution scheme).

A contingent benefit order refers to benefits payable under the rules of the pension scheme if the member dies during the employment to which the scheme relates. Benefits include lump sum benefits (including fund value) and benefits payable to dependants on the death of the member.

A PAO which relates to contingent benefits ceases once the member leaves the job to which the scheme relates. A non-member seeking such an order must not have remarried or registered a new civil partnership, and must apply for the contingent benefit order within 12 months of the decree being granted.

Separate PAOs must be made for retirement benefits and contingent benefits in a company pension scheme, and for each private pension arrangement.

Pension rights and entitlements may involve:

1) a pension at retirement age (or earlier if in ill health);
2) a spouse's pension on the death of the scheme member (before or after retirement);
3) a tax-free lump sum at retirement of up to one-and-a-half times final salary (depending on the length of service in the pension scheme) or 25 percent of the fund value;
4) contingent (life assurance) benefits, commonly of two to four times' salary;
5) an income for dependent children aged under 18 (or up to 23 if in full-time education); or
6) an Approved Retirement Fund or Approved Minimum Retirement Fund.

The court does not have to make a pension adjustment order. It must first consider whether adequate or reasonable financial provision exists (or can be made) for the dependent spouse by any other order.

'Defined Benefit' and 'Defined Contribution'

Many employees are members of an occupational pension plan and their pension rights are generally regarded as 'deferred pay'. Equal pay legislation means many working women have also accumulated their own pension rights. The two main types of pension scheme are 'defined benefit' and 'defined contribution'.

In a defined benefit scheme, retirement benefits are based on an individual's final pay and service with the employer. Benefits generally accrue at a set 'pension fraction', such as 1/60th of pay for each year of service. This means a worker can predict in advance what percentage of his final pay will be received as a pension.

The actuarial or transfer value of pension benefits depends on the member's salary, the type of pension scheme (public service or private sector), the amount of benefits, years of service in the scheme up to the date of the decree and the scheme's funding status. In many cases, the value of a pension in transfer terms may be greater than the value of the family home.

Public service-type defined benefit schemes are unfunded, so no transfer value will be obtainable. Orders will relate to the members' benefits and will commence whenever the member begins receiving his benefits.

A defined benefit scheme's funding status will have a bearing on the transfer or actuarial value of a member's benefit. If the value of the accrued benefits to date amounts to, say, €100,000 and the scheme is only 50 percent funded, the transfer value will be reduced to €50,000.

A defined contribution scheme usually works more like a conventional savings plan. The employee and employer both contribute to a fund which increases (or decreases) over the period leading to retirement, depending on whether the investments go up or down. The eventual value of these benefits is unpredictable, as it will be influenced by the amount of contributions, as well as the performance of the investment.

Many employees also make additional voluntary contributions (AVCs), which generally operate on a defined contribution basis.

People who are self-employed, or not covered by an employer's occupational scheme, can take out 'personal pensions' (or, more accurately, retirement annuity contracts) with insurance companies. These work on the principle of a defined contribution, with tax relief allowed up to a set total of contributions in each tax year.

Individuals working in family businesses may be members of either occupational or personal pension schemes, depending on the source of their earnings.

ARFs and AMRFs

An Approved Retirement Fund is a post-retirement scheme which allows members to invest the balance of their funds after they have taken a tax-free cash lump sum. An ARF allows members to continue to invest their retirement funds and draw an income (subject to income tax) at their convenience. Funds can grow tax-free. The minimum annual withdrawal from age 60 is five percent.

An ARF operates in a similar way to a defined contribution scheme, in that its value is determined by the performance of the investments. All the funds can be withdrawn from an ARF at any time, but subject to income tax.

An Approved Minimum Retirement Fund is similar to an ARF. However members cannot access the original capital until their 75th birthday or until they can satisfy the minimum annual income requirement of €12,700 from guaranteed sources. Funds can be withdrawn, subject to income tax. An annuity can be bought at any time with the proceeds of the AMRF.

Trustees

Pension schemes are run by trustees whose responsibilities are set out in the scheme's trust deed and rules, together with general trust law and the requirements of the Pensions Acts. A spouse or dependant may also be a potential beneficiary of the pension scheme and also has a right to information under the Pensions Acts.

Employees should consult the trustees or scheme administrator to obtain details of their pension rights, although other experts—such as actuaries and consultants—may also be involved.

Benefits payable under pension schemes will vary, but generally consist of a:

- retirement pension payable to the member;
- pension payable to the member's spouse if the member dies *after* retirement;
- cash lump sum and pension payable to the member's spouse (or dependants) if the member dies *before* retirement; or
- cash lump sum and the right to put the balance of the funds into an ARF or AMRF.

Middle-income workers are likely to have built up a reasonable level of pension rights by the time they're middle-aged. In the case of the self-employed or those working in family businesses, much of their personal wealth may still be secured in the business, rather than through a pension plan, so pensions may not be such an important issue.

Until 1995, the courts could not divide up pensions as a specific asset on separation, although couples could make their own arrangements as part of an overall maintenance agreement. But the family law acts set out rules to deal with pension rights on judicial separation. The Divorce Act also gives the courts power to divide pension assets in the same way as other financial assets.

Pensions may become a contentious issue if agreement can't be reached on splitting other assets, such as the home and any other property or financial holdings.

All pension rights may be taken into account on divorce or separation, including those accumulated before the marriage. The court can order that part of the pension rights be paid to the spouse or to dependent children. If a dependent spouse has already died, payment can be made to his or her estate.

The court can make orders about the pension benefits of either spouse. Generally, a pension will be split at the time of a decree, but either spouse can apply to the court for a pension adjustment order at any time during the lifetime of the pension scheme member. The application may also be made by a person acting on behalf of any dependent members of the family.

The court may:

- transfer pension rights from one spouse to the other (a 'clean break' approach); or
- set aside benefits due to be paid in the future ('earmark assets').

Pension adjustment orders may be made against self-employed people and those in non-pensionable employment, as well as against members of occupational pension schemes.

Example 1

Catherine, a self-employed woman, takes out a pension contract at 25. At 30, she marries Mike. Ten years later, they separate. The court awards Mike 50% of the pension. Catherines's total contributions come to €20,000. The value of the fund is now €28,000. Mike therefore receives €14,000.

Example 2

Brendan joined his employer's pension scheme when he was 20. He married Vera ten years later but they separated when he was 40. The court awards Vera 50% of the pension that accrued during their married life. Under the company scheme, Brendan gets 1/60th of his salary for each year of service up to age 60. Vera's benefit when Brendan retires will be one twelfth of his salary (50% x 10/60 x final salary). At normal retirement age, Brendan will be entitled to 40/60 (or two thirds) of his final salary, less Vera's share, leaving Brendan with a pension of seven-twelfths of his final salary.

Where pension assets are split at the time of divorce under the clean break approach, part of the pension rights may be transferred to:

- the spouse's own pension arrangements (if a member of an occupational scheme);
- an insurance company bond in the name of the receiving spouse; or
- an ARF or AMRF in the name of the receiving spouse.

Specialist advice will be required to work out the value of the amounts to be transferred, to represent the current value of future entitlements.

As well as a retirement pension, the court can also order the pension scheme member to provide for a lump sum to be paid to the former spouse if the member dies before retirement. This benefit would cease if the receiving spouse remarried or died before the pension scheme member.

If a worker leaves his pensionable employment, the court will decide how much is due to the former spouse. The benefits can be kept in the pension scheme and paid later, or may be transferred to the spouse's scheme or an insurance bond. If a spouse leaves a pension scheme, the trustees must notify the other spouse and the court.

If a former spouse dies, the accumulated benefits (as decided by the court) must be paid to the estate within three months of the date of death. Depending on the arrangements made about death-in-service benefits, the lump sum and accumulated pension benefits may become payable to the former spouse at this stage.

A contingent benefit PAO will cease for contingent benefits but not retirement benefits if the non-member remarries or registers a civil partnership.

Letter of Authority

In order to assess the pension situation, the scheme member should give his solicitor a letter of authority addressed to the trustees authorising them to release information about the scheme and entitlements.

LETTER OF AUTHORITY

To whom it may concern

I_____ am a member of the _____ pension scheme. I hereby request and authorise the scheme trustees to provide such information about the scheme and my entitlements as may be requested by _____ _____.

Signed: _____

Date: _____

Tax Situation

A change in marital status will also affect a person's tax position. The Finance (No 3) Act 2011 followed the passing of the Civil Partnership and Certain Rights and Obligations of Cohabitants Act 2010. The Act provides that civil partners in a registered partnership are entitled to the same tax treatment as married couples. Cohabitants are assessed to tax as single individuals.

Married couples or civil partners living together may choose to be assessed for income tax by:

- single assessment;
- joint assessment; or
- separate assessment.

Spouses or civil partners are not considered to be living together if they are separated by formal agreement or court order, or if their separation is likely to be permanent.

The 1983 Finance Act dealt with income tax assessment for separated spouses. Where a legally-enforceable maintenance agreement existed before 8 June 1983, the payer deducts tax at the standard rate from maintenance payments. The recipient is taxed on the original gross amount, but receives a credit for the tax deducted at source.

If the maintenance agreement was made after 8 June 1983, the payer does not withhold income tax, but receives a deduction for payments made to a spouse. The recipient's payment is treated as income for tax purposes. Payments for children are disregarded.[1]

Parents who are not entitled to a married allowance may be entitled to a single parent allowance for children who live with them for all or part of the year. Child allowance is also payable for disabled children. Mortgage relief is limited to the single person's mortgage allowance, but may be allowable on loans for two properties.

Single treatment automatically applies when spouses separate unless they both request in writing to be assessed as if they were still living together.

---

[1] *FF v PF* [2012] IEHC 581.

This does not apply to divorced couples or in the case of civil nullity. Both parties must be resident in the state and one spouse must be making payments under a maintenance agreement.

The spouses submit their own individual tax returns and are entitled to their own personal allowances but pay tax only on their own income. Any unused personal allowances can be transferred to the other spouse. Any maintenance payments are not taken into consideration, as there would be no such payments between a married couple, and the couple are taxed on a separate assessment basis.

If a person remarries, the Revenue Commissioners will recognise the new marriage, even if it is not recognised under the Domicile and Recognition of Foreign Divorces Act.

Different capital gains tax rules apply for separated couples in relation to their principal private residence, property transfers, share interaction, remarriage and death. The position of separated couples may also change with regard to capital acquisitions tax and stamp duty.

Qualified cohabitants do not enjoy the same tax treatment as married spouses or civil partners.

Spouses intending to separate or divorce, or civil partners planning to separate or seek a dissolution of their relationship, should ask their solicitor to refer them to an experienced tax accountant.

WILLS

Introduction

Marriage—or remarriage—revokes any previous will, unless the will was made in contemplation of that marriage, so people who change their marital status should also change their wills. The Civil Partnership and Certain Rights and Obligations of Cohabitants Act 2010 also amends 20 sections of the 1965 Succession Act, so it would be wise for anyone entering a civil partnership also to consider drawing up a new will.

Wills can be very straightforward where a couple intend leaving all their property to the other or in equal shares between their children. Separation, divorce or remarriage introduce all sorts of complications. Anyone who has already made a will—or, indeed, anyone who has not yet made a will—and intends to separate or remarry should take legal advice before drawing up a new will.

The Succession Act 1965, which sets out the requirements for a valid will, says that a spouse and children have a right to a certain share in the property of a deceased parent or spouse, whether a will was made or not.

This also applies now to civil partners. Orders 79 and 80 of the Rules of the Superior Courts have been amended[1] to allow surviving civil partners to obtain a grant of administration.

Where a person dies leaving a spouse or partner and no children, the spouse or civil partner has a right to half the estate, whatever the will might say and even if the parties have lived apart for a long period. If there are children of a marriage, the spouse has a right to one third of the estate. This is known as the 'legal right'.

Legal Right

The so-called 'legal right' may be renounced in writing by a spouse or civil partner at any time, before or after marriage, but the courts would need to be quite sure that a person received proper legal advice before giving up the right, and was not subjected to any pressure.

In the case of an intestacy, where there is no valid will and no children, a spouse or civil partner is entitled to the whole estate. If there are children or grandchildren, the spouse or civil partner is entitled to two thirds of the estate, with the remainder going to the children or grandchildren.

If both spouses or civil partners are dead, the children share the estate. If there is no surviving spouse or civil partner and no issue, the estate goes to his parents or is divided according to ss 68-73 of the 1965 Act.

In the case of *O'Dwyer v Keegan*,[2] a testator had died leaving IR£2.4 million. His wife, who was in a coma at the time, died 12 hours later, leaving IR£370,000. The husband had not provided for his wife in his will. The couple had no children and the wife had not renounced her legal right.

The High Court ruled that the surviving spouse did not automatically receive the estate of the deceased spouse, but the legal right was merely a right which the wife could have exercised if she wished. However, on

[1] SI No 348 of 2011.
[2] [1997] 1 ILRM 102.

appeal, the Supreme Court said the legal right was automatically exercised when one spouse died.

The legal right has priority over any other bequests, but may be extinguished by the court following a judicial separation or dissolution, and disappears after a divorce.

A spouse or civil partner may try to evade the provisions of the statute by giving away all his property, but if he dies within three years of such dispositions, the gifts are void if they were made for that purpose. Of course, it might not always be possible for the other partner to recover such void 'gifts'.

A separation agreement may also include a clause renouncing succession rights. Where a divorced spouse dies, the other spouse may apply within six months of the grant of probate to be provided for out of the estate, taking into account the rights of anyone else. The court will not make such an order for someone who has remarried.

Law of Probate

The law of probate, relating to wills, is largely contained in the Succession Act 1965 and orders 79 and 80 of the Rules of the Superior Court.

For a will to be valid, the person making the will (known in legal terms as the testator, or testatrix if female) must be 18 years old or over, or have been married. He must also be acting of his own free will and be of "sound disposing mind".[3]

A person who is entitled to appoint a guardian of a child may do so by will, even if he is under 18 and single.

In the 19th century, Chief Justice Cockburn said no "insane delusion" should influence the making of a will, so a testator must:

1) understand the nature and effects of making a will;
2) know the extent of his property (for example, he must not bequeath property which he had already given away); and

---

[3] s 77(1)(b), Succession Act 1965.

3) be able to recall the people who might be expected to benefit from his bounty (or to call to mind those who might have a claim against, or expect to benefit from, his estate).[4]

In *Scally v Rhatigan*,[5] Laffoy J confirmed that this test also applied in Ireland.[6]

Testamentary Capacity

A will may be challenged on the basis that the testator did not have 'testamentary capacity', that is the mental ability to make a valid will. Testamentary capacity may be proved by an affidavit from a doctor or solicitor who was present when the will was made but, in the last resort, testamentary capacity is a matter for the courts, as the Supreme Court ruled in *Glynn v Glynn*.[7]

In that case, the testator's sister challenged his testamentary capacity after he left his residue to a cousin. He had already instructed a parish priest to draw up his will for him, but two months later he suffered a stroke which left him dumb. When the will was read back to him in hospital, he was only able to shake and nod his head. He marked an 'X' at the end of the will.

A doctor testified that the deceased did not have testamentary capacity at the time, but the priest said he did. The High Court declared the will valid and the Supreme Court upheld that decision on appeal.

In the case of *Blackall v Blackall*,[8] a 99-year-old woman had made a will leaving her property equally between her four children. When her solicitor read the will over to her, the testatrix commented: "I think that's fair, one of them is a bit fiery". The judge said he was satisfied that was the comment of someone who knew what had been read to her, and that the testatrix did have testamentary capacity.

---

[4] *Banks v Goodfellow* [1870] LR 5.
[5] Unreported, High Court, 21 December 2009.
[6] See also *O'Donnell v O'Donnell*, unreported, High Court, 24 March 1999, and *Flannery v Flannery* [2009] IEHC 317.
[7] [1990] 2 IR 326.
[8] Unreported, Supreme Court, 1 April 1998.

In *Carroll v Carroll*,[9] Denham J said the court could set aside a voluntary gift, unless it was proved that the gift was a "spontaneous act" in the free exercise of the donor's independent will.

In a case in August 2013,[10] the president of the High Court said he was satisfied that testatrix Mary Coffey "was of sound mind and knew what she was doing" when she left her 80-year-old brother only €45,000 in her €3.5 million will.

Coffey made dozens of charitable bequests ranging from €100 to €50,000 to the poor, the deaf and blind, hospices and the Samaritans. Her solicitor said she had drawn up the will herself and was, in his opinion, "perfectly capable of making her will". Her family doctor said Coffey had never shown symptoms of suffering "any mental deficit".

Kearns J rejected Joseph Dee's challenge to his sister's will on the grounds that she was mentally incapable, was easily led and had been badly advised.

In *C & anor v C & ors*,[11] the Supreme Court upheld a High Court decision that the nephew of a ward of court had exercised undue influence over his aunt, and setting aside alleged gifts from her to him of more than €900,000.

Duress and Undue Influence

It may be acceptable to persuade a testator to change his will, but it is not acceptable to put undue pressure on him. In the English case of *Hall v Hall*,[12] the judge said:

> Persuasion is not unlawful, but pressure of whatever character, if so exerted as to overpower the volition without convincing the judgment of the testator, will constitute undue influence, though no force is either used or threatened.

---

[9] [1999] 4 IR 241.

[10] Aodhan O'Faolain, Ray Managh, 'Brother fails in bid for greater share of sister's €3.5m estate', *The Irish Times*, 26 August 2013; available from http://www.irishtimes.com/news/crime-and-law/courts/brother-fails-in-bid-for-greater-share-of-sister-s-3-5m-estate-1.1506187; accessed 7 January 2014.

[11] [2013] IESC 36.

[12] LR 1 P & D 481.

In the High Court, Murphy J said that undue influence in the context of probate was more closely aligned to common law duress.[13]

The Law Reform Commission's Consultation Paper on the Law of the Elderly[14] said that, while a solicitor might be able to decide after a single interview whether a testator had the capacity to make a will, it would often be more difficult to detect undue influence without a "detailed understanding of complex relationships between family members".

Law Society guidelines say that solicitors should not accept instructions which they suspect have been given by a client under duress or undue influence. "Particular care should be taken where a client is elderly or otherwise vulnerable to pressure from others," said the Law Society.

However, if a testator receives independent legal advice, that can rebut any allegation of undue influence. In *Carroll v Carroll*,[15] the Supreme Court set aside a conveyance, holding that a presumption of undue influence arose when a donor had not obtained independent legal advice. But in *Naylor v Maher*,[16] where an 80-year-old Tipperary farmer used a new solicitor to change his will, the High Court rejected a claim of duress and undue influence.

Validity

A valid will must be in writing and signed (or marked) at the end by the testator, or by someone in his presence and by his direction. The signature must be written or acknowledged before two witnesses, both present at the same time, and the witnesses must sign in the presence of the testator, though not necessarily in each other's presence.

A witness may be an executor of the will, or even a child, although this may cause problems if he is required to swear an affidavit while he is still a minor. The incompetence of a witness does not invalidate a will.

---

[13] *Lambert v Lyons* [2010] IEHC 29.
[14] June 2003.
[15] [1999] 4 IR 243.
[16] [2012] IEHC 408.

Neither a witness nor his spouse may benefit under a will, except where:

1) the legacy is a legal or moral duty, such as a debt;
2) the benefit is given to a named beneficiary but in trust for someone else;
3) the beneficiary and the witness married after the will; or
4) the legacy is bequeathed in an additional clause to which the witness to the will is not a witness.

'Signature' can include the initials of the testator or, in the case of an illiterate or severely disabled person, a mark. In the 1987 *Glynn* case, an X was accepted as a signature. In another case,[17] the court proved a will signed simply "Your loving mother".

A will is not necessarily invalidated just because the signature does not immediately follow the last word or is after the witnesses' signatures, but any writing after the testator's signature is normally excluded. The court decided in the English case of *Beadle*[18] that a document was not a will where the testatrix signed at the top of the page.

A will which does not comply with all these provisions will be valid if it complies with the law:

1) of the place where the testator made it;
2) of the testator's nationality (either when he made the will or at his death);
3) of the place where the testator was domiciled or habitually resident when he made the will or died;
4) of the place where immovable property is situated; or,
5) when a will is made on a ship or plane, where it had its most real connection.

A will should contain:

1) the testator's name and address;
2) a revocation clause;
3) a clause appointing executors (preferably, but not necessarily, two or more);

---

[17] *In Bonis Cook* [1960] 1 WLR 353.
[18] [1974] 1 All ER 493.

4) details of general and specific legacies (gifts of money or goods);
5) details of devises (gifts of real property);
6) a residuary clause, disposing of the remainder of the estate;
7) the date;
8) the testator's signature;
9) the attestation clause or *testimonium*; and
10) the witnesses' signatures.

The revocation clause must revoke all other codicils and earlier testamentary dispositions, as well as former wills. The executors should be clearly identified. 'I appoint AB and CD as my executors' or 'I appoint AB as my executor or, if he predeceases me, I appoint CD in his place' are acceptable, but 'I appoint AB or CD as my executor' would be void for uncertainty.

If any of the specific gifts should fail, for example, under the doctrine of lapse, the property involved would fall into the residue. If the will has no residuary clause, any property not specifically mentioned passes according to the rules of intestacy in the Succession Act.

A will may contain only an executor clause and a residue clause, and still be valid if it expresses the wishes of the testator. If the executors have died or cannot (or will not) act, the person entitled to the residue can administer the estate.

The lack of a date on a will does not invalidate it, but the probate office will require an affidavit from one of the witnesses confirming that the document was executed before the testator died.

The testimonium might read:

> Signed by the testator as and for his last will and testament in the presence of us, both present at the same time, and signed by us in the presence of the testator.

The witnesses normally sign under this clause, but the will is not invalid if they sign elsewhere on the document. If the will does not contain a testimonium, the probate office will require an affidavit from one of the witnesses.

Wills "speak from death", and are interpreted as if they had been executed immediately before the death of the testator, unless the will itself specifies otherwise.

If any children of the testator die before him, property bequeathed to them will automatically pass to their children. If two or more people die together, for example in a plane crash, and it is not possible to establish who died first, they are deemed to have died simultaneously.

Any obliteration, insertion or alteration in a will after its execution is invalid unless:

1) the testator and witnesses sign near the alteration;
2) the changes are proved to have been in the will before its execution;
3) the alterations are mentioned in the recital clause; or
4) there is a properly-executed codicil or memorandum referring to the alterations.

If the will refers to any documents which existed when the will was executed, they should be produced. An official copy of any will or grant of administration may be obtained from the probate office or district probate registry.

Removal of Succession Rights

A spouse or civil partner who has deserted or 'who has been guilty of the murder, attempted murder or manslaughter' of another person, or who has committed a serious offence against the testator or the testator's children in the case of a marriage, loses any right to a share in the estate, except under a will made after the offence.

In *Nevin & anor v Nevin*,[19] Kearns P said the absence of the phrase "found guilty" in s 120(1) of the legislation was an "extraordinary omission" but, as the sub-section was "punitive and conclusive", it had to be strictly construed. He said the sub-section only went so far as to state public policy that a murderer should not benefit from her crime.

A husband and wife's mutual rights to succeed to each other's estates may also be extinguished by the court at any time on or after a decree of judicial separation, under the 1995 Family Law Act. Succession rights are automatically extinguished after a divorce, as the couple are no

---

[19] [2013] IEHC 80.

longer man and wife, though a spouse may apply under s 18 of the Divorce Act for provision from the estate of a former spouse. Where a marriage is void, the partners are not spouses and these provisions do not apply.

Revocation of Will

A will may be revoked by:

1) a subsequent marriage—unless the will is made in contemplation of that marriage;
2) a later will or codicil which expressly revokes all earlier testamentary dispositions;
3) declaring in writing an intention to revoke the will, and executing the document in the same way as a will; or
4) the testator (or someone in his presence and at his direction) burning, tearing or destroying the will with the simultaneous intention of revocation.

If a testator writes to the person who holds the will asking him to destroy it, that would revoke the will, whether or not it was actually destroyed. If no other will is executed, this would result in an intestacy.

Revocation of a will does not revive any earlier will; that may only be done by re-execution or a properly-executed codicil. However, there may be an implied revocation of an earlier will if the later will is clearly inconsistent with it—for example if the testator disposes of all his assets in the later will.

Representation

When a person dies, his estate is administered by a personal representative who can be either an executor (nominated in a will or codicil) or an administrator (appointed by the court).

A personal representative holds the whole estate as trustee for anyone entitled to the property. Where someone dies without leaving a will (or executor), his estate vests in the President of the High Court until the probate office grants administration.

There is no legal requirement to extract a grant of representation to an estate but a grant is usually necessary to be able to sell property or collect assets. Applications for a grant of probate or letters of administration may be made 14 days or more after the death of the deceased.

An executor may be removed by the court for misconduct. In the case of *Flood v Flood*,[20] the executor had borrowed money from the testator and refused to repay it. The judge said the court could remove an executor in the case of "serious misconduct and/or serious special circumstances".

Caveats

Anyone challenging the terms of a will should lodge a warning notice or caveat in the probate office. The caveat should say:

> Let nothing be done in the estate of (*name*), late of (*address*), who died on (*date*) at (*address*), unknown to me, (*your name*) of (*address*) having interest. Signed: (*your name and address*)

The caveat remains in force for six months and may be renewed.

Anyone who wants to prove the will must issue a 'warning to caveat' requiring the caveator to enter an appearance in the probate office within six days to state his interest in the estate. A will may only be challenged by someone who would be entitled to benefit if it was struck down. A caveator may, for instance, have been a beneficiary in an earlier will or, if he is the testator's next-of-kin, it might be in his interests to create an intestacy.

Construction of Will

There is a presumption that wills are properly executed and that the testator had testamentary capacity so, if the will appears valid, it is presumed to be so.

If the terms of a will are clear, the court will not allow extrinsic evidence about its construction. In the case of *O'Connell v Bank of Ireland*,[21] a widow

---

[20] [1999] 2 IR 234.
[21] [1998] 2 IR 596.

told several people that she had left her house and contents to the plaintiffs, but the will only mentioned the contents, not the house. The judge said he was satisfied that the testatrix had intended to leave her house to the plaintiffs, but he could only construe the will in accordance with its terms. The decision was upheld by the Supreme Court.

If the will is unclear, extrinsic evidence may be allowed to show the intention of the testator. In the case of *Lindsay v Tomlinson*,[22] the testatrix left IR£25,000 to a non-existent charity, the "National Society for the Prevention of Cruelty to Animals (Dogs and Cats Home), 1 Grand Canal Quay in the city of Dublin". To confuse matters further, the Dublin Society for the Prevention of Cruelty to Animals and the Irish Society for the Prevention of Cruelty to Animals had formerly shared premises at 1 Grand Canal Quay.

The judge allowed evidence that the testatrix was a dog-lover, that she subscribed annually to the Dublin Society which operated the "Dogs and Cats Home" when it was situated at Grand Canal Quay. On the balance of probabilities, the judge said the scales came down in favour of the Dublin Society.

Section 117 Applications

If a testator died wholly or partly testate, any of his children may bring an application under s 117 of the Succession Act claiming that he failed in the moral duty to make proper provision for his children. This action may be brought by a child of any age, whether adopted or not, whether born inside or outside the marriage and whether dependent or not. It may not be brought by a person who was guilty of a serious offence against the testator, punishable by more than two years' imprisonment.

The principles on which a s 117 application will be decided were set out by Kearns J in the High Court in *XC v RT (Succession; Proper Provision)*[23]:

(a) The social policy underlying s 117 is primarily directed to protecting those children who are still of an age and situation in life where they might reasonably expect support from their

---

[22] Unreported, High Court, 1996.
[23] [2003] 2 IR 250.

parents, against the failure of parents who are unmindful of their duties in that area.

(b) What has to be determined is whether the testator, at the time of his death, owed any moral obligation to the children and, if so, whether he has failed in that obligation.

(c) There is a high onus of proof placed on an applicant for relief under s 117, which requires the establishment of a positive failure in moral duty.

(d) Before a court can interfere, there must be clear circumstances, and a positive failure in moral duty must be established.

(e) The duty created by s 117 is not absolute.

(f) The relationship of parent and child does not itself, and without regard to other circumstances, create a moral duty to leave anything by will to the child.

(g) s 117 does not create an obligation to leave something to each child.

(h) The provision of an expensive education for a child may discharge the moral duty, as may other gifts or settlements made during the lifetime of the testator.

(i) Financing a good education so as to give a child the best start in life possible and providing money which, if properly managed, should afford a degree of financial security for the rest of one's life, does amount to making 'proper provision'.

(j) The duty under s 117 is not to make adequate provision, but to provide proper provision in accordance with the testator's means.

(k) A just parent must take into account, not just his moral obligations to his children and to his wife, but all his moral obligations, e.g. to aged and infirm parents.

(l) In dealing with a s 117 application, the position of an applicant child is not to be taken in isolation. The court's duty is to consider the entirety of the testator's affairs and to decide upon the application in the overall context. In other words, while the moral claim of a child may require a testator to make a particular provision for him, the moral claims of others may require such provision to be reduced or omitted altogether.

(m) Special circumstances giving rise to a moral duty may arise if a child is induced to believe that by, for example, working on a farm, he will ultimately become the owner of it, thereby causing him to shape his upbringing, training and life accordingly.

(n) Another example of special circumstances might be a child who had a long illness or an exceptional talent which it would be morally wrong not to foster.

(o) Special needs would also include physical or mental disability.

(p) Although the court has very wide powers both as to when to make provision for an applicant child and as to the nature of such provision, such powers must not be construed as giving the court a power to make a new will for the testator.

(q) The test to be applied is not which of the alternative courses open to the testator the court itself would have adopted if confronted with the same situation, but rather whether the decision of the testator to opt for the course he did, of itself and without more, constituted a breach of moral duty to the plaintiff.

(r) The court must not disregard the fact that parents must be presumed to know their children better than anyone else.

In relation to (n) and sick children, in the case of *K & ors v D & anor*,[24] which had "a long and unfortunate history", the High Court said the testator had not made proper provision for his severely epileptic daughter, who was a ward of court.

The testator's two sons and his daughter, suing by her mother, challenged the testator's decision to leave land to his partner, who tended him for the three years before his death. She also received a house on half an acre by right of survivorship.

The testator left a commercial yard to his partner and children in equal shares, and half-acre sites to his sons if they got planning permission within two years. However, the testator's partner blocked the planning applications, which were not granted.

The personal representatives agreed that proper provision had not been made for the daughter, and the amount left to her in the will was "somewhat meagre". Even the testator's partner agreed that her share of the estate should be adjusted to make extra provision for the daughter.

---

[24] [2011] IEHC 22.

Birmingham J said he was "firmly of the view that there was a clear failure on the part of the testator to make proper provision for his daughter". The position of the two sons was "less clear cut", and the provision that the testator sought to make for them appeared "unimpeachable".

He ordered that all the assets in the estate should be converted into cash and half given to the daughter, with the balance divided between the two sons and the partner.

In the case of *FM v TAM*,[25] the judge said the court would consider:

1) the amount left to the surviving spouse (or the value of the legal right);
2) the number of the testator's children;
3) the ages and positions in life of the children at the testator's death;
4) the means of the testator;
5) the age of the applicant;
6) the financial position and prospects of the applicant; and
7) any other provision already made by the testator for the applicant.

Age

Any child of any age can make a s 117 application, though a testator has no legal obligation under s 117 to stepchildren.[26]

In 1998, in the case of *EB v SS*,[27] the judge said:

> Since the legislature, no doubt for good reasons, declined to impose any age ceiling which would preclude middle-aged or even elderly offspring from obtaining relief, the courts must give effect to the provision, irrespective of the age which the child has attained.

A solicitor does not have to inform a beneficiary about the possibility of a s117 application.[28] Costs are at the court's discretion, though the applicant's costs are normally allowed, even if he is unsuccessful, as long as there was a statable case.

---

[25] (1972) 106 ILTR 82.
[26] *Naylor v Maher* [2012] IEHC 408.
[27] [1998] 4 IR 527.
[28] *Rojack v Taylor & Anor* [2005] IEHC 28.

The moral duty of a testator to make proper provision for his children must be proved. In *AC (A minor) v JF, FG & PMcE*,[29] Clarke J said a deceased person may owe a moral duty to people other than those to whom he owes a legal obligation.

The court will consider the claim from the point of view of a "prudent and just parent", taking into account any payments made during the testator's lifetime and the situation of any other children, but disregarding the testator's attitude to the applicant.

In *MPD v MD*,[30] Carroll J held that the court must consider the value of the entire estate at the date of death and at the date of hearing.

The court ruled in the case of *PMcD v MN*[31] that it could also take into account a plaintiff's behaviour towards his parent.

In *Browne v Sweeney*,[32] the plaintiff's mother bequeathed IR£5,000 to each of her grandchildren and divided the residue of her estate—worth about IR£1.3 million—between five charities. The plaintiff and his three siblings had each received about IR£275,000 five years before their mother's death. The plaintiff was an addict and had wasted the money. The judge said that, in the circumstances, the testatrix had discharged her moral duty and he dismissed the claim.

A child who has been found guilty of an offence against the deceased, or against any spouse or child of the deceased, punishable by two years' imprisonment or more, may not make an application under s 117.

Time Limits

Section 117 applications must be made within six months of the first taking out of representation of the estate,[33] that is a grant of probate or administration with the will annexed, not grant of administration *ad litem*.[34] This limitation period cannot be extended by the court and applies whether or not it is raised as a defence. If the deadline is missed,

[29] [2007] IEHC 399.
[30] [1981] ILRM 179.
[31] [1999] 4 IR 301.
[32] Unreported, High Court, July 1996.
[33] *MPD & Ors v MD* [1981] ILRM 179.
[34] *S1 v PR1 & Ors* [2013] IEHC 407.

consideration might be given to claiming a constructive trust instead. Care should be taken that any alternative claim based on, for example, promissory estoppel should be brought promptly to avoid being statute-barred.[35]

Discovery of documents in a s 117 application may be limited by the court. In *GP v GR and PM*,[36] a daughter of the testator brought a s 117 action claiming that neither she nor any of her three siblings from her father's first marriage had ever obtained any financial help from him. On the other hand, her father had paid for her two stepsisters' college education and had given the girls presents all their lives, including cars, houses and holidays.

She asked the court to order the defendants to produce 13 categories of documents, including ten years' tax returns for the testator's widow and her daughters, a list of all gifts worth more than €500 received from any source, and details of the daughters' qualifications, education, employment history and medical condition since the testator's death.

However, the testator's solicitor pointed out that the testator had left everything to his second wife if she survived him by 30 days, which she did. Neither of the daughters was a beneficiary of the estate, so any provision made for them during their father's life was irrelevant to a s 117 application. As GP had not asked the court to declare the will to be a disposition disinheriting the testator's children, documents relating to gifts received by the widow were irrelevant. However, the widow agreed to swear an affidavit of her means at the time of her husband's death.

Laffoy J asked whether all the documents sought were relevant and necessary for disposing fairly of the case, or for saving costs. She said it was difficult to see how the daughters' assets were relevant, as neither had benefited under the will and both were independent adults at the time of their father's death. The "burden, scale and cost" of producing the documentation demanded from the daughters, "even if it was relevant, which it is not, would be likely to be disproportionate". She dismissed the application for discovery of documents relating to the daughters.

---

[35] *FDC v AC & Ors* [2012] IEHC 537.
[36] [2013] IEHC 333.

In relation to the documents sought from the widow, she adjourned the motion to enable the widow to swear her affidavit of means and to give GP's legal advisers time to examine it.

The danger of making a series of wills was illustrated by the High Court case of *Felix Smyth v John Joseph Halpin and Regina Stokes*.[37]

The father of Felix Smyth made a number of different wills in 1966, 1976, 1986, 1991 and 1992. Smyth, who was told that he would inherit his father's house, asked the High Court to declare that he was entitled to the house after the death of his mother.

Mr Justice Geoghegan referred to the English case of *Inwards v Baker*[38] where a father had suggested to his son that he build on his land, which the son did, at his own expense. The Court of Appeal held that the son had an equitable right to remain in the house for the rest of his life, even though the father had left all his property to a lady with whom he had lived for some years.

The judge ruled that Smyth had "clearly established that he falls within these (equitable) principles" and he directed that the remainder interest in the house be vested in Smyth.

---

[37] "Expenditure on property on foot of testator's promise creates an equity" *The Irish Times* (archived), 31 March 1997, [1997] 2 ILRM 39.
[38] [1965] 2 QB 29.

LEGAL AID

Introduction

Using the services of a solicitor or barrister can be cripplingly expensive, particularly where both sides have to pay their own costs, as in most family law proceedings. To help those who can't afford private legal representation, legal aid was introduced.

The Legal Aid Board came into operation in December 1980, following the decision of the European Court of Human Rights in *Airey v Ireland*.[1] The ECHR ruled that the absence of a legal aid scheme in Ireland to help the applicant bring judicial separation proceedings was a barrier to access to justice and a violation of her rights under Article 6 of the European Human Rights Convention.

The purpose of the Legal Aid Board is to provide legal aid and advice by solicitors and barristers to people who have little or no money. Costs of the scheme are met by government grant which totalled €24.125 million in 2011. The grant in 2012 came to €32.922 million, but included funding for the Family Mediation Service which was transferred to the board in November 2011.

Contrary to popular opinion, civil legal aid is not free; applicants make some contribution, depending on their means. But state funding of civil legal aid has always been an issue. In 1990, board chairman Nial Fennelly (later a Supreme Court judge) resigned in protest at the lack of funding.

---

[1] (1979) 2 EHRR 305.

The Civil Legal Aid Act 1995 established the board on a statutory basis and provided, for the first time, a statutory entitlement to civil legal aid. Most legal aid services are provided by full-time legal aid solicitors at 30 law centres around the country. The board also uses private solicitors for domestic violence, maintenance, guardianship and custody/access matters in the District Court. The services of barristers are also available, under a different scheme.

In the five years from 2006-2011, there was a 93 percent cumulative increase in demand for Legal Aid Board services.

In 2012, the number of applicants was slightly down on the historically high 2011 figure. A total of 16,870 clients, excluding applicants for refugee legal services, applied for legal services. The overwhelming majority of civil legal aid cases are concerned with family law. In 2012, the board provided legal aid in 5,322 divorce, separation or nullity cases, 2,568 other family law matters and 1,178 child care cases, with only 628 cases relating to other civil matters.

The board aims to ensure that applicants are given an appointment within four months of completing their application. But the popularity of the scheme and the effects of the economic downturn mean there can be lengthy waiting lists in some centres.

In September 2013, more than 5,300 people were waiting for a first appointment with a solicitor, although there is a priority service for people seeking legal services in cases of domestic violence, childcare, child abduction and other matters where there are statutory time limits. The target waiting time is two to four months, but the reality is that applicants may be waiting for up to 12 months; the average wait in September 2013 was ten months. The board has now introduced a 'triage' service aimed at providing early legal advice to all applicants.

Means Test

Applicants for legal services from the Legal Aid Board must satisfy a means test. The required contributions from applicants increased from September 2013.

Financial limits are subject to change but, at the time of writing, applicants' disposable income must be less than €18,000 per annum and disposable capital (other than their home) less than €100,000. For legal advice, applicants pay between €30 and €150. The minimum contribution for legal aid is €130 and applicants may also be liable for a capital contribution, depending on their disposable capital.

The maximum allowances which may be set against income for calculating eligibility are:

- Dependent spouse or partner €3,500;
- Dependent child or adult €1,600;
- Child care up to €6,000 per child;
- Accommodation up to €8,000;
- Income tax—full amount;
- Social insurance and Universal Social Charge—full amount
- *Ex gratia* payments €1,040.

If the case goes to court, the Legal Aid Board will also take into account the value of the applicant's capital resources, such as his house, land, car or savings, and may require payment of a capital contribution.

Examples of Operation of Means Test

1) Single mother with two young children. Her only income, other than child benefit, is a weekly One Parent Family payment of €204.40. She pays €25 a week rent for her local authority accommodation. She has no assets.

   - 2 children €3,200
   - Rent €1,300

Disposable income: €6,128.80. Contribution payable for legal advice is €30 and for legal aid €130.

2) A salaried employee earning €44,497 and paying income tax of €5,430, PRSI of €1,760 and USC of €2,952. His spouse / partner is not dependent on him. He pays €200 a week childcare costs for his two dependent children. His mortgage, which he pays, is €580 a month, including life assurance cover. His car is worth €8,500 and he has shares worth €20,000. He has no other assets.

   - 2 children €3,200
   - Childcare €10,400
   - PAYE €5,430
   - PRSI €1,760
   - USC €2,952
   - Accommodation €6,960

Disposable income: €13,795. Contribution payable: €150 for legal advice and €704 for legal aid. This is calculated by taking the applicant's disposable income, deducting €11,500 and, for the purpose of legal advice, taking 10 percent of the remainder and adding the minimum contribution of €30. However, the maximum advice contribution is set at €150, so this figure applies to the example. The aid contribution is assessed by taking 25 percent of the difference between the applicant's disposable income and €11,500 and adding the minimum legal aid contribution of €130.

The minimum contribution is payable by a person whose disposable income does not exceed €11,500 a year. An applicant who has more than €4,000 in disposable capital will also have to pay a contribution for legal aid of up to €1,250, plus five percent of any amount over €54,000. However, the board may waive any contribution or accept a lower contribution if to do otherwise would cause undue hardship.[2] This may apply where the applicant:

- depends entirely on supplementary welfare;
- is on "shared payments"; or
- is bringing proceedings to compel payment of a maintenance order.

In the example, the applicant's assets total €28,500 and a notional allowance of 10 percent is allowed for realisation costs. This leaves €25,650. The first €4,000 of assets are exempt. The contribution is assessed on the basis of 2.5 percent of the value of the assets up to €54,000. In the example, the capital contribution is assessed at €541. Thus, an applicant with these details who is granted a legal aid certificate will have to pay a total contribution of €1,245.

For someone with a large amount of disposable capital, it may well be cheaper—and quicker—to consult a good family law solicitor. However, even if an applicant's income and assets are low enough to qualify, legal services will not be granted unless the applicant also passes a merits test.

---

[2] s 29(2)(b), Civil Legal Aid Act 1995, as amended by s 80, Civil Law (Miscellaneous Provisions) Act 2008.

Criteria for Granting Legal Aid

The general criteria for granting legal aid[3] State that a person shall *not* be granted legal aid or advice unless the board believes that:

a) a reasonably prudent person would be likely to seek such services at his own expense, even if the cost represented a financial obstacle, though not undue hardship, and
b) a solicitor or barrister acting reasonably would be likely to advise him or her to obtain such services at his or her own expense.

The board will grant a legal aid certificate if it believes that:

1) the applicant has reasonable legal grounds for instituting, defending or being a party to the proceedings;
2) the applicant is reasonably likely to succeed; and
3) it is reasonable to grant the certificate when balancing the probable cost to the board against the likely benefit to the applicant.[4]

A certificate may be terminated at the discretion of the Legal Aid Board:

a) at the request of the legally-aided person;
b) where a legally-aided person has failed to comply with any condition, especially where any required contribution is more than 21 days in arrears;
c) if the legally-aided person's solicitor reports that the certificate should be terminated;
d) where the legally-aided person is no longer eligible for legal aid on financial grounds;
e) where the legally-aided person is behaving unreasonably or it is unreasonable (on grounds including cost) that the person should continue to receive legal aid; or
f) where the legally aided person made an untrue statement about his resources or deliberately failed to disclose any material fact.

---

[3] s 24, Civil Legal Aid Act 1995.
[4] s 28(2), Civil Legal Aid Act 1995.

Refusal or Termination of Legal Aid

In *H v Governor of Wheatfield Prison & Anor*,[5] a foreign national applied for legal aid in relation to her husband's appeal against being jailed over maintenance arrears. The Legal Aid Board rejected her application.

But in *Forrest v The Legal Aid Board & Ors*,[6] O'Hanlon J said that judicial separation proceedings and matters connected with the welfare of children of a marriage were in a "completely different category from conventional disputes between litigating parties". Once it is established that either spouse cannot afford to be legally represented, particularly in proceedings about the custody, access and maintenance of infant children,

> it would only be in wholly exceptional circumstances which I cannot now envisage—and which do not, in my opinion, exist in the present case—that legal aid could be denied.

On appeal, the Supreme Court set out the principles applicable to legal aid in family law cases involving children in *MF v Legal Aid Board*.[7]

In cases involving the custody, guardianship and welfare of a child of married parents, it is only necessary for the Legal Aid Board to conclude that there is a "reasonable likelihood" that the judge will take into account the applicant's point of view and submissions. The "benefit of the applicant" in the statute should be interpreted as meaning the applicant's interest in the welfare of a child. The same principles would apply to appeals or variations of orders relating to children.

In *Kavanagh v Legal Aid Board & Ors*,[8] a woman who had applied for legal aid in connection with a judicial separation had to wait nearly two years for her application to be granted.

The separation proceedings were eventually instituted in April 2000 and had been concluded by the time of her High Court application. Elizabeth Kavanagh sought damages for the board's failure to consider her application within a reasonable time, as required by the 1995 Legal Aid Act.

---

[5] [2011] IEHC 492.
[6] Unreported, High Court, 4 December 1992.
[7] [1993] ILRM 797.
[8] Unreported, High Court, 24 October 2001.

The judge said that the Act required the provision of legal aid and advice "within the board's resources". The board said that meant, not just financial resources, but also the availability of personnel.

Refusing the claim for damages, the judge said:

> The words [of the Act] simply mean that legal aid shall be provided within the board's resources and I am fully satisfied...that that is precisely what the board did in this case. The board had a method of dealing with cases in a certain order of priority and, within that scheme, the applicant was given equal treatment to all other applicants.

But in *O'Donoghue v Legal Aid Board and Others*,[9] Mr Justice Peter Kelly said that the 25-month delay in obtaining legal aid breached the applicant's constitutional rights to access to the courts and fair procedures.

However, a delay in obtaining legal aid does not mean that a party is entitled to an adjournment of proceedings. In *M v Judge Ó Donnabháin*,[10] the Supreme Court dismissed an appeal against a decision of a High Court judge refusing *certiorari* of a decision by the Circuit Court to adjourn a nullity petition pending an application for legal aid.

If the board's solicitor employee believes that a case does not have a reasonable chance of success, he must tell the board. It is a matter for the solicitor whether he recommends termination or not.

In *O'Duffy v Legal Aid Board*,[11] the applicant was granted a legal aid certificate in 2007 to bring proceedings to overturn what he claimed was a fraudulent deed of assignment for the family home. The board terminated the certificate four years later and the applicant appealed, but the board's appeal committee upheld the decision. He then sought a court order to overturn the decision.

The board said the certificate was terminated in accordance with regulation 9(3)(c) of the Civil Legal Aid Regulations 1996. His Legal Aid Board solicitor had recommended that the certificate be terminated on the basis that the case would not be successful.

---

[9] Unreported, High Court, 21 December 2004.
[10] [2011] IESC 22.
[11] [2012] IEHC 38.

In judicial review, the courts will not interfere with the decisions of administrative bodies such as the Legal Aid Board on grounds of unreasonableness or irrationality unless satisfied that:

1) no information before the board could reasonably have led to the decision;
2) the decision maker failed to take into account relevant material; or
3) the decision flew in the face of "fundamental reason and common sense".[12]

In this case, the judge said there was no evidence to suggest that either the decision by the board or by the appeal committee was irrational or contrary to common sense.

FLAC

Those who cannot afford a solicitor may also be able to obtain help from the Free Legal Advice Centres, FLAC. The volunteer barristers and solicitors will advise on legal problems, but will not act or write letters for clients or represent them in court.

FLAC provides a general legal advice service through a network of part-time clinics. During office hours, the head office in Dublin also operates a telephone information and referral line.

---

[12] *Gannon v Information Commissioner* [2006] IEHC 17.

ALTERNATIVES TO COURT

Introduction

No couple should put an end to their relationship without first trying to salvage the partnership. But it's not necessary to go to court.

Couples can also use ADR, normally known as alternative dispute resolution, to try and resolve their problems. Alternative dispute resolution covers a broad range of dispute resolution processes, including mediation, collaborative law and counselling.

The benefit of ADR is that both parties can feel they have contributed to the eventual agreed solution, which can then be 'ruled' by the court. This is particularly important where children are involved. In litigation, on the other hand, both parties may feel that the judge has failed to understand them and has imposed an unacceptable agreement on them, including limited access to the children, selling property, paying maintenance, moving home or living on a much-reduced income.

Of course, mediation or other ADR processes may not work, as both parties may not enter a preliminary ADR process in good faith. They may hold back for tactical reasons, as they anticipate a 'second act', so to speak. But what happens in an unsuccessful mediation will remain confidential. In *MP v AP*,[1] mediation was attempted for a period, but eventually proceedings were issued in the High Court seeking a judicial separation.

---

[1] [2005] IEHC 326.

A judge will perhaps guess that mediation has been attempted, but will not know anything else, so the parties will not be prejudiced.

In *BB v AA*,[2] Hogan J said that it was "very desirable" that a dispute about a child's schooling "might be resolved through mediation, rather than the acrimony which is inevitably generated through the judicial process".

In *CF v JDF*,[3] McGuinness J said, in relation to a Supreme Court appeal from the High Court, that the wisest course would be for the parties to endeavour to reach an agreed settlement, even at that late stage.

> I would now reiterate that advice in the strongest possible terms. It is of no advantage to either party to expend further resources on litigation.

But couples can't be forced to mediate or negotiate; alternatives to litigation work only if the participants are both willing and able to take part in the process. As Mr Justice Peter Kelly told the 2013 Irish Commercial Mediation Association conference: "It is not possible to force people to go to mediation and, if one does so, it is unlikely to be successful."

However, in *I v I*,[4] after 70 court appearances in a child custody and judicial separation case, the judge ordered a husband and wife to go to mediation before bringing any further court proceedings. In *V v U*,[5] a father who had chosen to use the courts rather than ADR had "a profound sense of grievance" that a child custody dispute had been before the courts 51 times.

Mediation Legislation

In 2008, the Law Reform Commission (LRC) published a consultation paper on alternative dispute resolution and a draft mediation bill. Another draft Mediation Bill, published in 2012 by the Department of Justice, is being finalised following proposals at committee stage.

Under the draft legislation, solicitors and barristers must inform and advise clients about mediation, while the solicitor must advise the client

---

[2] [2013] IEHC 394.
[3] [2005] IESC 45.
[4] [2011] IEHC 411.
[5] [2011] IEHC 519.

about the estimated costs and time that litigation or mediation would take.

Section 11 of the draft bill says it is up to the parties to decide whether a mediation agreement is to be enforceable. But Article 6 of the 2008 European Mediation Directive says that, if both parties so request, member states must ensure that mediation agreements can be made enforceable.[6] The directive was given effect in Irish law by the Rules of the Superior Courts (Mediation and Conciliation) 2010.[7]

Order 56A of the Rules of the Superior Courts allows the court to invite parties to consider mediation, conciliation or another dispute resolution process approved by the court (but not arbitration). If one side refuses ADR "without good reason", the judge can take this into account when awarding costs, even if that person wins the case.[8]

Family Mediation Service

The Family Mediation Service offers separating couples, or couples who have already separated, the opportunity to negotiate their own agreements with the help of a mediator.

The service was set up in 1986 as a pilot service and placed on a permanent footing in 1993. Responsibility for the service was transferred to the Legal Aid Board in 2011 following the enactment of the Civil Law (Miscellaneous Provisions) Act 2011.

There are 16 FMS offices around the country, with waiting times for a consultation at the end of 2012 varying from two months in Waterford to five months in Cork.

The professional, confidential service is free and is available to married and non-married couples. It is not marriage counselling nor a legal advice centre. The underlying principle is that couples solve their own problems with the assistance of a professionally-trained mediator, rather than have decisions made for them by someone else.

---

[6] European Communities (Mediation) Regulations 2011, SI No 209 of 2011.
[7] SI No 502 of 2010.
[8] *McCarthy v O'Sullivan*, unreported, High Court, March 2012, and *Earl of Malmesbury v Strutt & Parker* [2008] EWHC 424 (QB).

Any legal proceedings that have already been issued must be adjourned or suspended for six months. Successful mediation is likely to take between two and six one-hour sessions.

All issues are open to negotiation, including child custody and access, living arrangements, the family home, financial support, property, education and health. Both sides must make a full and frank exchange of information at mediation if the process is to be successful.

On their first visit to a mediator, the parties sign a mediation agreement which sets out the principle of confidentiality. The mediator is in charge of the process, but may not be required to give evidence or produce documents in any subsequent court proceedings.

The couple swear a declaration of assets. Normally all areas of agreement are written down at each session and are signed by both parties, thus progressively reducing the areas of disagreement.

All discussions are confidential and the neutral mediator will not discuss the case with anyone else. Neither spouse will be allowed to produce in evidence any matters discussed or written down during an attempted reconciliation or mediation.

Either party (or the mediator) may withdraw from the discussions at any time without giving a reason. If agreement is reached, the parties are advised to have the agreement checked by their solicitors. The mediation document is not legally binding on the parties, but frequently forms the basis for a formal separation agreement which can be drawn up by the couple themselves or by their solicitors or a mediator.

A separation agreement can incorporate agreements about custody and access, financial matters, taxation, pension and succession rights. If the parties agree, a separation agreement may be ruled by a court, which gives all its elements the force of court orders.

Most couples want to mediate four main issues: children, the family home, finances and property. Others have already agreed some issues and want to mediate the remainder.

The next stage is to explore the issues and develop the options. One issue at a time is dealt with. The couple are asked to keep their preferred option under consideration until the final session on negotiation and decision-making. In the meantime, both parties can consult experts such as a solicitor or an auctioneer, who can value the family home.

Finally the mediator will produce a written agreement setting out the decisions of the couple. The document may be modified after further consideration or after either side has consulted a solicitor. If the final document is perceived to be illegal, unfair to one partner or drawn up in bad faith, the mediator may withdraw from mediation.

Having come to an agreement, married couples are invited to bring in their children for a joint session, explaining that they intend to split up as husband and wife, but remain jointly as parents. They may invite suggestions from older children about the parenting plan.

Six months after the final session, a review session is held to discuss how the agreement has worked and to consider any necessary changes.

Mediation services are also available from organisations such as Mediation Northside in Dublin and Gingerbread Ireland, which has branches in Dublin, Blanchardstown, Wexford, Cork, Limerick and Drogheda.

Under s 6(2) of the 1996 Divorce Act, lawyers are obliged to give potential litigants a list of conciliators and mediators and to discuss the possibility of reconciliation, using a mediator or engaging in negotiation.

Whatever form of ADR is chosen, it's sensible to use an adviser who is a member of a recognised professional organisation, such as the Mediators Institute of Ireland or the Association of Collaborative Practitioners.

On the negative side, mediation may give one parent time to hide assets, initiate litigation in a more sympathetic country, manipulate third parties or alienate the other parent and the children. In those circumstances, it might be a good idea to begin court proceedings, but ask the judge for an adjournment so that ADR may be attempted.

Collaborative Law

A relatively recent ADR option is collaborative law, where the couple, with lawyers representing each of them, take part in negotiations to try and resolve any outstanding issues. The unusual element of collaborative law is that a 'disqualification clause' signed by the lawyers before the sessions ensures that, if the case eventually ends up in court, they will not represent their clients in any way, or even appear as witnesses.

In the collaborative process, the couple initially sign a 'participation agreement' setting out the nature and scope of the dispute and agreeing to seek to reach a mutually-agreeable settlement in good faith. At the first sign of bad faith, the process may be terminated.

They voluntarily disclose all relevant information and material. Other experts, such as accountants, estate agents or pension experts, may be jointly engaged by agreement to assist the parties to reach agreement.

Initially there are lawyer-to-lawyer and lawyer-to-client meetings, after which all the parties—clients and lawyers—sit round a table to try and thrash out the so-called 'hot spots'. Affidavits of discovery or means and vouching documents (and welfare, if necessary) are exchanged early on in the process on an 'open basis', so they can be used in any subsequent court proceedings if the collaborative process is unsuccessful.

The affidavit of discovery must specifically include a paragraph confirming that the

> obligation on a party giving discovery is to discover all documents and electronically-stored information...which may enable the party receiving the discovery to advance its own case or to damage the case of the party giving discovery, or which may fairly lead to a train of inquiry which may have either of those consequences.[9]

Collaborative law practitioners (most of whom are currently solicitors) charge by the hour, so the parties are constantly aware how much the process will cost.

Counselling

Counselling services exist throughout Ireland to help couples who want to try and resolve their difficulties with the aim of staying together.

Accord (formerly the Catholic Marriage Advisory Council) can help clients resolve conflict and difficulties in their relationships. Counsellors discuss the couple's problems in a non-directive way to enable them to

---

[9] SI No 93 of 2009.

make their own decisions. Counselling services are also available for those of other religions (or none).

Couples who may have sexual problems in their marriages or difficulties in having children may use Accord's marital sex therapy or fertility management services.

Accord's 800 counsellors and facilitators provide marriage and relationship counselling services in 60 centres nationwide. In 2011, more than 9,900 people used the service, involving 49,000 hours of counselling—up 12 percent on the previous year.

The fastest growing area of problems is the amount of time being spent by one partner on the internet, and more than one in four couples cited the use of texting as a problem in their relationship. In 2011, there was also a 10 percent increase in the number of clients experiencing financial difficulties, with money problems now affecting two thirds of those coming for counselling.

Cost

ADR can also be less expensive, especially if you can't get help from the Legal Aid Board either because of a lengthy waiting list or because you don't qualify. The court process can result in a large financial bill, particularly if proceedings are heard in the High Court or there are numerous applications.

Although parties in family law legislation are often ordered to meet their own legal costs, this is by no means a requirement, and a judge may order one party to pay the entire legal bill, which may run into hundreds of thousands of euro.

In *SD v BD*,[10] for example, costs were close to €1,000,000 in a 15-day High Court hearing. Abbot J ordered the husband to pay his wife's costs, especially as he had not filed an up-to-date affidavit of means.

In the case of *BD v JD*,[11] a Supreme Court judge said that the estimate given to the High Court of one side's costs (well above €100,000) caused

---

[10] [2007] IEHC 492.
[11] *ibid*.

him "surprise and disquiet", even though the case was "of some, but not extreme, complexity".

Hardiman J said the costs in family law actions were sometimes out of proportion to what was involved, even in an 'ample resources' case. "They can be very burdensome, especially—but not exclusively—in less prosperous circumstances," he said. Instruction fees and brief fees should be "related to the work done and not directly to the asset value in a case".

Costs in civil cases normally 'follow the event': that is, the loser usually pays. But that is not necessarily the rule in family law cases.

In *MK v JPK (No 3) (Divorce: Currency)*,[12] McCracken J said there was a "pool of assets" in family law cases which were to be used to make proper provision for both spouses and any dependants and to pay the legal costs of both parties. "There is no question of either party having further assets which could be used to pay costs," he said. "In my view, therefore, the general rule does not necessarily apply in family law proceedings."

In *Dunne v Minister for the Environment*,[13] former Chief Justice John Murray said the rule of law that costs normally follow the event had "an obvious equitable basis". But he said the court had a discretion to vary that rule or depart from it in the interests of justice.

He noted in *Roche v Roche*[14] that matrimonial litigation

> often gives rise to particular circumstances in which the courts consider it just and equitable to depart from the general rule of costs following the event.

In *WYYP v PC*,[15] Denham CJ dismissed an appeal against a decision by the High Court not to award costs to either party in a family law dispute. She said the High Court judge considered the general rule and his discretion not to follow it, "especially in the context of matrimonial proceedings".

"The award of costs is an exercise of discretion of the trial judge, who has considered all the circumstances of the proceedings before her or him, and decided the issues," she said. "This court is very reluctant to interfere with the exercise of such discretion."

---

[12] [2006] IESC 4.
[13] [2007] IESC 60.
[14] [2010] IESC 10.
[15] [2013] IESC 12.

YOUR DAY IN COURT

Introduction

For many people involved in marriage breakdown, the thought of going to court may fill them with apprehension. Judges recognise that. As Mr Justice Gerard Hogan said in *DX v Judge Buttimer*[1]:

> Legal proceedings are, of course, stressful occasions for the parties, and this is especially true of family law proceedings.

> While it is true that the interests of most litigants are represented by legal professionals, many litigants nonetheless find the entire experience so daunting that they would wish to have the company of a friend to provide support and reassurance quite independently of legal advisers.

That's why the Oireachtas enacted s 40(5) the Civil Liability and Courts Act 2004. Section 40(5) of the 2004 Act provides that

---

[1] [2012] IEHC 175.

> nothing contained in a relevant enactment shall operate to prohibit a party to proceedings to which the enactment relates from being accompanied, in such proceedings, in court by another person, subject to the approval of the Court and any directions it may give.[2]

Perhaps the fear of the courtroom is why such a large proportion of cases is settled on the steps of the court. However, it's not quite as bad as it may seem. The court registrar can be very helpful at explaining in advance what will happen and how to prepare an application, though he won't give legal advice.

In general, family law matters are heard *in camera*, that is in private, unlike other civil law matters. In *Sheehy v Talbot*[3] Edwards J refused a defendant's application to have Partition Act proceedings held *in camera*. He said the parties were not married and there was no statutory provision which would entitle the defendant to have the proceedings heard *in camera*.

Traditionally, the only people allowed in court—apart from the judge and the spouses—were the lawyers (possibly a barrister and solicitor on each side), the registrar, the judge's tipstaff and maybe a stenographer. Witnesses who have given evidence leave court when they have finished testifying.

However, the Civil Liability and Courts Act 2004 and the Courts and Civil Law (Miscellaneous Provisions) Act 2013 amended the rules for *in camera* hearings.

The 2004 Act allowed barristers, solicitors and other groups specified by the justice minister to attend family law cases and publish reports about them, subject to not identifying the parties or any children. Regulations in 2005 specified that those attending and reporting on family law cases could also include:

- Family mediators accredited to the Mediators' Institute Ireland, nominated by the Family Support Agency and approved by the minister;
- Family law researchers nominated by the Law Reform Commission, the Economic and Social Research Institute or academic institutions listed in the regulations and approved by the minister; and
- Reporters engaged by the Courts Service.

---

[2] SI No 247 of 2005.
[3] [2008] IEHC 207.

Privacy of Proceedings

Normally, the substance of family law proceedings may not be revealed to anyone not connected with the case, to preserve the privacy of the parties. In *Tesco (Ire) Ltd v McGrath*,[4] for example, Morris P held that family court orders about the sale of property could not be released, even where the orders might be critical as far as the title of other people was concerned. Likewise, in *RM v DM*[5] Murphy J held that the *in camera* rule precluded the disclosure of pleadings to a professional disciplinary body in a complaint against a lawyer.

But in *LD v MA*,[6] the court permitted a variation from the *in camera* rule so the court order could be produced to financial or legal advisors to enable properties to be sold.

The parameters of the *in camera* rule were set out by Barr J in *Eastern Health Board v Fitness to Practise Committee of the Medical Council*[7]:

1) Court proceedings relating to the alleged abuse of children are normally held *in camera*, as an exception to the general rule that justice shall be administered in public.
2) The primary reason for the *in camera* rule in such cases is to protect minors from harmful publicity.
3) Judicial discretion to allow disclosure in appropriate circumstances can only be displaced by specific statutory authority.
4) No Irish statutory provision provides an absolute embargo in all circumstances on publishing information about *in camera* proceedings.
5) The court has a discretion to allow the dissemination of information from *in camera* proceedings where it is in the interests of justice to do so.[8]
6) The paramount consideration is to do justice.

---

[4] Unreported, High Court, 14 June 1999.
[5] [2000] IEHC 140.
[6] [2012] IEHC 584.
[7] [1998] 3 IR 399, see also *Re R Ltd* [1989] IR 126 and *Health Service Executive v McAnaspie* [2011] IEHC 477.
[8] See *PSS v Independent Newspapers (Ireland) Ltd*, unreported, High Court, 22 May 1995.

7) Evidence from an *in camera* hearing may be used, not only in related litigation, but also in non-judicial proceedings.[9]

8) It is a contempt of court for anyone to disseminate information from an *in camera* hearing without prior authority from a judge.

9) Whether the *in camera* rule is mandatory or by way of judicial discretion, the court may still permit disclosure of information where justice requires.

10) The court can impose whatever conditions it considers necessary to protect the interests of minors and others who are intended to have the benefit of the *in camera* rule.

Section 40(4) of the Civil Liability and Courts Act 2004 now allows the disclosure to third parties of extracts of court orders in family law proceedings.

Mackenzie Friends

Although either party may be represented by a solicitor or barrister, it is possible to represent yourself, in which case you may be accompanied by a so-called 'Mackenzie friend'. The idea of a McKenzie friend originates in the decision of the Court of Appeal in England in *McKenzie v McKenzie*.[10]

Davies LJ recalled the statement of Lord Tenterden CJ in *Collier v Hicks*[11]:

> Any person, whether he be a professional man or not, may attend as a friend of either party, may take notes, may quietly make suggestions, and give advice; but no one can demand to take part in the proceedings as an advocate, contrary to the regulations of the court as settled by the discretion of the justices.

That description of the role of a McKenzie friend is generally accepted by the Irish courts. It was considered in the High Court by Macken J in *RD v McGuinness*,[12] which involved family law proceedings. She concluded that a litigant in person was

---

[9] See *A County Council v W* [1997] 1 FLR 574.
[10] [1970] 1 P 33.
[11] (1831) 2 B & Ad 663.
[12] [1999] 2 IR 411.

entitled to be accompanied in court by a friend who may take notes on his behalf and quietly make suggestions and assist him generally during the hearing, but...may not act as advocate.

But she said this common law principle was overridden by the statutory prohibition that existed at that time.

Fennelly J in a costs judgment[13] said a judge may occasionally invite the McKenzie friend to explain some point of fact or law which was not clear, but that was always a matter for the sole discretion of the judge. The McKenzie friend has no right to address the court unless invited to do so by the judge.

In *DX v Judge Olive Buttimer*,[14] DX sought an order of *certiorari* to quash a decree of judicial separation granted by Circuit Judge Buttimer in 2011. DX claimed that Buttimer was in breach of fair procedures and s 40(5) of the Civil Liability and Courts Act 2004 in the judicial separation proceedings by refusing to allow his friend in court, even though he was legally represented.

DX and his wife represented themselves in the judicial review proceedings, but DX was also helped by a friend, as he'd had a laryngectomy in 1997 and could speak only with considerable difficulty.

In the High Court, Hogan J said *in camera* proceedings must normally be "confined to 'special and limited cases prescribed by law' in the relatively narrow sense of that term".

Section 40(5) of the Civil Liability and Courts Act 2004 now provided that a litigant could be accompanied in court by another lay person, subject to the approval and directions of the court. The court could, for example, require an undertaking to respect the confidentiality of the proceedings.

Hogan J said that the legislation

clearly presumptively favours the right of a litigant to choose a friend to accompany them in court, irrespective of whether that litigant is already legally represented.

---

[13] [2013] IESC 11.
[14] [2012] IEHC 175.

He ruled that the judge had erred in excluding DX's friend.

Hogan also said that litigants with a physical disability should not be put at a disadvantage compared with their "able-bodied opponents", so the exclusion of DX's friend from the hearing was *ultra vires*, though this did not affect the validity of the Circuit Court order.

District Court

The District Court handles the majority of family law cases, with the exception of judicial separation or divorce applications, which are made in the Circuit Court (or, in big money or 'ample resources' cases, in the High Court).

The District Court is a court of local jurisdiction, which means that cases are allocated to courts in the area where the applicant lives or works. Ireland is divided into 23 districts—22 provincial districts and the Dublin Metropolitan District. The president of the District Court and his 50 judges sit at 200 venues around the country.

The powers of the District Court and the amounts which it can award are limited by statute. The court deals with a range of family law matters, including domestic violence applications, maintenance orders (up to €500 a week for a spouse and €150 a week for each child), applications for custody, access and guardianship and declarations of paternity.

Proceedings in the District Court usually begin with the issue of a summons or notice of application. A summons must give the name and address of the applicant and the name and address of the person against whom the application is being made, called the respondent.

Details of the applicant's claim and the grounds for making it must be set out in the summons, which also stipulates where and when the summons will be heard. The summons is dated and signed by the judge or District Court clerk and must be lodged in the District Court office.

A summons or notice of application must be served on the respondent at least 14 days—or, by registered post, at least 21 days—before the date of the court hearing. The summons or notice and a declaration of service is lodged with the District Court clerk at least four days before the hearing. Time limits vary, depending on the type of application.

Court procedures were described by Miss Justice Iseult O'Malley in *LC v Judge Hugh O'Donnell & anor*.[15] She said:

- Courts normally act on evidence;
- The party applying for an order must establish grounds for the making of the order;
- Where there is consent, it will not usually be necessary to hear evidence;
- It is not necessary to prove again matters that have previously been established;
- Where new information is not accepted by the other party, it should normally be given as sworn evidence.

A decision of the District Court may be appealed to the Circuit Court within 14 days for a full re-hearing, but there is no further appeal to the High Court, except on a point of law. The notice of appeal and affidavit of service must be filed in the Central Office within ten days of the order made by the Circuit Court judge.

Circuit Court

In Dublin, the Circuit Family Court sits in Smithfield, near the Four Courts. Around the country, family law matters are generally heard on different days from other civil and criminal matters.

Apart from District Court appeals, the Circuit Court deals with a wide range of family law matters including nullity, judicial separation, divorce and applications to dispense with the three-month waiting period for those planning to marry.

In the context of divorces and judicial separation applications, the Circuit Court can also deal with many of the same matters as the District Court, including barring orders, child custody, guardianship and access, maintenance, financial orders (including lump sums, pensions and succession rights) and property orders.

---

[15] [2013] IEHC 268.

Circuit Court family law proceedings usually involve a family law civil bill, affidavit of means, affidavit of welfare (where there are children) and a notice to trustees of any pension scheme.

The documents, which are lodged in the court office, must be properly served on the other side, who will have an opportunity to answer any allegations before the eventual hearing.

Any further application to the Master of the High Court for further and better discovery should be limited to specific examples of non-disclosure. The Master pointed out in *FD v PJD*[16] that discovery in matrimonial proceedings was really further and better discovery, as evidence had already been provided in the affidavit of means. He said there ought to be "fairly clear evidence that a party may have concealed a materially significant portion of income or wealth" before the court would grant a further and better discovery order.

In *M v M*,[17] the Master criticised an application for discovery as being

> casual to the point of irresponsibility. After all, a request for discovery is the first step in a process which could lead to the jailing of a respondent who does not comply, and the court should never be used to oppress.

The progression of the case will be monitored by the county registrar who makes sure that everything has been done properly and in accordance with the rules. On the day of the hearing, the parties will either negotiate a settlement or the case will be heard by a judge.

Appeals

In *MD v EHD*,[18] White J said, that where family law proceedings were initiated in the Circuit Family Court and appealed to the High Court, and that court varied the Circuit Court order, any motion to enforce the order could be brought to either the Circuit Court in the original county or the High Court.

---

[16] Master of the High Court, 28 July 2004.
[17] MR3, Master of the High Court, 19 October 2011.
[18] [2012] IEHC 580.

He said a motion to review or vary an order under s 18 of the Family Law Act 1995 or s 22 of the Family Law (Divorce) Act 1996 must be brought to the court of first instance (in this case the Circuit Court), to ensure the right of appeal is maintained.

An appeal may be struck out because of delay or disobedience to court orders. In *GS v PS*,[19] a wife was in breach of Circuit Court orders relating to the custody of and access to a child. She lived in England, but emailed the court to say that she could not come to Ireland because she was pregnant and also could not afford to travel. She also said she would face committal to prison if she travelled to Ireland.

The wife appealed against the Circuit Court order but never prepared a book of appeal or attended court. Abbot J said the wife had been guilty of delay and oppressive conduct in pursuing her appeal. The husband had had no access to the child as a result of her disobedience, and the judge struck out the wife's appeal.

In *LT v JT*,[20] White J said the High Court and the Circuit Court had a concurrent jurisdiction to grant reliefs under the Judicial Separation and Family Law Reform Act 1989 and the Family Law Act 1995. If the proceedings were taken in the Circuit Court at first instance, there is a right of appeal to the High Court with a full re-hearing. If the proceedings were first brought taken in the High Court, there is a right of appeal to the Supreme Court.

From the autumn of 2014, it's expected that the Supreme Court will deal only with appeals of exceptional public importance, leaving other appeals to be handled by the new civil Court of Appeal.[21]

But as Murray CJ pointed out in *P Clohessy v P Clohessy*[22]:

> [The Supreme Court] does not have jurisdiction to entertain appeals from the High Court where the decision of the High Court is on an appeal from the Circuit Court. That has been the clear and stated law for a very long time.

---

[19] [2011] IEHC 122.

[20] [2012] IEHC 588.

[21] In a referendum on 4 October 2013, 795,008 (65.2 percent) people voted in favour of the proposed new court, while 425,047 (34.8 percent) voted against.

[22] Unreported, Supreme Court, 31 July 2008.

To ensure finality in litigation, the Supreme Court will vary or set aside its own final judgments and orders only:

a) where there has been an accidental slip in the judgment;
b) where the judgment as drawn up does not correctly state what the court intended and decided;
c) in separate proceedings for fraud;
d) or in rare and exceptional cases to protect constitutional rights or natural justice.

In *NB v MB*,[23] the husband asked the Supreme Court to extend time for an appeal against a High Court order made on appeal from the Circuit Court.

The wife had claimed a decree of divorce and property orders, but the husband argued that the couple's property rights had been disposed of in proceedings many years earlier. He said the application to the Circuit Court was an abuse of process.

The Supreme Court said the husband was aggrieved by the fact that there appeared to be no finality to his matrimonial problems but there was no doubt about the legal principles applicable: the Supreme Court had "no jurisdiction to hear an appeal from the High Court exercising its appellate jurisdiction in respect of decisions of the Circuit Court".[24]

In *Talbot v McCann Fitzgerald Solicitors & ors*,[25] the High Court had refused an application for leave to apply for judicial review of Circuit Court judicial separation and divorce orders. The Supreme Court upheld the High Court decision.

The lack of appeal to the Supreme Court from an order made by the High Court on appeal from the Circuit Court was "well established," said Denham J "This Court has no jurisdiction." There can also be no judicial review of a High Court order.

---

[23] [2002] IESC 31.
[24] *P v P* [2001] IESC 76.
[25] [2009] IESC 25.

High Court Appeals

Very few family law cases start out in the High Court, but if the rateable valuation of your family home exceeds €254, you may elect to have the matter heard in the High Court. Family law cases generally go to the High Court if the husband or wife are very wealthy or if the case is particularly complex.

As McGuinness J said in *CF v JDF*[26]:

> Where the parties in family law proceedings are, to use the current phrase, of 'high net worth', and many millions of euros are at stake, it may be necessary to invoke the jurisdiction of the High Court.

Any notice of appeal against a High Court decision must be served on the other side within 21 days of the court order being perfected (or signed). The appeal must be filed in the Supreme Court office, together with a copy of the High Court order certified as a true copy, within seven days of service. Once the appeal has been lodged, books of appeal must be prepared and lodged.

An appeal from the High Court is heard in the Supreme Court or Court of Appeal.

Court of Appeal

The proposed Court of Appeal is expected to be in operation by the autumn of 2014 following its approval in a referendum in October 2013. It will hear most appeals from the High Court, leaving the Supreme Court free to deal with constitutional cases, those involving an important point of law and appeals from the Court of Appeal.

In exceptional circumstances, the Supreme Court will hear appeals from the High Court provided they involve a matter of "general public importance" or in the "interests of justice".[27]

---

[26] [2005] IESC 45.

[27] "Court of Appeal—Main Changes", Referendum Commission, available from http://referendum2013.ie/court-of-appeal-main-changes/, accessed 27 January 2014.

Supreme Court

According to figures published in July 2013, 605 appeals were lodged with the Supreme Court in 2012—a 21 percent increase on 2011. It gave judgment in 121 cases, compared to 64 in the US Supreme Court and 85 in the English Supreme Court.

But there is a huge backlog of appeals, so appellants can expect a long wait. In 2003, the waiting time for an appeal in the State's highest court was four months. Ten years later, it was four years.

Lay Litigants

Many of the appellants—for costs and other reasons—go it alone, without a lawyer. According to the Courts Service annual report, litigants without legal representation made up 26 percent of all applicants to the Supreme Court in 2012, up around eight percent since the previous year. The *Law Society Gazette*[28] said the "significant rise" in the number of lay litigants had led in some cases to "the complication or prolonging of proceedings".

'Lay litigants', as they are called, may be given a degree of latitude when it comes to pleadings or court appearances. In *Talbot v McCann Fitzgerald Solicitors & ors*,[29] a lay litigant was given "great latitude" in his oral and written submissions, was allowed to submit many documents and then made two hours of oral submissions to the Supreme Court.

If the lay litigant is poor at drafting pleadings, the court may make allowances. In *JO'N v SMcD & ors*,[30] Birmingham J said:

> Clearly, there can be no questions of a lay litigant being deprived of his right of access to the courts by reason of any lack of skill as a draftsman. It is also important to avoid a situation where the tone and style of the pleadings so grate on one that it leads to an assumption on the part of the reader that the pleadings are frivolous or vexatious.

Parties in family law cases may have to endure several appearances in court. There may be a series of urgent interim applications relating to such

---

[28] May 2011 edition, p11.
[29] [2009] IESC 25.
[30] [2013] IEHC 135.

matters as barring, maintenance, access or property which have to be dealt with before the substantive hearing.

But in most cases, particularly where there is agreement between the parties or in consent applications, there will only be one short court hearing.

It is always better if litigants can reach agreement—even if neither gets everything they want—rather than let a judge make a decision which both may find unsatisfactory. If a deal can be hammered out before a court hearing, it can be 'ruled' by the judge and given the force of a court order.

If, despite the best efforts of everyone, agreement cannot be reached, a court hearing becomes inevitable. But judges will not be happy with a plaintiff who uses "proceedings and the threat of proceedings to harass and intimidate".[31]

The Hearing

Parties should normally arrive at court before 10am to meet their solicitor and barrister. The lawyers will explain the usual sequence of events and may indicate what matters are likely to be raised, though they may not coach witnesses.

At 10.30 am, there is normally a call-over of the day's cases, at which stage all the lawyers appear in court to inform the judge sitting that day either that the case has been settled, that it requires an adjournment or that it is going ahead.

After the call-over, short matters (such as consent divorces and marriage exemptions) may be heard first to allow the lawyers in those matters to leave. For the rest of the cases on the list, it can be a very long day, with no guarantee that matters further down the list will even be reached.

Anyone appearing in court should dress appropriately. When called into the courtroom, the applicant and respondent will sit separately at the back of the court while the lawyers will sit at a table at the front. Normally, the

---

[31] *JO'N v SMcD & ors, ibid.*

barristers will face the judge, while the instructing solicitors will sit on the other side of the table with their backs to the judge, facing the barristers. In complicated cases or in the High Court, there may be senior and junior counsel.

The case is opened by the barrister (or solicitor) for the applicant who will outline the matter to the judge.

The applicant's case is heard first and the applicant will be called to give sworn evidence in the witness box. A witness who is not religious may affirm, rather than take the oath. The applicant's barrister may not 'lead' by asking questions which suggest a certain answer. If a barrister does ask leading questions, the respondent's barrister may object.

At the end of the examination-in-chief, the respondent's barrister will cross-examine the witness. If new matters are raised in cross-examination, the applicant's barrister may briefly re-examine the witness at the end of the cross-examination. Finally, the judge will clarify any unclear matters and the applicant will then be allowed to 'stand down' or leave the witness box.

All the witness's answers to questions should be directed in a loud, clear voice to the judge who, since 2006, has been addressed simply as 'Judge' in all courts. If a question is unclear, the lawyer should be asked to repeat or explain it.

Apart from the spouses, other witnesses may be called. Children may give evidence in certain circumstances. Other witnesses may include doctors, psychologists, accountants, estate agents and gardaí.

Interruptions

Spouses should not interrupt the proceedings, even if they disagree with the evidence being given. In *JE v DE*,[32] a husband seeking a variation of a High Court access order refused to stop raising "certain matters" about his wife after the court had warned him not to do so.

Sheehan J said the court had taken into account the way the man had conducted his case and his contempt in the face of the court, even though

---

[32] [2013] IEHC 379.

he had later apologised. He said the man had not established that it was in the best interests of either of his children for the Court to vary the supervised access order.

It is important to mention everything that may be relevant, but not to raise irrelevant matters. A woman who gave a gratuitous and one-sided account of her differences with her husband in judicial review proceedings in the Supreme Court was criticised for her vexatious and "absolutely unfair" conduct.[33]

If something urgent should be drawn to counsel's attention, a note should be discreetly passed to the solicitor. It is not in a litigant's interest to interrupt the concentration of his lawyers unless the matter is really important.

Giving evidence can take hours—or, in some cases, days. The courts normally sit from 11am to 1pm, then rise for lunch and sit again from 2pm to 4pm. If the court adjourns during a person's evidence, the legal team may not discuss the evidence with the witness during the break.

Sometimes settlement talks may resume in the middle of a case when one side begins to see sudden unanticipated strengths or weaknesses on the other side. A judge will always allow time for talks if requested to do so. Similarly, if one side decides that the talks are at an end, the judge must resume the case.

If the matter is very complicated, the judge may reserve judgment, that is deliver a written judgment on a later date (a book-length 61,000-word judgment in the case of *AB v CD*[34]!) Alternatively, he may decide at any stage to adjourn the proceedings, as he has discretion to do.[35] Either side may appeal a judgment.

While written judgments should be carefully scrutinised in the case of an appeal, a minor error may not invalidate the lower court's findings. In *AS v CS*,[36] Macken J said the "infelicitous use of one or another word

---

[33] *Per* Hardiman J in *Collins & Ors* [2004] IESC 38.
[34] [2012] IEHC 543.
[35] See judgment of Keane CJ in *RB v AS (Nullity; Domicile)* [2002] IR 428.
[36] [2009] IESC 77.

or phrase" may not affect the correctness of a judge's findings, especially when read in their correct context.

Appearing in court may be very stressful, but it's important to remember that family law judges and lawyers are used to courtroom nerves. They should do what they can to make the difficult occasion as straightforward as possible.

MARRIAGE REGULATIONS

Introduction

The European Convention on Human Rights says:

> Men and women of marriageable age have the right to marry and to found a family according to the national laws governing the exercise of this right.[1]

But it is necessary to fulfil all the necessary requirements if the marriage is to be legally valid. The Civil Registration Act 2004, which came into force in November 2007, introduced major changes to the procedures for solemnising and registering marriages in the Republic of Ireland.

Marriage by civil ceremony is a civil contract. In 2012, 29 percent of the 20,694 marriages that took place in the state were civil ceremonies. But marriage by certain religious denominations is also recognised in civil law as being a civil contract.

The main changes in relation to religious marriages were that:

- all couples attend in person at the registrar's office to give notification, establish their identity and freedom to marry and sign declarations of no impediment;

---

[1] Art 12.

- all couples must be issued with a marriage registration form (MRF) by a registrar before the marriage; and
- anyone solemnising marriages after 5 November 2007 must be on the register of solemnisers, which is maintained by the General Register Office.

The Act allows temporary registration in cases such as an overseas priest who is marrying a relative or a priest who is a short-term substitute for another.

For a marriage to be valid, the man and woman must be free to marry, they must have the required physical and psychological ability to "enter into and sustain a normal marital relationship" and they must marry voluntarily. Even if these conditions are fulfilled, they may still fall foul of regulations relating to age, notice or other requirements, the absence of which may invalidate the marriage.

As Dunne J said in *Zappone and Anor v Revenue Commissioners and Ors*,[2] the state had "a legitimate interest in circumscribing and regulating the requirement in respect of contracting a valid marriage".

Age

Both parties to a civil marriage in the Republic of Ireland must be over 18 years old on the day of the marriage. Evidence of age must be provided if requested by a registrar. If such evidence is not produced on request, the official may not go ahead with the marriage.

Until 1972, the minimum age for marriage in the Republic was based on canon law (the law of the Catholic Church) and was 14 years for boys and 12 years for girls. In 1972, the government passed the Marriages Act, which raised the minimum marriage age to 16 for boys and girls alike. Anyone aged between 16 and 21 had to have their parents' written consent to marry.

The 1995 Family Law Act raised the minimum age to 18. Under that Act, any marriage—civil or religious—which did not comply with the rules could not be registered as a valid civil marriage.

---

[2] [2006] IEHC 404.

The 1995 Act allows the Circuit Family Court or the High Court to grant an exemption from the age limits or the notification requirements if both applicants show that this is justified by serious reasons and is in the couple's best interests. It is an informal procedure and couples may apply in person without using a solicitor. There is no charge for such an application.

Anyone knowingly performing a marriage ceremony for a person under 18 is guilty of a criminal offence and liable to be fined up to €2,000 and jailed for up to six months. The law applies to all marriages in the Republic of Ireland. The minimum age requirement also applies to marriages in any other country if either of the spouses is normally resident in Ireland.

Notice

The couple must also give three months' prior written notification to a registrar. The courts may exempt a couple from either of these requirements, but a written exemption order must be obtained *before* the marriage takes place.

The three months' notification of a marriage may be given by either:

1) both parties writing—jointly or separately—to the registrar of the district in which they are to marry, giving the names and addresses of both parties, the name of the church or place where the ceremony will take place, the proposed date of the marriage and the dates of birth of the couple (or confirmation that they are both over 18), or

2) filling in a pre-printed form and returning it to the local registrar. (If only one form is sent in, both parties must sign it.)

If the couple write jointly to the registrar, they must both sign the letter. If they write separately, the required three months runs from the receipt of the second letter. The notice required is a full three months.

Limitation periods are calculated differently under English and Irish law. In *McCann v An Bord Pleanála*,[3] the High Court said that, under s 11 of the 1937 Interpretation Act, where a period of time is reckonable from a

---

[3] [1997] 1 IR 264.

certain day, that day is *included* in the limitation period unless a contrary intention appears. So, for example, a person giving notice on 1 April would be able to marry on June 30.

It is not necessary for anyone giving written notification to give the registrar documentary proof of their age (such as a birth certificate) at the notification stage. If required, the registrar will subsequently request the documents. There is no need to obtain parental consent for a marriage if the parties are both over 18.

Where either party to a civil marriage has been divorced, a certified copy of the decree absolute is required at the time of serving notice, together with the birth certificates of both parties to the divorce if born outside the state. If the decree is in a foreign language, a certified translation must be provided. The divorced party will also have to complete two questionnaires, one concerning each of the divorced spouses. The documents are subject to a check by the Registrar General, which can take five weeks or more.

Where either party is widowed, a certified copy of the death certificate and the original marriage certificate must be produced at the time of serving notice.

Where either party has been granted a civil nullity decree, a certified copy of the decree must be produced when serving notice, together with a statement from the Supreme Court (or appropriate court in any other EU country) that no appeal has been lodged against the decree.

Only original documents with original signatures may be accepted for notification of intention to marry. The registrar will issue an official receipt confirming the date of the application, which must be produced on request to the person solemnising the marriage.

The couple must pay the registrar the notification fee and provide evidence of their identity, addresses, ages, marital status and nationalities, including:

- passport or driving licence with photo;
- original final decrees of any previous divorce or death certificate of any previous spouse and civil marriage certificate for the first marriage;

- names, addresses and dates of birth of the two proposed witnesses;
- name and address of the solemniser; and
- PPS numbers (where either has one).

The couple have to state the date they wish to marry, whether they want a civil or religious ceremony, the names and dates of birth of their witnesses, and details of the proposed solemniser and venue.

They will also both have to complete a declaration stating that they are not aware of any lawful civil impediment to the proposed marriage. This declaration may be made up to two days before the wedding, but has to be made in the presence of the solemniser and the witnesses. The fact that the marriage may be no more than a marriage of convenience does not constitute a civil impediment.[4]

Once the legal requirements have been met, the couple are issued with a marriage registration form (MRF) which is effectively a civil marriage licence. But a court may not order a county registrar to issue a marriage registration form where there is inadequate evidence of identity

In *Tahir & Sheehan v Registrar for Co Cork & An tArd Chláiritheoir*,[5] Tahir claimed to be a Somali national. But a detective from the Garda National Immigration Bureau told the registrar that her fingerprints appeared on a visa application in the name of a Tanzanian national. Hedigan J said it was clear that Tahir had "at least two identities" and was guilty of a "distinct lack of candour". He refused to order the registrar to issue an MRF.

The registrar will confirm the date of the receipt of the notification. If either party is seriously ill or resident outside the state, a marriage notification may be posted to the registrar by prior agreement. But the couple must still attend the registrar's office in person at least five days before the marriage to complete their declarations of no impediment, produce the required documents and be issued with their MRF.

---

[4] *Izmailovic & Anor v Commissioner of An Garda Síochána & Ors* [2011] IEHC 32.
[5] [2012] IEHC 191.

Postal notifications of intention to marry should not be returned to the General Register Office, but to the registrar who authorised the postal notification. If either party was previously married, they must send the original final divorce decree or death certificate of the former spouse with the notification.

Marriage notification can be given to any registrar, not just in the area where the marriage is to take place or where the couple are living. To find your local registrar, check the list of HSE registration offices

Civil Ceremonies

Marriages by civil ceremony may take place at the office of a Registrar of Civil Marriages or at a venue which has been approved in advance by the registrar. If you want to have a civil ceremony somewhere other than in a register office, contact the nearest registration office to the venue and ask to have it approved for the ceremony.

The registrar may need to inspect the venue, so you should make these arrangements well in advance of your notification appointment. In 2012, 37 percent of the 20,694 marriages in the state were outside registrars' offices. There are additional fees for civil marriages at venues other than register offices.

The Civil Registration (Amendment) Act 2012 amended the 2004 Act by extending the categories of bodies and organisations, including secular groups, that can apply to the Registrar General for registration to solemnise marriage. Until that Act, only the Health Service Executive and religious groups could apply.

A secular, ethical or humanist group applying for registration must have been in existence for at least five years, meet regularly and have at least 50 registered members. The section excludes bodies such as terrorist organisations, political parties, trade unions, chambers of commerce or organisations that promote purposes contrary to public morality.

All marriages must be in a place open to the public, except where one or both parties are seriously ill and a doctor has certified that they cannot attend at a place open to the public. In such cases, the local superintendent registrar may grant approval for the marriage to take place at a venue such as a private house or hospice.

Religious Ceremonies

For Catholic marriages, applicants should complete a registration form after the church ceremony which must be returned to a registrar for the marriage to be civilly registered. The priest solemnising the marriage must be on the register of solemnisers.

For non-Catholic religious marriages, the local registrar should be contacted for a completed marriage registration form. The person solemnising the marriage must also be on the register of solemnisers.

If a couple marry in church without complying with the requirements of the Act, they must subsequently marry in a civil ceremony, or they will remain unmarried as far as the state is concerned. That means that neither 'spouse' can make use of marital legislation which applies only to married couples. Their children will be 'non-marital' children and they will be unable to divorce because, as far as the civil courts are concerned, they were not married in the first place.

The 1995 Act allows either spouse to ask the court to rule that their marriage is null and void, although it may not be necessary to make such an application if the facts are beyond dispute. The 1995 regulations are in addition to previous regulations.

Religious marriages may be performed according to the customs and ceremonies of the Church or religious body carrying out the ceremony. However, the couple must first obtain an MRF which they must show to the person solemnising the marriage.

Any marriage that takes place without an MRF cannot be civilly registered.

The venue for religious marriages is a matter for the authorities of the Church or religious body, but the venues for all marriages, civil or religious, must normally be open to the public.

The ceremony must be performed by a registered solemniser—recognised by the religious body of which he or she is a member—in the presence of two witnesses, both over 18, and the couple must declare that:

- neither of them knows of any impediment to the marriage; and
- they accept each other as husband and wife.

The solemniser must be satisfied that the couple understand the nature of the marriage ceremony and the declarations they have made. The legislation says all these are "substantive requirements for marriage".[6]

At the end of the ceremony, the solemniser, the couple and two witnesses must all sign the MRF. The completed MRF should be given to any registrar within one month of the ceremony for the marriage to be civilly registered. A civil marriage certificate will not be available until the MRF has been returned to a registrar.

If the MRF is lost, destroyed or damaged, the registrar may complete another MRF and arrange to have it signed. Any errors in the register of marriages (or the register of civil partnerships) may be corrected.[7] Anyone who believes there is an error in the register may apply in writing to the Superintendent Registrar for the area in which the marriage was solemnised. Even though a clerical error may be corrected, the entry with the clerical error is also retained.

If the bride or groom, either witness or the solemniser does not understand the language of the ceremony, the couple must arrange for an interpreter to be present.

Foreign Divorce

The Domicile and Recognition of Foreign Divorces Act 1986 allows the recognition of UK divorces where *either* spouse was domiciled in the UK. Where *neither* spouse was domiciled in Ireland, a foreign divorce will be recognised here if it is recognised in the country where either spouse was domiciled. Generally speaking, the validity of a marriage in another country is exclusively governed by the law of the place in which the marriage was solemnised.[8]

In the case of *Paul Lambert v The Registrar General of Marriages*,[9] Mr Lambert was domiciled in Ireland with his wife and children. In 1984, she left him and went to live in England with the children. Two years later she divorced him in England.

---

[6] s 51(5), Civil Registration Act 2004.
[7] SI No 668 and SI No 672 of 2010.
[8] *Hamza v Minister for Justice* [2013] IESC 9.
[9] *Lambert v An tArd-Chláraitheoir* [1995] 2 IR 373.

Mr Lambert wanted to marry someone else in Ireland, but the Registrar General refused to issue a certificate because he said he wasn't satisfied that the former Mrs Lambert was domiciled in England at the time of the divorce. Mrs Lambert swore a declaration to say that she had intended to live permanently in England.

In the High Court, the judge said the registrar was entitled to investigate the circumstances of the divorce, but the question of the former wife's domicile was partly a matter of law—which was a matter for the courts, not the registrar. The judge said the court was entitled to act on Mrs Lambert's uncontradicted declaration, and he ruled that Mr Lambert was free to remarry.

On the other hand, the courts may refuse to recognise a foreign decree where neither spouse was domiciled in the jurisdiction of the court granting the divorce. In 2008, an Irish businessman whose Dutch divorce was not recognised in Ireland lost his eight-year effort to prevent the Irish courts deciding how much maintenance he should pay his wife.[10]

The couple had married in Ireland in 1980 and had three children, all now grown up. They lived in the Netherlands for five years for work reasons but the wife returned to Ireland with the children in the early 1990s to send them to Irish schools.

She initiated maintenance proceedings in the Netherlands and obtained an interim order from a Dutch court. Under Dutch law, she then had four weeks to start divorce proceedings if she wanted the maintenance order to continue to be enforceable, but she did not do so.

In 1994, the husband started divorce proceedings in the Dutch courts but he returned to Ireland later that year to work. The Dutch court granted a divorce decree which included maintenance for the wife, but the court said it had no authority to rule on custody or maintenance for the children.

The wife initiated judicial separation proceedings in Ireland in 2000. She argued that the Dutch divorce should not be recognised here and she sought maintenance for the children. The Irish High Court rejected the husband's claim that the Irish courts should recognise his Dutch divorce, and he appealed to the Supreme Court.

---

[10] *DT v FL* [2008] IESC 48.

In 2003, the Supreme Court upheld the High Court decision because, at the time of the divorce, the man was not domiciled in the Netherlands.

In 2004, the man brought further proceedings to have the Irish courts decline jurisdiction in relation to his wife's proceedings. He lost in the High Court in 2006 and then appealed to the Supreme Court.

The case centred on the interpretation of the European Brussels I, Brussels II and Brussels II *bis* regulations concerning the recognition and enforcement of judgments of other EU Member States.

The court said that the man was not domiciled in Holland when he got the divorce, and enforcement of the Dutch court's maintenance order would conflict with the earlier Supreme Court judgment.

Mr Justice Nial Fennelly said that many of the man's arguments were "unfounded and, in many respects, without merit". He refused to refer questions to the European Court of Justice for interpretation because the man tended to "use legal procedures" to delay matters, which caused injustice to his wife.

The five-judge court unanimously rejected his argument that the Irish courts should refuse jurisdiction for his wife's maintenance proceedings.

A divorce or nullity decree granted in any EU country except Denmark after 1 March 2001 is automatically recognised in Ireland. Article 14.2 of EC Regulation 1347/2000 says that

> no special procedure is required to update the civil records of a member state on the basis of a final judgment relating to divorce, legal separation or marriage annulment given in another member state (after March 1 2001).

If the divorce was granted by a court in another State and is in a foreign language, an English translation must be provided, certified by an official body or recognised translation agency. If the divorce comes within EU regulations, it is sufficient to confirm that both parties to the divorce were notified about the proceedings and had a chance to give evidence to the court which granted the divorce. Where EU regulations do not apply, the parties must complete a questionnaire which is forwarded to the General Register Office for consent to the marriage.

A Catholic Church annulment does not have any effect in civil law and anyone who has obtained a Church annulment, without a divorce or civil nullity decree, is not free to remarry in civil law.

Foreign Marriage

Marriages which take place outside the state are normally registered in the country where they are celebrated and are not registered in Ireland. If you are marrying abroad, make sure that you meet all the legal requirements of the country in question, such as the age requirement (though this normally remains 18 for parties who are habitually resident in Ireland). Ask the appropriate embassy or religious authorities how to obtain a marriage certificate from that country.

A certificate of freedom to marry (also known as a *certificate de coûtume* or certificate of *nulla osta*) may be required in some countries. The certificate, which states that a person is not already married, may be obtained from the consular section of the Department of Foreign Affairs. Irish citizens living abroad may obtain the certificate from their nearest Irish embassy.

A marriage certificate in a foreign language is normally accepted for official purposes in Ireland if you have an official translation.

A marriage involving Irish residents will not be valid if:

- either party is under the age of 18, unless a court exemption has been obtained;
- either party is already validly married;
- either party is incapable of understanding the meaning of marriage because of mental handicap or illness; or
- both parties are the same sex.

Restrictions on Marriage

In *Zappone and Anor v Revenue Commissioners and Ors*,[11] Dunne J said that s 2(2)(e) of the Civil Registration Act 2004 had set out

> what was previously the common law exclusion of same sex couples from the institution of marriage. Is that not of itself an indication of the

---

[11] [2006] IEHC 404.

prevailing idea and concept in relation to what marriage is and how it should be defined? I think it is.

A person may also not marry within the forbidden degrees of relationship by kindred (consanguinity) or marriage (affinity).

Under the heading of kindred, a man may not marry his:

- Grandmother
- Mother
- Father's or Mother's sister (aunt)
- Father's or mother's daughter (sister or half-sister)
- Daughter
- Son's or daughter's daughter (granddaughter)
- Brother's or sister's daughter (niece)

A woman may not marry her:

- Grandfather
- Father.
- Father's or mother's brother (uncle)
- Father's or mother's son (brother or half-brother)
- Son
- Son's or daughter's son (grandson)
- Brother's or sister's son (nephew)

According to the law on affinity, a man may not marry his:

- Grandfather's wife (step-grandmother)
- Father's wife (stepmother)
- Father's or mother's brother's wife
- Son's wife
- Son's or daughter's son's wife
- Brother's or sister's son's wife
- Wife's grandmother (grandmother-in-law)
- Wife's mother (mother-in-law)
- Wife's father's or mother's sister
- Wife's daughter (stepdaughter)
- Wife's son's or daughter's daughter
- Wife's brother's or sister's daughter

A woman may not marry her:

- Grandmother's husband (step-grandfather)
- Mother's husband (stepfather)
- Father's or mother's sister's husband
- Daughter's husband
- Daughter's or son's daughter's husband
- Brother's or sister's daughter's husband
- Husband's grandfather (grandfather-in-law)
- Husband's father (father-in-law)
- Husband's father's or mother's brother
- Husband's son (stepson)
- Husband's son's or daughter's son
- Husband's brother's or sister's son

Any queries about the requirements for a civil marriage should be directed to the marriages unit at the General Register Office, Convent Road, Roscommon, phone LoCall 1890-252076, +353(0)9066-32945/7/8/9, -32964 or -32970, or email the General Register Office.

EUROPEAN LEGISLATION

Introduction

The 2000 Brussels II Regulation was the first EU legal measure directly concerning family law.

In a paper delivered to the Judicial Studies Board in London, solicitor Geoffrey Shannon said the measure was "arguably the most dramatic development in the field of family law since the establishment of the EEC".

The Brussels II Convention, which was adopted as a Regulation on 1 March 2001,[1] took precedence over the 1996 Hague Convention, which continues to apply outside the EU and in Denmark.

The 'Brussels II Regulation' set out the rules on jurisdiction and the recognition and enforcement of judgments in matrimonial matters and in matters of parental responsibility for children of both spouses. Matrimonial matters includes divorce, annulment and legal separation, but do not include, for example, property issues and the grounds for divorce.

The Regulation applied to all applications for divorce, legal separation or annulment, and any declaration or other order concerning parental responsibility for the children of both spouses in connection with those proceedings.

---

[1] Council Regulation 1347/2000 OJ L160/19 on jurisdiction and the recognition and enforcement in matrimonial matters and in matters of parental responsibility for the children of both spouses.

The aim of the Regulation was to standardise the rules about the jurisdiction of courts in divorce, legal separation and nullity proceedings and to establish that the court which first heard the case retained jurisdiction.

As a result, spouses tried to ensure that their case would first be heard in a 'friendly' State, particularly in disputes regarding foreign property. Shannon said the danger with this was that

> the parties to a transnational marital breakdown will be lured into a 'race' to see who can get to court first...This militates against the statutory provisions encouraging parties to engage in mediation and other forms of alternative dispute resolution.

This Regulation was replaced by Regulation 2201/2003 ('Brussels II *bis*') for cases arising from 1 March 2005 but the rules relating to matrimonial matters are virtually unchanged. Brussels II *bis* prevents forum shopping, except in matters relating to parental responsibility.

Under Brussels II *bis*, divorce decrees are recognised throughout the EU, but the main significant changes relate to jurisdiction, recognition and enforcement of measures relating to the protection of children including:

- custody and access;
- guardianship;
- anyone in charge of the child or his property, or representing the child;
- foster families or institutional care; and
- the administration, conservation or disposal of the child's property.

Brussels II *bis* covers biological and adopted children, as well as stepchildren and non-marital children. Agreements between couples which are enforceable in a member state will be recognised and enforced in other member states.

Habitual Residence

The Irish courts can hear a matter relating to divorce, legal separation or marriage annulment where:

- the spouses, at the time of the application, are habitually resident in Ireland;

- the spouses were last habitually resident together in Ireland (as long as one remains habitually resident there);
- the respondent is habitually resident in Ireland;
- if the parties make a joint application, where either spouse is habitually resident in Ireland;
- the applicant has been habitually resident in Ireland for at least one year immediately before making the application;
- the applicant has been habitually resident in Ireland, lived there for six months before the application and is either an Irish national or is domiciled in Ireland.

Article 8(1) of Brussels II *bis* gives the Irish courts jurisdiction in matters of parental responsibility over a child who is habitually resident in Ireland at the time the court first deals with the matter. This is a significant change from the original Brussels II Regulation.

The courts in the state of the child's habitual residence have jurisdiction to rule on custody and access rights, except where the child has been living with the non-custodial parent for more than a year, and the custodial parent has not requested the child's return.

In *G(U) (Minor), B(E) (applicant) v G(A)*,[2] Finlay Geoghegan J refused to return a child to its father in Latvia, as she said the child was habitually resident with its stepfather in Ireland and had not acquired a habitual residence in Latvia.

The ECJ ruled in the case of *A*[3] that habitual residence must take into account:

1. the child's nationality;
2. the child's knowledge of the country's language;
3. the place and conditions of the child's attendance at school;
4. the child's family and social relationships in that State;
5. the family's reasons for moving to that State;
6. the duration, regularity, conditions and reasons for the child's stay in the State; and
7. the degree of the child's integration in a social and family environment

---

[2] Unreported, High Court, 4 March 2009.
[3] Case C-523/07, 2 April 2009.

A court can also vary an existing judgment about access for three months after the child acquires a new habitual residence, as long as the person with access rights continues to maintain a habitual residence in that country.

Custody Rights

In the case of a wrongful removal or retention of a child, the courts of the child's former habitual country of residence retain jurisdiction until the child has acquired a habitual residence in another Member State and:

a)   anyone with custody rights has acquiesced to the removal or retention; or

b)   the child has lived in the other member state for at least a year after the person with custody rights should have known where the child was, the child is settled in the new environment and either:

   (i)   no request for return has been lodged or withdrawn within a year;

   (ii) the case before the court in the child's former country of habitual residence has been closed; or

   (iii) a custody judgment that does not involve the child's return has been made in the child's former country of habitual residence.

In *PL v EC (Child Abduction)*,[4] the Supreme Court said the decision about whether a child was "settled in a new environment" must take into account all the facts, including the physical and emotional element, family, home and school and the absence of contact with the applicant parent. But Fennelly J said that any "element of concealment or subterfuge on the part of the respondent" must also be considered.

The Supreme Court asked the Court of Justice of the European Union for a preliminary ruling on whether Council Regulation (EC) No 2201/2003 on the recognition and enforcement of judgments in matrimonial matters and matters of parental responsibility, precluded a member state from requiring by law that the father of a child who was not married to the

---

[4] [2009] 1 IR 15.

mother should have obtained a court order granting him custody in order to have "custody rights".[5]

The CJEU ruled[6] that a state was not precluded from granting a mother exclusive custody rights, and a natural father had custody rights only as the result of a court judgment. Such a requirement allowed a national court to decide on custody and access rights while taking into account the:

1. circumstances surrounding the birth of the child;
2. nature of the parents' relationship;
3. relationship of the child with each parent; and
4. capacity of each parent to take the responsibility of caring for the child.

In *Nottingham County Council v B*,[7] Finlay Geoghegan J said it was up to the High Court to decide whether or not custody rights existed when considering whether or not to order a child's return.

Exceptionally, a court may transfer a case—only once—to a court in another member state where the transferring court believes that the other court would be better placed to hear the case and this would be in the child's best interests. The second court must accept jurisdiction within six weeks. Judges who speak or understand a common language can contact each other directly, by phone, email or conference call, to discuss the case.

A court must issue a judgment on custody 'without delay', preferably within six weeks, and should consult the child, unless that is inappropriate because of the child's age and lack of maturity. A delay of 18 months is "unacceptable in child law matters, where circumstances change rapidly".[8]

The European Court of Human Rights ruled in 1999 in *T v UK*[9] and *V v UK*[10] that children normally have a right to participate in legal proceedings, particularly during child abduction proceedings.

---

[5] *JMcB v LE* [2010] IESC 48.
[6] Case C-400/10, 5 October 2010.
[7] [2010] IEHC 9.
[8] Remarks by author Geoffrey Shannon at launch of *Child Law* (1st ed, Round Hall, Dublin, 2005), Dublin Castle, 14 March 2005.
[9] 24724/94.
[10] 24888/94.

A court also cannot refuse to return a child unless the person who requested the child's return has had an opportunity to be heard, possibly through a video link.

For enforcement purposes, an access judgment that has been certified in the original member state will be treated as if it were delivered in the member state of enforcement. The access provisions apply not only to parents but also to those looking after a child, including grandparents.

Brussels II *bis* provides that a foreign divorce, separation and parental responsibility judgment (or decree, order or decision) from the courts of one EU member state must be recognised in all other member states without any special procedure, though spouses and children can contest the recognition of the foreign judgment.

A court which grants a judicial separation retains jurisdiction for converting the separation into a divorce, where possible under national law.

An Irish court cannot question the decision of a foreign court on the basis that the Irish judge would not have reached the same decision, or that such a judgment would not have been obtainable in Ireland.

The revised Regulation also provides for the recognition and enforcement of a costs order.

But a court does not have to recognise a decision that is "manifestly contrary to the public policy" of the Member State, such as an annulment based on falsified evidence,[11] or where a respondent was not served with the documents instituting the proceedings.

The Supreme Court rejected the application of estoppel to the issue of marital status in *CK v JK*.[12] However, in parental responsibility cases, a court can refuse to recognise a judgment if it cannot be reconciled with a later judgment of the member state in which recognition is sought, as orders relating to parental responsibility may be varied in the light of new circumstances.

---

[11] *Vervaeke v Smith* [1983] 1 AC 145.
[12] [2004] IESC 21.

In the case of a conflict between two judgments from other member states, the latter will prevail.

Judgments of non-Member States will be recognised only if they are judgments of the State in which the child is habitually resident and fulfil any other conditions necessary for it to be recognised in the state addressed.

If the enforcing court requires a certified translation of the documents, that must be provided. Any appeal against an enforcement decision must be brought within one month of service of the judgment if the defendant is habitually resident in the state where the decision is given, or two months otherwise.

An applicant to enforce a foreign judgment cannot be required to provide security for the other side's legal costs just because the applicant is a foreign national or is not domiciled or habitually resident in the State in which enforcement is sought.

Maintenance

In the area of maintenance, the European Communities (Maintenance) Regulations 2011 (SI No 274 of 2011) made provision for the operation of Council Regulation (EC) 4/2009, the Maintenance Regulation, which deals with maintenance obligations in a cross-border context. The regulations applied from June 2011.

An estimated 16 million EU citizens are married to spouses from another country, and there are an estimated one million divorces granted every year, so the regulations are vital in the case of parents who live abroad and refuse to provide financial assistance. Outside the EU, the 2007 Hague Maintenance Convention may be used to recover child support or maintenance from a person in another country.

The Maintenance Regulation aimed to enable a maintenance creditor to obtain an order which could be enforced throughout the European Union easily, quickly and generally free. It provided common rules in relation to jurisdiction, applicable law, recognition, enforcement, cooperation and standardised documents. It covers maintenance obligations which arise from family relationships, parentage, marriage or affinity.

The Central Authority (email mainrecov@justice.ie) will help applicants to send and receive applications, initiate related proceedings to establish or vary maintenance, and enforce a maintenance decision.

Property

New European Union rules to reduce legal headaches when a family member with property in another EU country died became EU law in July 2012.

The Regulation on cross-border successions will bring legal certainty to the estimated 450,000 European families dealing with an international will or succession every year, as more than 12 million EU citizens are resident in an EU country of which they are not citizens.

The new law provides a single criterion for determining both the jurisdiction and the law applicable in cross-border cases: the deceased's habitual place of residence. People will also be able to opt to have the law of their country of nationality apply to their entire estate.

The Regulation permits citizens to plan their succession with legal certainty. The law provides for an EU Certificate of Succession, which will allow people to prove that they are heirs or administrators of an estate without further formalities.

CASE PROGRESSION

Introduction

'Case progression' means preparing family law proceedings for trial to ensure justice, and ensuring that proceedings will be as fast and inexpensive as possible and that the best use is made of the court's time.

Anyone who has filed an appearance may apply to the county registrar for case progression. Except in the case of motions for judgment in default of appearance or defence in the Dublin Circuit, any motion for judgment in default of appearance or defence in proceedings not already subject to case progression, any matter remitted or transferred from the High Court and any motion for re-entry of proceedings is initially heard by the county registrar.

He or she holds a hearing not more than 70 days after the respondent has filed his defence, his affidavit of means and, where required, his affidavit of welfare.

The parties will be given enough time to vouch the items referred to in their affidavits of means. The registrar may give directions about vouching items where there is a dispute about the adequacy of any vouching. A party to the case may see a record of the case progression hearings.

Where either party is seeking a pension adjustment order, a notice to the trustees must be served, an affidavit of service filed and a copy of the notice and affidavit served on the other party before the case progression hearing.

Uncontested motions can be transferred to the court motions list or given a date for a case progression hearing. At that hearing, the county registrar can extend time for entering an appearance, or filing a defence or affidavit of means or welfare.

The county registrar will fix a timetable for completing preparation of the case for trial, and may make orders or give directions about:

- pleadings;
- the exchange of statements of issues;
- identifying disputed issues;
- particulars;
- discovery;
- interrogatories;
- inspection of documents or property;
- commissions; and
- examination of witnesses.

The county registrar also has a wide range of other powers at a case progression hearing, including adjourning the hearing for his orders to be carried out and awarding costs against a party—or even transferring a matter to the court if his orders are not obeyed promptly.

Any appeal against a decision or direction of a county registrar must be brought within ten days of the direction or the perfection of the registrar's order, and the notice of appeal must be served on the other party and filed in court, with an affidavit of service. The appeal can be served personally or by registered post and is heard by a Circuit Court judge.

High Court

In the High Court, a 2005 practice direction aimed to ensure that family law proceedings are decided in a "just, efficient and most cost effective" way, so that hearings can generally be completed within a year and the parties be given the earliest opportunity to start "productive discussions".[1]

Before the first hearing of a case, each party must properly vouch all the items in their affidavit of means, unless the other side foregoes this in writing. Vouching includes producing:

- all bank and credit card statements for three years before the proceedings;
- details of the assets and liabilities of each party during the three-year period;

---

[1] HC51 - Family Law Proceedings, 16 July 2009.

- copies of any guarantees/indemnities;
- all tax returns, with supporting documentation and balancing statements for three years;
- P60s for the three-year period and up-to-date pay slips;
- three years' accounts for any company, partnership, profession or business (except publicly-quoted companies);
- details of any grants, subsidies or public payments received in the past three years;
- details of any pension and insurance/assurance policies; and
- particulars of any trust or any benefits received under a trust.

A directions list return must be given to the family law registrar not more than two working days before the hearing date. An adjournment of up to 12 weeks may be allowed to allow the parties to prepare for trial. Proceedings are transferred from the directions list into a list to fix dates when the case is "substantially ready for hearing".

At the hearing to fix a date, each side must inform the court about anything which might delay or prolong the trial, and give the court a realistic schedule for the hearing.

A call-over will be held on the Friday three weeks before the hearing date. Not more than seven days beforehand, each side must give the other side a completed call-over return. Unless the court specifies otherwise, the case will also be called over on the Fridays two weeks and one week before the hearing.

The High Court can declare that separation or divorce proceedings should go ahead as an undefended action if there is "egregious non-compliance" with the practice direction.[2]

In *U v U*,[3] the husband sought a variation of a maintenance order, while his ex-wife applied to have him committed to prison for contempt for his failure to comply with a High Court order.

The husband asked the court to dismiss the application on the basis that committal could not be used to enforce maintenance payments in family

---

[2] *U v U* [2011] IEHC 228.
[3] *ibid.*

law proceedings. But the court said compliance with the divorce decree involved doing things other than just paying maintenance.

Abbott J said the husband's conduct, in terms of disclosure before and after the divorce decree, "amounted to litigation misconduct of the most serious kind". He said the court had the power to dismiss the ex-husband's application because of his conduct

> which could be regarded as contempt of court in the civil sense, insofar as he has flagrantly broken the order which he now seeks to have reviewed.

If a case is particularly complex, the court may specify a case management conference to be chaired by a judge.

DIRECTIONS LIST RETURN

(If necessary, continue on a separate sheet, referring to the item number)

Information to be supplied	Applicant's/ Petitioner's reply	Respondent's reply	Parties' agreed reply (see para 7 of Practice Direction)
1. Is the question of divorce/ judicial separation—other than in the context of proper provision—a live issue? If so, what is the position of each party on the issue?			
2. Is the question of custody/access of any dependent children a live issue? If so what is the position of each party on the issue?			
3. Are the pleadings properly closed and are any amendments expected? If so, what is their likely nature and how much further time is needed?			
4. Are the parties otherwise satisfied that the affidavits served are complete and in accordance with the rules? If not, what is the nature of the dispute?			

5. Are the parties satisfied that the information has been given and vouching done as required by the practice direction? If not, what is the nature of the dispute?			
6. Has there been (or will there be) agreement that any necessary *inter partes* discovery will be provided voluntarily?			
7. Do the parties envisage that third party discovery will be required?			
8. Are any orders being sought under s 12 or 13 of the Family Law Act 1995 or s 17 of the Family Law (Divorce) Act 1996? If so, have the trustees been served?			
9. Has any request being made by either party for particulars under s 38(7) of the Family Law Act 1995 or s 38(6) of the Family Law (Divorce) Act 1996?			
10. Will expert witnesses be giving evidence? If so, give details of (a) the expert, (b) the expert's professional standing and (c) the financial, medical, valuation or other matter about which the expert witness will be giving evidence.			
11. Will any social reports be sought under s 47 of the Family Law Act 1995?			
12. How long do you need for all the experts to complete their investigations and report on them?			
13. Is it agreed that:			

(a) the reports of each expert witness you intend to call will be exchanged between the parties?			
(b) if necessary, such witnesses will meet their counterparts to discuss meaningfully the issues on which they propose to give evidence and, if possible, reaching agreement on that evidence?			
(c) the parties will exchange a list of witnesses intended to be called?			
14. Would the trial as a preliminary issue of any question of fact, law or mixed fact and law facilitate the objective of this practice direction? If so, indicate the nature of such issue, the estimated length of any such hearing and the likely effect on the outcome on the substantive proceedings.			
15. Are written submissions required or desirable?			
16. Are any orders or directions being sought at this stage? If so, what is the scope and nature of any intended application?			
17. Should any other matters be brought to the attention of the court?			

CALL-OVER RETURN

(If necessary, continue on a separate sheet, referring to the item number)

Information to be supplied	Applicant's/ Petitioner's reply	Respondent's reply	Parties' joint reply (see paragraph 16 of the Practice Direction)
1. Are all witnesses intended or likely to be called, available for the entire hearing? If not, what is the difficulty?			
2. Is the question of divorce/ judicial separation—other than in the context of proper provision—a live issue? If so, what is the position of each party?			
3. Is the question of custody/access of any dependent children a live issue? If so, what is the position of each party?			
4. Has a report(s) under s 47 of the Family Law Act 1995 and/or medical reports, if applicable, been sent to the other party, or exchanged between the parties? If not, explain why and give the likely date of their availability/ exchange.			
5. What specific orders are being sought under Part II of the Family Law Act 1995 or Part III of the Family Law (Divorce) Act 1996?			
6. Have updated reports, including all documents referred to and relied on—including comparators where applicable—been exchanged (where relevant) between:			

Medical practitioners, psychiatrists or other medical personnel, psychologists or similar professionals?			
Valuers?			
Accountants or other financial experts?			
Agricultural consultants or similar professionals?			
Pension consultants?			
Other experts?			
7. Do such reports contain the substance of the evidence which the expert witness proposes to give at the hearing? If not, explain why.			
8. Have all the experts met and consulted their counterparts and discussed meaningfully the issues on which they propose to give evidence?			
If not, indicate why not and the likely date(s) for such meetings.			
Have the experts reached agreement on such evidence?			
If not, what is the scope and nature of all areas of disagreement?			
9. Have the experts prepared a memorandum (which will not be binding on the parties) signed by each of them, recording the outcome of their discussions? If not, explain why.			
10. Have the parties exchanged a list of witnesses intended to be called at the hearing?			

11. Have updated affidavits of means and particulars (verified by affidavit), and updated affidavits of welfare been exchanged between the parties? If not, indicate why not and the likely date for such exchange.			
12. Have written submissions been directed and, if so, have they been served and filed?			
13. If neither directed, served nor filed, are such submissions still required or desirable?			
14. Has the estimated length of the hearing changed?			
15. Should any other relevant matters be brought to the court's attention?			

FAMILY LAW (DIVORCE) ACT 1996 SYNOPSIS

s 1 (1) The short title of the Act is the Family Law (Divorce) Act.

s 1 (2) The Act came into operation on 27 February 1997.

s 2 (1) Interpretation section.

s 3 Repeal of s 14 (2) of the Censorship of Publications Act 1929, restricting the media's right to publish full details of divorce, nullity or separation cases.

s 4 Administration of the Act to be financed by the Oireachtas.

Part II - Obtaining a decree of divorce

s 5 (1) The court may grant a divorce where it is satisfied that:

(a) when the proceedings began, the spouses had lived apart for at least four of the preceding five years;
(b) there is no reasonable prospect of reconciliation; and
(c) there is proper provision for the spouses and dependent children.

s 5 (2) The court may give directions concerning the dependent children's welfare, custody and access.

s 6 (1) The person applying for the divorce is called the applicant.

s 6 (2) Before proceedings begin, the applicant's solicitor must discuss with him the possibility of:

(a) reconciliation and give him the names and addresses of people qualified to help reconcile the couple;
(b) mediation to help the couple agree the basis of their separation or divorce, and give him the names and addresses of qualified mediators; and
(c) a written separation agreement.

s 6 (3) If the couple are not judicially separated, the applicant's solicitor must tell him about judicial separation as an alternative to divorce.

s 6 (4) The solicitor acting for the applicant must:

(a) sign a certificate confirming he has complied with sub-sections (2) and, if necessary, (3) and must hand in that certificate with the original petition, or else the court may adjourn the application; and

(b) leave a copy of the certificate with any copy of the petition served on anyone else or left in a court office.

s 6 (5) The certificate must be in the form required by the rules of court.

s 6 (6) The minister may make regulations for the establishment of a register of professional organisations whose members are qualified to help reconcile spouses. The register would give the names of members of the organisations and procedures for regular updating of the membership lists.

s 7 (1) The spouse who is not the applicant is called the respondent.

s 7 (2) As soon as any solicitor acting for the respondent receives instructions, he must tell her about the possibility of:

(a) reconciliation and give her the names and addresses of people qualified to help reconcile the couple;

(b) mediation to help bring about a separation or divorce on an agreed basis, and give her the names and addresses of qualified mediators; and

(c) a written separation agreement.

s 7 (3) If the couple are not already judicially separated, the respondent's solicitor must tell her about judicial separation as an alternative to divorce.

s 7 (4) The solicitor acting for the applicant must:

(a) sign a certificate confirming he has complied with sub-sections (2) and, if necessary, (3) and must hand in that document with the original petition, or else the court may adjourn the application; and

(b) leave a copy of the certificate with any copy of the petition served on anyone else or left in a court office.

s 7 (5) The certificate must be in the form required by the rules of court.

s 8 (1) If both spouses wish, the court may adjourn divorce proceedings at any time, to allow the couple to consider reconciliation.

s 8 (2) If the court believes the spouses can't be reconciled, it may adjourn proceedings (if both spouses wish) to let them try and reach agreement on some, or all, of the terms of the proposed divorce.

s 8 (3) If proceedings are adjourned for talks on reconciliation or divorce terms, and one spouse wants them resumed, the court will resume the proceedings.

s 8 (4) The powers in s 8 are additional to any other power the court may have to adjourn proceedings.

s 8 (5) Where the court does adjourn proceedings under s 8, it may advise the couple to seek the help of a third party.

s 9 If the couple seek assistance for the purpose of reconciliation or to reach agreement on the terms of a divorce or separation, any oral or written communication between either spouse and a third party (whether or not the other spouse knows about it), and any record of such a communication by either spouse or the third party, will not be admissible in evidence.

s 10 (1) A decree of divorce dissolves the marriage and the spouses are free to remarry.

s 10 (2) A divorce decree does not affect the right of a father or mother to be joint guardians of their child.

Part III - Preliminary and ancillary orders during or
after divorce proceedings

s 11 Before the court grants a divorce, it may make one or more of the following orders without an application under the relevant Act:

(a) a safety order, barring order, temporary barring order or protection order;

(b) an order for the custody, access or maintenance of a dependent child;

(c) an order to protect the family home, its contents or any money from its sale.

s 12 (1) The court may order either spouse to pay maintenance for the other spouse and any dependent children from the date of the application until the court's final decision. Alternatively, a spouse may be ordered to pay lump sums.

s 12 (2) The court may decide appropriate terms and conditions for such payments.

s 13 (1) When the court grants the divorce, on an application by either spouse (or on behalf of a dependent child), the court may make any of the following orders during the lifetime of either spouse:

(a) a periodical payments order; that is an order

(i) for one spouse to make payments to the other, as often, and for as long as, the court orders (See s 13(4)); or

    (ii) for either spouse to make payments to another person for the benefit of a dependent child, as often, and for as long as, the court orders (See s 13(4))

  (b) a secured periodical payments order, that is an order

    (i) for one spouse to secure payments to the other to the court's satisfaction; or

    (ii) for either spouse to secure payments to another person for a dependent child, to the court's satisfaction or

  (c) an order

    (i) for one spouse to make a lump sum payment (or payments) to the other at specified time(s); or

    (ii) for either spouse to make a lump sum payment (or payments) to another person for a dependent child at specified time(s)

s 13 (2) The court may order a spouse to pay a lump sum to:

  (a) the other spouse to meet any reasonable liabilities or expenses incurred before that spouse applied for a periodical payments order; or

  (b) a specified person to meet any reasonable liabilities or expenses incurred before a periodical payments application was made on behalf of a dependent child.

s 13 (3) The court may order that the lump sum be paid by specified instalments, and that payment be secured.

s 13 (4) Periodical payments shall not start before the application for the divorce and shall not continue beyond the death of either spouse or any dependent child in whose favour the order is made.

s 13 (5)

  (a) Periodical payments shall stop when a spouse remarries, except for any arrears due.

  (b) If a spouse remarries after the divorce, the court will not make a periodical payments order in his or her favour.

s 13 (6)

  (a) At the same time as a court makes a periodical payments order, subject to any secured order, it shall make an attachment of earnings order if the spouse earns wages. (See s 10(2) of the Family Law (Maintenance of Spouses and Children) Act 1976)

(b)   Before making an attachment of earnings order, the court shall take into account the spouse's views in relation to:

(c)   whether

   (i)   he is paid earnings and

   (ii)   he would pay the periodical payments.

(d)   References to a periodical payments order include references to an order which has been appealed or varied (See s 22).

s 14 (1) At any time after granting a divorce, on an application by either spouse (or on behalf of a dependent child), the court may—during the lifetime of either spouse—make a property adjustment order providing for one or more of the following:

(a)   the transfer of property by either spouse to the other spouse, to a dependent child or to another person for the benefit of a dependent child;

(b)   the satisfactory settlement of specified property for the benefit of the other spouse and/or any dependent child;

(c)   the variation of any pre-marriage or post-marriage settlement made on the couple (including any settlement in a will), for the benefit of either spouse and/or any dependent child;

(d)   the extinguishment or reduction of the interest of either spouse under such a settlement.

s 14 (2) The court may restrict or refuse to allow future variations of orders made under paragraphs (b), (c) or (d).

s 14 (3) If a spouse remarries after obtaining a divorce, the court will not make a property adjustment order in his or her favour.

s 14 (4) Where a property adjustment order relates to land, the registrar or clerk of the court shall lodge a certified copy of the order in the Land Registry or Registry of Deeds.

s 14 (5) Where a person

(a)   is ordered to execute a deed or document in relation to land and

(b)   refuses or fails to do so, (or if the court considers it necessary),

the court may order another person to execute the deed or document, and that execution shall be valid.

s 14 (6) The court will apportion any costs in relation to a property adjustment order between the spouses.

s 14 (7) If a spouse remarries after a divorce, the court will not make a property adjustment order in relation to the home where that spouse lives with his or her new partner.

s 15 (1) When the court grants a divorce, on an application by either spouse (or on behalf of a dependent child), the court may—during the lifetime of either spouse—make any of the following orders:

   (a)   an order

         (i)   giving one spouse the right to live in the family home for life or any other period, to the exclusion of the other spouse; or
         (ii) directing the sale of the family home and the division of the proceeds between the spouses and anyone else with an interest in the property (See s 15(2) and s 15(3)).

   (b)   deciding the ownership of any property,
   (c)   dispensing with the consent of a spouse who refuses to agree to the sale of the home, an order to protect the home, an order relating to arrears of mortgage or rent, an order restricting the disposal of household chattels,
   (d)   a safety, barring, interim barring or protection order on the application of a spouse of the respondent, person who lives with the respondent, parent of the respondent, co-habitee or health board,
   (e)   partition of the property,
   (f)   custody or access or other order relating to the welfare of a child.

s 15 (2) In relation to orders under sub-section (1)(a), the court shall consider the welfare of the spouses and any dependent children and, in particular, shall take into consideration:

   (a)   that a couple cannot live together after they have divorced; and
   (b)   that dependent children and dependent spouses should be provided with proper secure accommodation.

s 15 (3) If a spouse remarries after a divorce, sub-section (1)(a) does not apply to the family home where that spouse lives with his or her new partner.

s 16 (1) At any time after the court grants a divorce, on an application by either spouse (or on behalf of a dependent child) during the lifetime of either spouse, if the court considers:

   (a)   that the financial security of the applicant spouse or child can be improved; or
   (b)   that compensation should be made to the applicant or child for giving up a benefit, such as a pension,

the court may make a financial compensation order requiring the other spouse to do one or more of the following:

(i) take out a life insurance policy for the benefit of the applicant or child,

(ii) assign some or all of the benefit of an existing life insurance policy to the applicant or child,

(iii) continue to pay life insurance premiums. (See s 16(2)(d))

s 16 (2)

(a) The court can make a financial compensation order as well as (or instead of) all or part of the orders under sections 13, 14, 15 or 17, but it must take into account whether, in the circumstances, proper provision exists (or can be made) for the spouse and child concerned.

(b) A financial compensation order ceases to apply to the applicant if she dies or remarries.

(c) The court shall not make a financial compensation order in favour of a spouse who has remarried.

(d) In relation to a life insurance policy, the court may vary any order concerning the disposal of

(i) an amount equal to the accumulated value of a policy taken out under sub-section (1)(i) or

(ii) the interest or part-interest in a policy under sub-section (1)(ii).

s 17 (1) Pension adjustment orders interpretation section.

s 17 (2) If either spouse is a member of a retirement benefit scheme, either may apply at any time after a divorce decree (during the member's lifetime) for an order to pay

a) the member's spouse or, in case of death, the personal representative or

b) anyone specified, for the benefit of a dependent child

all (or part) of the benefit which has accrued at the time of the divorce decree. The application may also be made by someone on behalf of a dependent child. The order will specify

(i) the period of reckonable service of the member before the divorce and

(ii) the percentage of the benefits accrued during that period to be paid to the applicant.

s 17 (3) On application by either spouse (or a person on behalf of a dependent child) within one year of the divorce decree, the court may order that all (or a specified percentage) of any death-in-service benefit be paid on the member's death to

    (a) the other spouse and/or

    (b) anyone specified, for the benefit of a dependent child.

The court will decide what share each applicant is to receive.

s 17 (4) Where a pension adjustment order is made, and payment of the retirement benefit has not yet started, the applicant will be entitled to an equal amount of money from the scheme (a "transfer amount"), as calculated by the scheme's trustees.

s 17 (5) Where a pension adjustment order is made, and payment of the retirement benefit has not yet started,

    (a) on application by the spouse in whose favour the order was made and

    (b) after being provided with any information required by that spouse

the scheme's trustees shall use the transfer amount either

        (i) to provide the spouse with a benefit of the same actuarial value (if the trustees and spouse agree), or

      (ii) to make a payment, at the spouse's discretion, to

            (I) another occupational pension scheme of which the trustees agree to accept the payment or

          (II) pay off any money owed by the trustees under an approved insurance policy.

s 17 (6) Where the pension scheme is a *defined contribution* scheme, and a spouse has not applied for a transfer amount, the trustees may, if they see fit, make a payment

    (a) to another occupational pension scheme where the trustees agree to accept the payment or

    (b) to pay off any money owed by the trustees under an insurance policy.

s 17 (7) Where

    (a) a pension adjustment order is made and

    (b) the member dies before payment of benefits has started,

the trustees must—within three months of the death—pay an equal transfer amount to the person in whose favour the order was made, calculated in accordance with relevant guidelines.

s 17 (8) Where

    (a)   a pension adjustment order is made and

    (b)   the member leaves the scheme (other than dying),

the trustees may apply the transfer amount in accordance with the guidelines

        (i)   to provide a benefit of the same value under the same scheme (if the trustees and spouse agree) or

      (ii)   to make a payment

           (I)   to another occupational pension scheme which will accept the payment or

         (II)   to pay off any money due under an insurance policy,

whichever the trustees prefer.

s 17 (9) Where

    (a)   a pension adjustment order is made and

    (b)   the recipient spouse dies before payment of benefits has started,

within three months of the death, the trustees shall pay an equal transfer amount to the spouse's personal representative.

s 17 (10) Where

    (a)   a pension adjustment order is made and

    (b)   the recipient dies *after* payment of benefits has started,

the trustees shall pay to the personal representative—within three months of the death—an amount equal to the value of the balance of the benefit which would have otherwise been paid to the spouse during the member's lifetime.

s 17 (11) Where

    (a)   a pension adjustment order is made in favour of a child and

    (b)   the child dies before payment of benefits has started,

that part of the order shall have no further effect.

s 17 (12) Where

    (a)   a pension adjustment or death-in-service order is made in relation to an occupational pension scheme and

    (b)   the trustees of the scheme have not transferred the amount concerned and,

    (c)   after the order was made, the member leaves the scheme, within a year of his leaving, the trustees shall notify the clerk of the court and the other spouse.

s 17 (13) Where the trustees make a transfer under sub-sections 6 or 8, they must notify the member's spouse (or other person concerned) and the court, giving particulars of the scheme and the amount transferred.

s 17 (14) Where a pension adjustment or death-in-service order is made, the benefit (or transfer amount) is payable out of the scheme concerned and must be paid in accordance with the rules of the scheme, unless the order says otherwise.

s 17 (15) Where a pension adjustment order is made, the amount of retirement benefit payable to the member shall be reduced by the amount of benefits payable under the order.

s 17 (16)

    (a)   Where a death-in-service order is made, the amount of benefit payable to the member is reduced by the amount of death benefit payable to the spouse.

    (b)   Where a pension adjustment order is made and the member dies before payment of benefits begins, the amount of death benefit payable to the member is reduced by the amount payable under sub-section 7.

s 17 (17) Where a pension adjustment order is made and the trustees make a payment under any one of sub-sections 5 to 10, they do not have to make any further payments under any other of those sub-sections.

s 17 (18) A person who applies for a pension adjustment or death-in-service order, or a change in an existing order, must notify the trustees, and the court shall take note of the representations of the trustees, the member and anyone else specified by the court before making the order.

s 17 (19) A death-in-service order shall cease to have any effect on the death or remarriage of the member's spouse or child.

s 17 (20) At any time after the making of a pension adjustment order, the court may give the trustees directions which contravene the scheme rules or the Pensions Act 1990. The trustees shall not be liable for any loss or damage caused by their compliance with the court's directions.

s 17 (21) The registrar or clerk of the court must serve the trustees with a copy of any pension adjustment order.

s 17 (22)

    (a)   The court will decide whether the costs incurred by the trustees (in relation to making representations, obeying court directions, making calculations or complying with a pension adjustment order) should be met by the member, the other spouse or both of them. If there is no order, the costs are shared equally.

(b) If a person fails to pay his share of the costs, the trustees may apply to the court for the share to be deducted from any pension adjustment or death-in-service payment.

s 17 (23)

(a) No pension adjustment order shall be made in favour of a spouse who has remarried.

(b) A pension adjustment order may be made instead of, or as well as, any periodical payments, lump sum, property adjustment, financial compensation or family home order. Before making a pension adjustment order, the court must decide whether proper provision has been made for the spouse and children by the other orders.

s 17 (24) S.54 of the Pension Act 1990 (dealing with the disclosure of information about schemes) shall apply, with any necessary modifications, to a scheme where a member is involved in divorce proceedings.

s 17 (25) The court may direct the trustees within a certain time to calculate

(a) the value and amount of the retirement or death-in-service benefit that had accrued when the order was made (or the benefit that would have been payable if there had been no divorce) and

(b) the amount of death-in-service benefit payable.

If either spouse (or anyone else concerned) requests the information, the court must direct the trustees to provide it.

s 17 (26) An order under this section may restrict or exclude any future variation.

s 18 (1) Where a divorced spouse dies, and on application by the other spouse within six months of the grant of probate, the court may order that the applicant be provided for out of the estate, taking into account the rights of anyone else with an interest in the estate. The court must specify in the order that the deceased spouse did not make proper provision for the applicant within his lifetime under ss 13-17, having regard to his circumstances, for some reason other than the applicant's conduct.

s 18 (2) The court shall not make an order under this section for someone who has remarried.

s 18 (3) Before making any order, the court shall consider all the circumstances, including:

(a) any property adjustment order or lump sum payments to the applicant

(b) any bequest made to the applicant by the deceased spouse.

s 18 (4) Taking into account any lump sum or property adjustment order, the applicant may not receive more than he or she would have been entitled to under the Succession Act if there had been no divorce. The value of any lump sum or property adjustment order is taken as its value on the date of the original order.

s 18 (5) The applicant must give notice of the application to the spouse of the deceased person and to anyone else the court may direct, and the court shall take account of their views.

s 18 (6) The personal representative of the deceased spouse shall make a reasonable attempt to inform any potential applicant about the death of the deceased spouse and, if an application is made, the personal representative shall not dispose of any of the estate without the court's permission until the court has ruled on the application.

s 18 (7) Where the personal representative of a deceased spouse has given notice to the surviving spouse and

(a)   the spouse intends to apply for an order under this section,
(b)   the spouse has already applied for an order or
(c)   an order has already been made,

the surviving spouse must notify the personal representative within a month of the notice or else the assets may be distributed among the people entitled to them.

s 18 (8) In the case of such a distribution, the personal representative shall not be liable to the surviving spouse for the assets.

s 18 (9) Even if the assets have been distributed, the surviving spouse may still try and get them back.

s 18 (10) At any time after the court grants a decree of divorce, it may order (on the application of either spouse) that neither spouse be entitled to apply for an order under this section.

s 19 (1) At any time after the court makes a secured periodical payments, lump sum or property adjustment order, it may order the sale of property in which either of the spouses has an interest.

s 19 (2) The court will not order the sale of a family home where it has already ordered that a spouse should have the right to occupy the home.

s 19 (3)

(a)   An order for sale may contain other appropriate provisions.
(b)   An order for sale may also specify:
    (i)   the manner and conditions of sale,

(ii)   the person(s) to whom the property must be offered,

(iii) the date when the order is to come into effect,

(iv) payment(s) to a specified person from the proceeds of sale, and

(v)   the division of the proceeds.

s 19 (4) Periodical payments to a spouse out of the proceeds of sale shall cease on the death or remarriage of that spouse, except for any arrears due.

s 19 (5) The court must take note of representations by anyone other than the spouse who has an interest in the property or the proceeds of sale.

s 19 (6) This section does not apply to a family home where a divorced spouse ordinarily lives with his or her new spouse.

s 20 (1) The court must ensure that, in all the circumstances, the spouses and dependent children are properly provided for when making an order under sections 12, 13, 14, 15 (1)(a), 16, 17, 18 or 22.

s 20 (2) In particular, the court shall also consider:

(a)   the income, earning capacity, property and other financial resources of each spouse at the time or in the foreseeable future,

(b)   the financial needs, obligations and responsibilities of each spouse at the time or in the foreseeable future (whether in the case of remarriage or not),

(c)   the standard of living enjoyed by the family before the proceedings began or the spouses started to live apart,

(d)   the age of the spouses, duration of marriage and length of time they lived together,

(e)   any physical or mental disability of either spouse,

(f)   the contribution which each spouse has made (or is likely to make) to the welfare of the family, including contributions to the income, earning capacity, property and financial resources of the other spouse, and any contribution made by looking after the home or caring for the family,

(g)   the effect of marital responsibility on the earning capacity of either spouse while they were living together, and particularly the degree to which a spouse's future earning capacity was affected by giving up the possibility of paid work to look after the home or care for the family,

(h)   any income or benefits to which either spouse is statutorily entitled,

(i)   the conduct of either of the spouses, if it would be unfair, in all the circumstances, to disregard such conduct,

(j)   the accommodation needs of either spouse,

(k)   the value to either spouse of any benefit (such as a pension) which would be lost because of the divorce,

(l)   the rights of anyone else, including a new husband or wife.

s 20 (3) The court shall consider the terms of any separation agreement still in force. [Note that this sub-section does not refer to pre-nuptial or post-nuptial agreements and is "an expression of a very broad discretion".[1]]

s 20 (4) In relation to any dependent child, the court shall particularly consider:

(a) his financial needs,
(b) his income, earning capacity, property or other financial resources,
(c) any physical or mental disability,
(d) any income or benefits to which he is statutorily entitled,
(e) the parents' proposed education or training of the child,
(f) the matters specified in paragraphs (a), (b) and (c) of sub-section 2 and sub-section (3), and
(g) his accommodation needs.

s 20 (5) The court shall not make any order under sub-section (1) unless it would be in the interests of justice to do so.

s 21 (1) In an order for periodical payments, the court may direct that:

(a) payments shall be backdated to the date proceedings began,
(b) any retrospective payments should be paid in a lump sum by a set date,
(c) any payments made between the start of proceedings and date of the decree may be deducted from the lump sum.

s 21 (2) The right to order retrospective payments does not affect the court's right to order payment of any other lump sum.

s 22 (1) This section applies to the following orders:

(a) maintenance pending suit,
(b) periodical payments,
(c) secured periodical payments,
(d) lump sums by instalments or by secured instalments,
(e) the settlement of specified property and variation or extinguishment of any settlement,
(f) a right of residence in the family home or for the sale of the family home and division of the proceeds,
(g) financial compensation,
(h) pension adjustment,
(i) an order under this section.

---

[1] *SN v PO'D* [2009] IESC 61.

s 22 (2) Subject to specified restrictions, on application by

(a) either spouse,
(b) on the death of either spouse, by anyone else with a sufficient interest or on behalf of a dependent child or
(c) by a new spouse in the case of remarriage,

in the light of changed circumstances or new evidence, the court may temporarily or permanently change, suspend, revive or discharge an order, and may require a person to give up property obtained under such an order.

s 22 (3) Periodical payments shall cease when a child reaches the age of 18 (or 23 if in full-time education) and the court shall discharge such an order if the child has ceased to be dependent.

s 22 (4) The power of the court to change an order settling property, or extinguishing or varying a settlement (subject to any restriction in the order) is a power

(a) to vary the settlement in favour of anyone or to extinguish or reduce anyone's interest and,
(b) in the light of such variation, to make any appropriate additional provision (including another property adjustment or lump sum order)

and s 19 will apply to any variation of an order under sub-section (2) and to any property adjustment order.

s 22 (5) The court shall not vary an order settling property, or extinguishing or varying a settlement if it believes such a variation would prejudice the interests of anyone who

(a) has acquired a right or interest as a result of the original order and
(b) is not a spouse or dependent child.

s 22 (6) This section will apply to any legal documents executed as a result of any variation orders.

s 22 (7) Where the court varies a property adjustment order relating to land, the registrar or clerk of the court shall lodge a certified copy in the Land Registry or Registry of Deeds.

s 23 The court will disregard the conduct of spouses when deciding whether to

(a) include a dependent child in an order for maintenance pending suit,
(b) make an order for periodical payments, secured periodical payments or a lump sum to a dependent child, or
(c) vary such orders.

s 24 (1) The court may order that payments shall be made by a specified method and subject to appropriate terms and conditions.

s 24 (2) This section applies to an order under

(a) s 11 (2)(b) of the 1964 Act (maintenance for an infant)
(b) ss 5, 5A or 7 of the 1976 Act (maintenance of spouses and dependent children and interim order)
(c) ss 7, 8 or 24 of the 1995 Act (maintenance pending suit, periodical payments, lump sum orders and maintenance pending relief) and
(d) ss 12, 13, 19 or 22 of this Act (financial or property orders).

s 25 Where there is an appeal against any such order (except in relation to lump sum payments, property sale or residence orders), there will be no stay on the order unless the court that made the order (or the appeal court) rules otherwise.

s 26 (1) Where an order is in force for

(a) maintenance, variation of maintenance or interim maintenance under the 1976 Act,
(b) periodical or lump sum payments, property adjustment, sale, transfer or partition, right to occupy the family home or guardianship under the 1989 Act,
(c) periodical or lump sum payments, property adjustment, sale, transfer or partition, the right to occupy the family home, guardianship, pension adjustment, extinction of succession rights or financial compensation under the 1995 Act,

the court may discharge it if the spouse in whose favour the order was made applies for a divorce or an order under Part III of this Act.

s 26 (2) If the court does not discharge the order when it grants a divorce, it will remain in force and s 22 of this Act will apply to it.

s 27 Amendment of the interpretation section of the Family Law (Maintenance of Spouses and Children) Act 1976.

s 28 Orders for maintenance pending suit, periodical payments or secured periodical payments may be made through the District Court clerk, with any necessary modifications, including that

(a) the reference in s 9(4) of the 1976 Act to the "maintenance creditor" means the person to whom payments are to be made,
(b) other references in s 9 to the "maintenance creditor" refer to the person who applied for the order and

(c)   the reference in s 9(3) to the "maintenance debtor" means the person required to make payments under the order.

s 29 The reference to "alimony" in the Defence Act 1954 includes orders for maintenance pending suit, periodical payments and secured periodical payments.

s 30 Amendment of Enforcement of Court Orders Act 1940.

Part IV - Income tax, capital acquisitions tax, capital gains tax, probate tax and stamp duty

s 31 Payments under this Act (other than pensions) shall be made without deduction of income tax.

s 32 Where a legally-enforceable maintenance agreement is made in a year of assessment by one spouse for the benefit of a divorced spouse and

(a)   both parties are resident in the state for tax purposes during that tax year and
(b)   neither spouse has remarried,

then both spouses will be separately assessed for income tax, as if they had not been divorced.

s 33 (1) Stamp duty will not be chargeable on a property transfer by either or both divorced spouses to either or both of them (See sub-section (3))

s 33 (2) Stamp duty (normally payable on gifts from one person to another) shall not apply to such a transfer.

s 33 (3) Subsection (1)

(a)   applies to an order under Part III of this Act,
(b)   does not apply to any property transferred to anyone else.

s 34 Any gift or inheritance that the court orders one spouse to give to the other shall be exempt from capital acquisitions tax and shall not be taken into account when computing such a tax.

s 35 (1) If the court orders either spouse to dispose of an asset to the other spouse on divorce, both spouses shall be treated, for the purposes of capital gains tax, as if there were no loss or gain on the disposal. (This does not apply if the asset was part of the stock in the trade of the disposing spouse or if it is acquired as trading stock by the other spouse.)

s 35 (2) In the case of any subsequent disposal of the same asset, the spouse making the disposal will be treated (for capital gains tax purposes) as if the other spouse's acquisition or provision of the asset was that of the disposing spouse.

s 36 (1) Abatement or postponement of probate tax payable by a surviving spouse (under s 115A(1) of the Finance Act 1993) shall apply (with any necessary modifications) to

    (a)   a spouse who has been granted an order providing a benefit from the estate of his or her deceased former spouse and

    (b)   any property interest which is the subject of such an order, in the same way as it applies to a person in s 115A who shares in the estate (or property interest) of a deceased spouse

Part V - Miscellaneous

s 37 (1) Interpretation section.

s 37 (2)

    (a)   If proceedings have *not* been decided, the court may—on the application of the person bringing the proceedings—

        (i)   restrain anyone from disposing of property or transferring it out of the state with the intention of defeating the applicant's claim

        (ii)   set aside any disposition of property which has been disposed of to defeat the applicant's claim. [This does not apply to a property bought in good faith from a party to proceedings.] (See s 37(2)(c))

    (b)   Where proceedings have been decided, if the court believes the other spouse (or anyone else) has disposed of property to defeat the applicant's claim, it may set aside the disposition.

    (c)   An application under paragraph (a) shall be brought as part of the relevant proceedings.

s 37 (3) The court shall include in any order under sub-section (2)(a) or (b) anything necessary for the order to be carried out, including the payment of money or disposition of any property.

s 37 (4) If the disposition of any property under sub-section (2) took place less than three years before the application, or where the other spouse proposes to dispose of property and the court is satisfied that the disposition,

    (a)   would defeat, or

    (b)   has defeated

the applicant's claim, the court will presume (unless proved otherwise) that the intention was to defeat the claim.

s 38 (1) The Circuit Family Court, as well as the High Court, may hear proceedings under this Act.

s 38 (2) Circuit Family Court proceedings relating to land with a rateable value of more than £200 (€254) must be transferred to the High Court on the application of anyone with an interest in the proceedings, but any order made by the Circuit Court before the transfer shall be valid unless the High Court decides otherwise. (See s 38(4))

s 38 (3) A Circuit Court judge may hear proceedings under this Act if any of the parties normally lives or works in the circuit area.

s 38 (4) If land has not been given a separate rateable valuation, the Circuit Court may decide its valuation.

s 38 (5) The Circuit Court shall hear proceedings under this Act in a different place (or different times or days) from other proceedings. Wigs and gowns will not be worn by judges or lawyers. The proceedings will be *in camera* and as informal as possible, consistent with the administration of justice.

s 38 (6) In proceedings under section 13, 14, 15 (1)(a), 16, 17, 18 or 22,

(a) each spouse shall give to the other spouse and to anyone representing the interests of a dependent child and

(b) any dependent child shall give any other dependent child, anyone acting on behalf of such a child and each spouse

any details of property and income that may reasonably be required.

s 38 (7) If a person fails to give such details, the court—on an application by anyone with an interest in the proceedings—may direct him to comply.

s 39 (1) The court may only grant a decree of divorce if

(a) either spouse was domiciled in the state on the date the proceedings were instituted or

(b) either spouse was ordinarily resident in the state for one year ending on that date.

s 39 (2) Where the court is hearing a divorce petition or appeal, it may grant a decree of judicial separation or nullity instead.

s 39 (3) Where the court is hearing a nullity petition or appeal, it may grant a decree of divorce instead.

s 39 (4) Where the court is hearing a judicial separation application or appeal, it may grant a decree of divorce instead.

s 40 Anyone bringing proceedings under this Act must give notice to

(a) the other spouse(s) concerned and

(b) anyone else specified by the court.

s 41 Where the court grants a divorce, it may declare that either of the parents is unfit to have custody of any dependent children under 18 and, if the other spouse dies, that parent shall not automatically have a right to the custody of those children.

s 42 The court may order social reports from a probation officer, health board or anyone else.

s 43 The cost of any mediation or counselling services for a spouse under this Act or the 1989 Act, or for a dependent child of such a spouse, shall be at the discretion of the court.

s 44 Where an engagement is broken off, the court will have power—as if the couple were married—to decide any dispute or claim to property in which either had an interest while they were engaged.

s 45 Amendment of the Judicial Separation and Family Law Reform Act 1989.

s 46 Amendment of the Succession Act 1965.

s 47 Amendment of the Pensions Act 1990.

s 48 Amendment of the Criminal Damage Act 1991.

s 49 Amendment of the Criminal Evidence Act 1992.

s 50 Amendment of the Powers of Attorney Act 1996.

s 51 Amendment of the Domestic Violence Act 1996.

s 52 Amendment of the Family Law Act 1995.

s 53 Amendment of the Maintenance Act 1994 (as amended by the Family Law Act 1995).

[Note: "Dependent child" in this synopsis includes those in full-time education up to the age of 23 and those who are dependent by reason of physical or mental handicap. "He" and "she" and like words are interchangeable.]

Legal Forms

Record No.

AN CHUIRT TEAGHLAIGH CHUARDA
(THE CIRCUIT FAMILY COURT)

NAME OF CIRCUIT   NAME OF COUNTY

IN THE MATTER OF THE FAMILY LAW (DIVORCE) ACT 1996

Between/

Your name

Applicant

-and-

Spouse's name

Respondent

DRAFT FAMILY LAW CIVIL BILL

INDORSEMENT OF CLAIM

YOU ARE HEREBY REQUIRED within ten days after the service of this civil bill upon you, to enter (or cause to be entered) with the registrar of the Circuit Family Court, at his office at (*address*), an appearance to answer the claim of (*your name and address*), the applicant herein as endorsed hereon.

AND TAKE NOTICE that, unless you do enter an appearance, you will be held to have admitted the said claim and the applicant may proceed therein and judgment be given against you in your absence without further notice.

AND FURTHER TAKE NOTICE that if you intend to defend the proceedings on any grounds, you must not only enter an appearance as aforesaid, but also, within ten days after entry of the appearance, deliver a statement in writing showing the nature and grounds of your defence. The appearance and defence may be entered by posting them to the registrar's office and by sending copies to the applicant and his/her solicitor by post.

Dated the   day of   20__

To: Respondent's solicitor

Signed:_____
Solicitor for the applicant (or applicant in person)

1) The applicant and respondent were married on the day of (*month and year*) at (*name and address of church or register office*).

2) The applicant and respondent have been living apart for XX years, since (*date*). During that time the applicant lived at (*full list of addresses*). The respondent lived at (*all addresses, if known*).

3) *Here give details of any previous matrimonial relief sought and/or obtained, with details of any separation agreement. Where relevant, a certified copy of any relevant court order, deed of separation or separation agreement should be annexed to this civil bill.*

4) There are XX dependent children of the marriage, namely (*list names, ages and dates of birth*) or There are no children of the marriage.

5) *Give details of present and past family homes, including manner of occupation/ ownership (eg ownership or lease).*

6) *Give a description of any land or premises referred to in the civil bill, and say whether it is registered or unregistered land.*

7) *Give the basis of the court's jurisdiction (such as the domicile, residence or place of work of the applicant or respondent, with the rateable value of any property – see s s 38(2) and (3) of the 1996 Act).*

8) *State the occupations of both parties.*

9) At the date of institution of these proceedings, the applicant and respondent had lived apart from one another for at least four of the preceding five years. There is no reasonable prospect of any reconciliation between the applicant and respondent. Proper provision, having regard to the circumstances, has been made for the respondent.

AND THE APPLICANT CLAIMS (*Include only the reliefs appropriate to your claim*):

1) An order pursuant to s 5(1) of the 1996 Act for a decree of divorce,

2) An order pursuant to s 5(2) of the 1996 Act for directions concerning the dependent children's welfare, custody and access,

3) An order pursuant to s 8(1) of the 1996 Act to adjourn proceedings to allow the parties to consider reconciliation (or an order pursuant to s 8(2) of the 1996 Act to adjourn proceedings to allow the parties to try and reach agreement on the terms of the proposed divorce),

4) An order pursuant to s 8(3) of the 1996 Act for the resumption of proceedings following talks on reconciliation or divorce terms,

5) An order pursuant to s 11 of the 1996 Act for

   (a) a safety, barring, temporary barring or protection order,

   (b) the custody, access or maintenance of a dependent child,

   (c) protection of the family home, its contents or any money from its sale, before proceedings have been issued under the relevant Act.

7) An order pursuant to s 12(1) of the 1996 Act for the respondent to pay maintenance or a lump sum for the support of the applicant and any dependent children from the date of the application until the date of the hearing,

8) An order pursuant to s 13(1) of the 1996 Act for

   (a) a periodical payments order,

   (b) a secured periodical payments order,

   (c) a lump sum payment,

9) An order pursuant to s 13(2) of the 1996 Act for payment of a lump sum to meet liabilities or expenses incurred before application for a periodical payments order,

10) An order pursuant to s 13(3) of the 1996 Act for payment of a lump sum by specified instalments and that payment be secured,

11) An order pursuant to s 13(6)(a) of the 1996 Act for an attachment of earnings order,

12) An order pursuant to s 14(1) of the 1996 Act for a property adjustment order providing for:

   (a) the transfer of property by the respondent to the applicant, to a dependent child or to another person for the benefit of a dependent child,

   (b) the satisfactory settlement of specified property for the benefit of the applicant and/or any dependent child,

   (c) the variation of any pre-marriage or post-marriage settlement made on the respondent (including any settlement in a will), for the benefit of the applicant and/or any dependent child,

   (d) the extinguishment or reduction of the interest of the respondent under such a settlement,

13) An order pursuant to s 14(2) of the 1996 Act restricting or refusing to allow future variations of orders made under paragraphs (b), (c) or (d),

14) An order pursuant to s 14(5) of the 1996 Act ordering a named person to execute a deed or document in relation to land,

15) An order pursuant to s 15(1)(a) of the 1996 Act

   (a) giving the applicant the right to live in the family home for life or any other period to the exclusion of the respondent or

   (b) directing the sale of the family home and the division of the proceeds between the spouses and anyone else with an interest in the property,

16) An order pursuant to s 15(1)(b) of the 1996 Act deciding the ownership of any property,

17) An order pursuant to s 15(1)(c) of the 1996 Act dispensing with the consent of the respondent to the sale of the family home, protecting the home, relating to arrears of mortgage or rent or restricting the disposal of household chattels,

18) An order pursuant to s 15(1)(d) of the 1996 Act for a safety, barring, interim barring or protection order,

19) An order pursuant to s 15(1)(e) of the 1996 Act for the partition of property,

20) An order pursuant to s 15(1)(f) of the 1996 Act for custody or access or relating to the welfare of a child,

21) A financial compensation order pursuant to s 16(1) of the 1996 Act requiring the respondent to:

   (a) take out a life insurance policy for the benefit of the applicant or child,

   (b) assign some or all of the benefit of an existing life insurance policy to the applicant or child,

   (c) continue to pay life insurance premiums,

22) A pension adjustment order pursuant to s 17(1) of the 1996 Act,

23) An order pursuant to s 18(10) of the 1996 Act that the respondent should not be entitled to be provided for out of the applicant's estate in the case of his/her death,

24) An order pursuant to s 19(1) of the 1996 Act for the sale of property in which the respondent has an interest,

25) An order pursuant to s 19(3)(b) of the 1996 Act specifying:

   (a) the manner and conditions of sale,

   (b) the purchaser(s),

   (c) the date when the order is to come into effect,

   (d) payment(s) to a specified person from the proceeds of sale, and

   (e) the division of the proceeds,

26) An order pursuant to s 21(1) of the 1996 Act in relation to periodical payments that:

   (a) payments shall be backdated to the date proceedings began,

   (b) any retrospective payments should be paid in a lump sum by a set date and

   (c) any payments made between the start of proceedings and date of the decree may be deducted from the lump sum,

27) An order pursuant to s 24(1) that payments shall be made by a specified method and subject to appropriate terms and conditions,

28) An order pursuant to s 26(1) discharging an order for

   (a) maintenance, variation of maintenance or interim maintenance under the 1976 Act,

   (b) periodical or lump sum payments, property adjustment, sale, transfer or partition, the right to occupy the family home or guardianship under the 1989 Act,

   (c) periodical or lump sum payments, property adjustment, sale, transfer or partition, the right to occupy the family home, guardianship, pension adjustment, extinction of succession rights or financial compensation under the 1995 Act,

29) An order pursuant to s 37(2)(a) of the 1996 Act to:

   (a) restrain anyone from disposing of property or transferring it out of the state with the intention of defeating the applicant's claim or

   (b) set aside any disposition of property which was intended to defeat the applicant's claim,

30) An order pursuant to s 37(2)(b) of the 1996 Act to set aside the disposition of any property after the granting of the divorce decree,

31) An order pursuant to s 38(4) of the 1996 Act for the court to assess the rateable valuation of any land,

32) An order pursuant to s 38(6) of the 1996 Act for the respondent to give the applicant details of property and income that may reasonably be required,

33) An order pursuant to s 41 of the 1996 Act that the respondent is unfit to have custody of any dependent children under 18 and that, if the applicant dies, the respondent shall not automatically have a right to the custody of those children,

34) An order pursuant to s 42 of the 1996 Act for social reports from a probation officer, health board or anyone else,

35) Any other order that may seem fitting to the court,

36) Costs.

AND FURTHER TAKE NOTICE that, in any cases where financial relief is sought by either party, you must file with the defence herein, or in any event within 20 days after the service of this civil bill on you, at the aforementioned Circuit Court office an affidavit of means (and, where appropriate, an affidavit of welfare) in the manner prescribed by the rules of this court, and serve a copy of same as provided by the rules of this court on the applicant or his solicitor at the address provided below.

Dated the   day of   20__

Signed:_____
Solicitor for the applicant (or applicant)

To: The registrar,
Circuit Family Court,
(*Address of local court*)

and

To: Respondent's solicitor

TAKE NOTICE that it is in your interest to have legal advice in regard to these proceedings. If you cannot afford a private solicitor, you may be entitled to legal aid provided by the state at a minimum cost to you. Details of this legal aid service are available at the Legal Aid Board, 47 Upper Mount Street, Dublin 2, tel: 1890 615 200 or 01 644 1900, email info@legalaidboard.ie, where you can obtain the addresses and telephone numbers of the legal aid centres in your area.

(Note: If you are seeking relief under s 18 of the 1996 Act, you must include the following details:

(i)   the date and place of marriage and the date of any decree of divorce/judicial separation. The marriage certificate and a certified copy of the decree of divorce/separation must be annexed to the civil bill (with authenticated translations, where appropriate);

(ii)   details of previous matrimonial relief obtained by you, particularly any lump sum maintenance orders and property adjustment orders;

(iii) details of any benefits previously received from (or on behalf of) your deceased spouse whether by agreement or otherwise, and details of any benefits accruing to you under the will of your deceased spouse or otherwise;

(iv) the date of your deceased spouse's death, the date on which representation was first granted in relation to the spouse and, if applicable, the date on which you were given notice of the death of your deceased spouse and the date on which you notified the personal representative of your intention to apply for relief under s 18(7) of the 1996 Act;

(v)   the nature and extent of any claim for relief, and the basis on which any such claim is being made;

(vi)   the marital status of your deceased spouse at the date of death, your marital status on the application date, and whether you have remarried since the divorce;

(vii)   details of all your deceased spouse's dependants at the date of death and of all your dependants on the date of the application, together with details of any other interested persons;

(viii) confirmation that no order under s 18(10) of the 1996 Act has previously been made;

(ix)   details of the value of the estate of your deceased spouse, if known, and

(x)   any other relevant facts.)

Record No.

AN CHUIRT TEAGHLAIGH CHUARDA
(THE CIRCUIT FAMILY COURT)

NAME OF CIRCUIT   NAME OF COUNTY

IN THE MATTER OF THE FAMILY LAW (DIVORCE) ACT 1996

Between/

Your name

Applicant

-and-

Spouse's name

Respondent

DRAFT AFFIDAVIT OF MEANS

I, (*name and occupation*), of (*address*), aged 18 years and upwards, MAKE OATH and say as follows:

1) I am the applicant in the above entitled proceedings and I make this affidavit from facts within my own knowledge, except where otherwise appears and, where so appearing, I believe the same to be true.

2) I have set out in the first schedule all the assets to which I am legally or beneficially entitled and the manner in which such property is held.

3) I have set out in the second schedule all income which I receive and the sources of such income.

4) I have set out in the third schedule all my debts and/or liabilities and the persons to whom such debts and liabilities are due.

5) My weekly outgoings amount to €   , and details of such outgoings have been set out in the fourth schedule.

6) To the best of my knowledge, information and belief, all pension information known to me relevant to these proceedings is set out in the fifth schedule (*or explain why the information has not been obtained*).

FIRST SCHEDULE

Assets

1) The property/ies known as (*address*), held in the name of (*name of owner or owners*)
2) Savings €
3) Car/s €
4) Personal items €
5) Any other assets

SECOND SCHEDULE

Income

1) Salary
2) Other income
3) Maintenance
4) Expenses

THIRD SCHEDULE

Debts and liabilities

1) Mortgage €
2) Loans €

FOURTH SCHEDULE

Weekly personal outgoings

Mortgage	€
Insurance (house, personal)	€
House repairs and maintenance	€
Food	€
Car (tax, insurance, running costs)	€
Fares	€
TV/Satellite	€
Clothing	€
Telephone	€
Television licence/cable TV/internet	€
Oil, gas and electricity	€
Family (birthdays, Christmas)	€

Newspapers	€
Holidays	€
Medical, dental expenses	€
Hairdresser	€
Social	€
Weekly total	€

FIFTH SCHEDULE

Pension

The applicant is a member of (*name of scheme*), a certified copy of which is attached (or *the applicant is not a member of any pension scheme*).

Sworn by the said (*your name*) before me, a practising solicitor/Commissioner for Oaths, on (*date*), at_____(*address*) and I know the deponent personally *or* the deponent has been identified by a named person personally known to me who certifies this *or* the identity of the deponent has been established by a photo in (type of document) (*strike out as necessary*).

Filed this ___ day of _____20__by (*name and address*), solicitors for the applicant (or by the applicant in person).

To: The registrar,
Circuit Family Court,
(*Address of local court*)

and

To: Respondent's solicitor

* The solicitor or commissioner for oaths must record here either that he knows the deponent or how that deponent is identified to him.

Record No.

AN CHUIRT TEAGHLAIGH CHUARDA
(THE CIRCUIT FAMILY COURT)

NAME OF CIRCUIT   NAME OF COUNTY

IN THE MATTER OF THE FAMILY LAW (DIVORCE) ACT 1996

Between/

Your name

Applicant

-and-

Spouse's name

Respondent

DRAFT AFFIDAVIT OF WELFARE

I, (*full name*) of (*address*), (*occupation*), aged 18 years and upwards, MAKE OATH and say as follows:

1) I am the applicant in the above proceedings and I make this affidavit of welfare from facts within my own knowledge, except where otherwise appears, and where so appearing, I believe the same to be true.

2) I say and believe that the facts set out in the schedule are true.

SCHEDULE
Part I - Details of the children

Give details of the children born to (or adopted by) the respondent and applicant, with forenames, surnames and dates of birth.
Give details of other children of the family, or children to whom either of the parties is in loco parentis.

Part II - Arrangements for the children of the family

Home details

The address(es) at which the children now live.
The number of living rooms, bedrooms at the above address(es).

Is the house rented or owned? Who is the tenant(s) or owner(s)?
Is the rent or mortgage being paid regularly? If so, by whom?
Give the names of everyone else living with the children, full-time or part time, and state their relationship to the children.
Will there be any changes to these arrangements? If so, give details.

Part III - Education and training details

Give details of the school, college or place of training attended by each child.
Do the children have special educational needs? If so, specify in detail.
Is the school, college or place of training fee-paying? If so, how much are the fees per term or year? Are the fees paid regularly and, if so, by whom?
Will there be any changes in these circumstances? If so, give details.

Part IV - Childcare details

Which parent looks after the children from day to day? If responsibility is shared, give details.
Give details of the work commitments of both parents.
Does someone look after the children when the parents are not there? If so, give details.
Who looks after the children during school holidays?
Will there be any changes to these arrangements? If so, give details.

Part V - Maintenance

Does the respondent pay towards the upkeep of the children? If so, give details. Specify any other sources of maintenance.
Is this maintenance paid under court order? If so, give details.
Has maintenance been agreed for the children? If so, give details.
If not, will you be applying for a maintenance order from the court?

Part VI - Details of contact with children

Do the children see the respondent? Give details.
Do the children stay overnight and/or have holiday visits with the respondent? Give details.
Will there be any changes to these arrangements? If so, give details.

Part VII - Details of health

Are the children generally in good health? Detail any serious disability or chronic illness suffered by any of the children.
Do any of the children have any special health needs? Give details of care needed and how it is to be provided.
Are the applicant or respondent generally in good health? If not, give details.

Part VIII - Details of care and other court proceedings

Are any of the children in the care of a health board or under the supervision of a social worker or probation officer? If so, give details.

Have there been any court proceedings involving any of the children? If so, give details. (All relevant court orders should be annexed.)

Sworn by the said (*your name*) before me, a practising solicitor/Commissioner for Oaths, on (*date*), at_____(*address*) and I know the deponent personally/the deponent has been identified by a named person personally known to me who certifies this/or the identity of the deponent has been established by a photo in (type of document) (*strike out as necessary*).

Filed this   day of   20__ by (*name and address*) solicitors for the applicant (or by the applicant in person)

To: The registrar,
Circuit Family Court,
(*Address of local court*)

and

To: Respondent's solicitor

Record No.

AN CHUIRT TEAGHLAIGH CHUARDA
(THE CIRCUIT FAMILY COURT)

NAME OF CIRCUIT   NAME OF COUNTY

IN THE MATTER OF THE FAMILY LAW (DIVORCE) ACT 1996

Between/

Your name

Applicant

-and-

Spouse's name

Respondent

DRAFT CERTIFICATE PURSUANT TO SECTION 6
OF THE FAMILY LAW (DIVORCE) ACT 1996

I, (*name*), the solicitor acting for the above applicant, hereby certify as follows:

1) I have discussed with the applicant the possibility of reconciliation with the respondent and I have given the applicant the names and addresses of persons qualified to help effect a reconciliation between spouses who have become estranged.

2) I have discussed with the applicant the possibility of engaging in mediation to help effect a divorce on a basis agreed between the applicant and the respondent, and I have given the applicant the names and addresses of persons qualified to provide a mediation service for spouses who have become estranged.

3) I have ensured that the applicant is aware of judicial separation as an alternative to divorce, no decree of judicial separation in relation to the applicant and the respondent being in force.

Dated the   day of   20__

Signed:_____
Solicitor
Address

Record No.

AN CHUIRT TEAGHLAIGH CHUARDA
(THE CIRCUIT FAMILY COURT)

NAME OF CIRCUIT   NAME OF COUNTY

IN THE MATTER OF THE FAMILY LAW (DIVORCE) ACT 1996

Between/

Your spouse' s name

Applicant

-and-

Your name

Respondent

DRAFT DEFENCE AND COUNTERCLAIM

TAKE NOTICE that the respondent, (*name and address*), disputes the claims made in the applicant's family law civil bill pursuant to sections (*list disputed sections*) of the 1996 Act, which was served on the respondent on (*date*).

AND FURTHER TAKE NOTICE that the respondent will rely on the following matters in disputing the applicant's claim:

Paragraphs ___ herein are denied (*List disputed paragraphs. Any paragraphs not listed are taken to be admitted.*)

COUNTERCLAIM

AND TAKE NOTICE that the respondent will rely on the following matters in support of his/her counterclaim:

1) The respondent repeats his/her answer herein.

2) The respondent and the applicant were lawfully married on (*date*) at (*address of church or register office*)

3) The respondent and applicant are, and were at the date of the said ceremony, domiciled in Ireland and are ordinarily resident within the jurisdiction of this court.

4)   The respondent and applicant have been living apart since (*date*) and there is no reasonable prospect of reconciliation between them. Proper provision has been made for the applicant herein.

5)   The grounds on which the respondent intends to rely in support of the claim(s) for ancillary relief are: (*specify the grounds*)

6)   There are X dependent children of the marriage, (*give names and dates of birth*)

7)   The family home is situated at (*address*), and is held in the joint names of the respondent and the applicant (*or give details*). The value of the property is approximately €XX. There is/is no outstanding loan on the property. The rateable value of the property is under €254.

AND THE RESPONDENT CLAIMS:

(See the list of claims by the applicant and select the reliefs *you* want)

Dated the   day of   20__

Signed:_____
Solicitor for the respondent (or by the respondent in person)

To: The Registrar,
Circuit Family Court,
(*address of court*)

and

To: Applicant's solicitor

MOTION FOR JUDGMENT

The applicant must write to the respondent at least 14 days before service of the notice, informing the respondent of the intention to serve the notice of motion for judgment. The applicant must also formally consent to the respondent's late filing of a defence within 14 days of the date of the letter.

If a defence is still not delivered, the applicant can serve a notice of motion for judgment in default of defence, returnable at least 14 *clear* days from the date of service of the notice. The notice of motion must be filed at least six days before the return date.

Record No.

AN CHUIRT TEAGHLAIGH CHUARDA
(THE CIRCUIT FAMILY COURT)

NAME OF CIRCUIT   **NAME OF COUNTY**

IN THE MATTER OF THE FAMILY LAW (DIVORCE) ACT 1996

Between/

Your name

Applicant

-and-

Spouse's name

Respondent

DRAFT NOTICE OF MOTION

TAKE NOTICE that on the   day of   20 , at the sitting of the court or as soon as possible thereafter, counsel on behalf of the applicant will apply to the Circuit Family Court sitting at court number XX at (*court address*) for judgment in the above-mentioned matter in default of appearance or defence, pursuant to Order 59 of the Rules of the Circuit Court

WHICH MOTION WILL BE GROUNDED ON this notice of motion and affidavit of service thereof, the original family law civil bill herein, the grounding affidavit of (*name*), the nature of the case and the reasons to be offered.

Dated

Signed
Solicitor for the applicant or respondent (or the applicant or respondent in person)

To the registrar of the Circuit Family Court,
And/
To the applicant respondent

Record No.

AN CHUIRT TEAGHLAIGH CHUARDA
(THE CIRCUIT FAMILY COURT)

NAME OF CIRCUIT   NAME OF COUNTY

IN THE MATTER OF THE FAMILY LAW (DIVORCE) ACT 1996

Between/

Your name

Applicant

-and-

Spouse's name

Respondent

DRAFT AFFIDAVIT OF (*your name*)

I, (*name, address and occupation*), aged 18 years and upwards, MAKE OATH and say as follows:

1) I am the applicant in the above proceedings and I make this affidavit from facts within my own knowledge, save where otherwise appears, and where so appearing, I believe the same to be true.

2) I beg to refer to the pleadings already had herein, when produced.

3) I say that the family law civil bill, affidavit of means and affidavit of welfare herein were served on the respondent on (*date*).

4) *Give details of entry (or non-entry) of appearance/defence, details of consent letter to extension of time for delivery of appearance/defence, and exhibit letter.*

5) I say that, notwithstanding the letter granting additional time for the entry of an appearance/filing of a defence, the respondent has failed and/or neglected to do so.

6) I therefore pray this court for relief as set out in the notice of motion hereto.

Sworn by the said (*name*) before me,
a practising solicitor/Commissioner for Oaths, on (*date*),
at_____ (*address*) and I know the deponent personally /
the deponent has been identified by a named person personally known to me who
certifies this / or the identity of the deponent has been established by a photo in
(type of document) (*strike out as necessary*).

Filed this   day of   20__ by (*name and address*), solicitors for the
applicant (or by the applicant in person)

To:
The registrar,
Circuit Family Court,
(*address*)

And/

To: Respondent's solicitor

SAMPLE SEPARATION AGREEMENT

This separation agreement made on 27 December 2013 between Catherine O'Brien of 1 Rotunda Crescent, Dun Laoghaire, in the County of the City of Dublin, (hereinafter called "the wife") and Liam O'Brien of The Mews, Henderson Street, Ballsbridge, Dublin 4, (hereinafter called "the husband"):

WHEREAS

> The husband and the wife were married to one another on 1 April 1999 at Sacred Heart Catholic church, Morehampton Road, Donnybrook, in the City of Dublin. There are two living children of the marriage, (hereinafter called "the children") namely Brendan, born on the 23rd day of October 2000 and Vera, born on the 12th day of August 2003. The husband and wife have been living apart from each other since 15 August 2013.

The parties have AGREED that, while living apart, the following provisions shall have effect and regulate their mutual rights and obligations:

1) The husband and wife shall live separate and apart from and free from the marital control of the other and neither the husband nor the wife shall in any manner annoy, disturb, molest or otherwise interfere with the other's manner of living, profession, business, friends, relations or acquaintances, nor use any force, violence or restraint on the other, with the intent that each shall live henceforth as if he or she were sole and unmarried.

2) Neither the husband nor the wife shall visit or be or stay in any place in which the other is for the time being resident, without the express invitation of the other.

3) The husband and wife shall remain joint guardians of the children. The wife shall have sole custody and the husband shall have such access to the children as may be from time to time agreed, including access at his home from 8am on Saturday until 10am on Sunday every week, and holiday access during July and/or August for two consecutive weeks, subject to three weeks' advance notice in writing to the wife. The husband shall also have access during all three days up to and including Easter Sunday and Christmas Day and access from 6pm to 8pm on the birthday of each child.

4) The husband and wife agree that they will consult each other as far as possible on matters affecting the children's upbringing, education, training, medical care and general welfare, and that they will immediately notify the other if either of the children should require the services of a doctor. The parent having care and control of the children at that time shall be absolutely entitled to obtain and provide such medical care,

including hospitalisation and any medical or surgical treatment as may be necessary. The husband and wife agree that both will receive copies of any school reports and both shall be entitled to attend parent-teacher meetings at the children's school.

5) Neither parent shall remove either child outside the jurisdiction of the courts of the Republic of Ireland without the prior written consent of the other, such consent not to be unreasonably withheld. The wife shall have custody of the children's passports.

6) Each parent shall refrain from interfering with or diminishing the love, affection and respect of the children for the other parent and shall not do or say anything which would tend to lower the other parent in the esteem of either of the children. Neither parent shall interfere with reasonable communication by telephone or post between either of the children and the other parent.

7) The husband and wife hereby agree to the following financial arrangements for the foreseeable future:

   a) That the husband will pay to the wife the sum of €350 per week for the support of the wife and the children, being €100 for the wife and €125 for each child. The first payment shall be made on 10 January 2014 and payments thereafter shall be made weekly on each subsequent Friday into the wife's building society account number 012345678 at Bank of Ireland, Grafton Street, Dublin 2.

   b) The maintenance payable by the husband shall be reviewed annually in the first week of January and shall be varied by a percentage either in accordance with the latest consumer price index published by the Central Statistics Office for the previous 12 months or in accordance with any variation in the husband's net income during the preceding tax year, whichever is the lesser, and such varied sum shall become due and payable to the wife weekly from the following Friday in the manner set out in clause 7(a) hereof.

   c) The maintenance payable for each child shall cease to be paid when that child attains the age of 18 years or, if still attending a full-time course at any university, college, school or educational institute, until the child attains the age of 23 years or completes full-time education, whichever is the earlier. Maintenance in respect of either of the children shall also cease if that child dies.

   d) If there is a significant change in the financial circumstances of either the husband or the wife, either party may serve notice on the other of an intention to seek an increase or decrease in the amount of maintenance payable under this agreement and specifying the amount of maintenance considered reasonable in the changed circumstances. On the service of such notice, both parties shall make available to the other within four weeks full details of his or her financial circumstances. If agreement is not reached on a revised sum of maintenance within four weeks of the receipt of such details, the parties agree to accept the decision of an arbitrator appointed by the chairman of the Bar Council as to the sum payable thereafter.

e)   The wife shall be entitled to continue to receive all social welfare benefits in respect of the children.

f)   The husband agrees to continue paying a monthly premium of €40 on the life assurance policy number 4949768 held with the Coach House Insurance Company and agrees that the wife shall continue to be the named beneficiary thereon.

g)   Maintenance payments shall cease in the event of any of the following:

  i.   the death of the husband,

  ii.   the death of the wife,

  iii. the wife going through a ceremony of marriage with another person at any time,

  iv.   the wife cohabiting with another person as if they were husband and wife for a continuous period of at least three months,

  v.   the court making a maintenance order which supersedes this agreement,

  vi.   the court granting a decree of nullity to the husband or wife.

8) In the event of the marriage of the parties hereto being dissolved by a decree of divorce, any property bought or money saved by the wife out of maintenance payments made to her by the husband shall belong solely to the wife, and the husband shall have no interest or claim therein, and s 21 of the Family Law (Maintenance of Spouses and Children) Act 1976 shall not apply thereto.

9) The husband and wife shall be separately assessed for income tax pursuant to s 3 of the Finance Act 1983, and shall be treated as single people in the future for all tax purposes.

10) The husband acknowledges that the household chattels remaining in the family home are, and will remain, the sole property of the wife.

11) The husband hereby agrees to assure to the wife the beneficial ownership of all his estate and interest in the family home at 1 Rotunda Crescent, Dun Laoghaire, in the County of the City of Dublin, free from encumbrances save the mortgage next referred, freed and discharged from all claims which he may have in respect of the same, whether under the Family Home Protection Act 1976 or otherwise, and the wife hereby agrees that, in consideration of such assurances, she will indemnify and keep indemnified the husband from and against all claims arising hereafter on foot of the building society mortgage

currently secured on the family home and the husband shall, prior to the execution of this agreement, deliver to the wife such deed of assurance and at any time thereafter, at the request of the wife or anyone acting on her behalf, shall execute such deed, document or consent required for the purpose of sale or otherwise for the purpose of giving full legal effect to this agreement.

12) The wife hereby agrees with the husband that she will, at all times in the future, support and maintain herself and the children out of the maintenance payments made by the husband pursuant to this agreement, together with any income received by her from any other source, and the husband and the wife agree that they will at all times keep the other indemnified from all debts and liabilities heretofore or hereafter contracted howsoever arising, and from all actions, costs, claims, damages, demands, losses and expenses in respect of any such debts or liabilities.

13) The husband and the wife hereby mutually surrender and renounce all succession rights due to either of them under the provisions of the Succession Act 1965 or any share or legal right in the estate of the other at any time, provided that either of them may take any legal action necessary to protect or defend the interests of the children in the estate of either the husband or the wife.

14) The husband shall pay the wife's costs in connection with the preparation, drafting and execution of this agreement, to be taxed in default of agreement on a solicitor/client basis.

15) The husband and wife agree that this agreement shall not be regarded as an approbation or ratification of a void or voidable marriage.

16) The husband and wife hereby agree for all purposes that this agreement is in *full and final settlement* of all present and future financial and property claims (except for periodic maintenance) which either shall have against the other under the Constitution of Ireland 1937, the Married Women's Status Act 1957, the Family Law (Maintenance of Spouses and Children) Act 1976, the Judicial Separation and Family Law Reform Act 1989, the Family Law Act 1995, the Family Law (Divorce) Act 1996, the Civil Partnership and Certain Rights and Obligations of Cohabitants Act 2010 or any amending Act of the Oireachtas or under similar legislation in this or any other jurisdiction, under the rules of equity or the common law or otherwise. The parties agree not to issue or maintain proceedings under any legislative provisions in this clause, except in respect of periodic maintenance.

IN WITNESS WHEREOF the parties hereto have hereunto set their hands and affixed their seals on the day and year first herein written

Signed, sealed and delivered by the said Liam O'Brien

Liam O'Brien

in the presence of:

A solicitor

Signed, sealed and delivered by the said Catherine O'Brien

Catherine O'Brien

in the presence of:

A solicitor

JOINT GUARDIANSHIP DECLARATION
FOR UNMARRIED PARENTS

Guardianship involves the collection of a parent's rights and duties towards a child. It includes the duty to maintain and properly care for the child, as well as the right to make decisions about a child's religious and secular education, health requirements and other matters affecting the child's welfare. The exercise of guardianship rights may be agreed between parents. If they disagree, either parent may ask the court to decide the matter.

The right to custody is one of the rights that arises under the guardianship relationship. Custody is the physical day-to-day care and control of a child. Even where one parental guardian has custody of a child, the other parental guardian is generally entitled to be consulted about matters affecting the child's welfare.

The mother and father of a non-marital child must both make this statutory declaration if they wish the father to become a guardian of the child jointly with the mother. If there is more than one child, a separate statutory declaration should be made for each.

If the parents of the child cannot agree about the father's appointment as joint guardian, the father can apply to the court to be made a joint guardian under s 6A of the Guardianship of Infants Act 1964.

A father who is appointed guardian by this joint statutory declaration can only be removed as guardian by court order. A father's duty to maintain his child and his right to apply to the court for custody or access to his child does not depend on his being made a guardian.

The appointment of a natural father as guardian will affect any adoption of the child. A child ceases to be subject to guardianship when he reaches the age of 18 or marries.

This declaration will seriously affect the legal position of both parents and it is advisable to obtain legal advice before making it. This is an important document and should be kept in a safe place when completed, as the state does not currently provide any register of guardianship.

In the matter of a declaration
under paragraph (e) of s 2(4) (inserted by the Children Act, 1997)
of the Guardianship of Infants Act 1964.

We

_____ *(father's name)*
of_____ *(father's address)*
and

_____ *(mother's name)*
of _____ *(mother's address)*

do solemnly and sincerely declare and say as follows:

1. We have not married each other.

2. We are the father and mother of_____ *(child's name)* who was born on the____day of _____

3. We agree to the appointment of _____ *(father's name)* as a guardian of _____ *(child's name)*

4. We have entered into arrangements regarding the custody of [and access to]*_____ *(child's name)* [*Strike out as necessary]*

We make this solemn declaration conscientiously believing the same to be true by virtue of the Statutory Declarations Act 1938 and pursuant to paragraph (e) of s 2(4) (inserted by the Children Act, 1997) of the Guardianship of Infants Act 1964.

Signed_____ *(father)*

Signed _____ *(mother)*

Declared before me by

_____*(father's name)* and_____ *(mother's name)*
who are personally known to me (or who are identified to me by
_____ who is personally known to me or whose identities have been established by photographs in (types of document)).

at

_____

on this_____day of_____ 20__

(Signature of practising solicitor/Peace Commissioner/Commissioner for Oaths/ Notary Public)

LEGISLATION

1. Married Women's Property (Ireland) Act 1865: permitted a wife to sue her husband in tort if separated or deserted.

2. Partition Acts 1868 and 1876: allowed courts to divide up property between spouses.

   http://www.bailii.org/nie/legis/num_act/pa1868134/ and http://www.bailii.org/nie/legis/num_act/pa1876134/

3. Matrimonial Causes and Marriage Law (Ireland) (Amendment) Act 1870: brought civil nullity rules in line with Church rules.

   http://www.bailii.org/nie/legis/num_act/mcamlaa1870446/

4. Married Women's Property Act 1882: allowed married women to hold property in their own name. Replaced by:

   http://www.bailii.org/nie/legis/num_act/mwpa1882290/

5. Married Women's Status Act 1957: made wives liable for their own debts and breaches of duty. Allowed courts to decide property disputes between spouses.

   http://www.irishstatutebook.ie/1957/en/act/pub/0005

6. Guardianship of Infants Act 1964: gave parents the right to joint guardianship of their children and allowed courts to make decisions on custody and access.

   http://www.irishstatutebook.ie/1964/en/act/pub/0007

7. Succession Act 1965: reformed the law relating to the estates of people who had died, especially the administration and distribution of property where there is no will. Specified the shares of spouses and children on intestacy.

   http://www.irishstatutebook.ie/1965/en/act/pub/0027

8. Marriages Act 1972: raised the minimum marriage age to 16 for boys and girls, retrospectively validated so-called "Lourdes marriages".

   http://www.irishstatutebook.ie/1972/en/act/pub/0030

9. Maintenance Orders Act 1974: allowed the reciprocal enforcement of maintenance orders between the Republic of Ireland, Northern Ireland, England and Wales and Scotland.

   http://www.irishstatutebook.ie/1974/en/act/pub/0016

10. Family Law (Maintenance of Spouses and Children) Act 1976: provided for periodical payments by one spouse to another in cases of failure to provide reasonable maintenance, with deductions of earnings at source and barring orders.

http://www.irishstatutebook.ie/1976/en/act/pub/0011

11. Family Home Protection Act 1976: protected the family home and required prior written consent of both spouses for sale of the family home or chattels.

http://www.irishstatutebook.ie/1976/en/act/pub/0027

12. Courts Act 1981: widened the jurisdiction in family law matters.

http://www.irishstatutebook.ie/1981/en/act/pub/0011

13. Family Law Act 1981: abolished actions for enticement of spouse and breach of promise to marry. Allowed courts to decide disputes over gifts after broken engagements.

http://www.irishstatutebook.ie/1981/en/act/pub/0022

14. Family Law (Protection of Spouses and Children) Act 1981: gave the Circuit and District Courts power to grant barring and protection orders.

http://www.irishstatutebook.ie/1981/en/act/pub/0021

15. Domicile and Recognition of Foreign Divorces Act 1986: confirmed independent domiciles of wives, recognised divorces granted where either spouse was domiciled.

http://www.irishstatutebook.ie/1986/en/act/pub/0024

16. Status of Children Act 1987: abolished status of illegitimacy and amended law on maintenance and succession for non-marital children. Allowed unmarried fathers to apply for guardianship of their children. Provided for blood tests to establish paternity.

http://www.irishstatutebook.ie/1987/en/act/pub/0026

17. Family Law Act 1988: abolished actions for the restitution of conjugal rights.

http://www.irishstatutebook.ie/1988/en/act/pub/0031

18. Children Act 1989: gave health boards powers to care for children.

http://www.irishstatutebook.ie/1989/en/act/pub/0018

19. Judicial Separation and Family Law Reform Act 1989: amended the grounds for judicial separation, assisted reconciliation between estranged spouses and provided for ancillary orders such as maintenance, property adjustment and custody of children.

http://www.irishstatutebook.ie/1989/en/act/pub/0006

20. Child Care Act 1991: gave powers to health boards to care for children who were ill-treated, neglected or sexually abused.

http://www.irishstatutebook.ie/1991/en/act/pub/0017

21. Child Abduction and Enforcement of Custody Orders Act 1991: dealt with wrongful retention of children. Implemented the Hague Convention 1980 and the Luxembourg Convention 1980.

http://www.irishstatutebook.ie/1991/en/act/pub/0006

22. Maintenance Act 1994: simplified procedures for recovering maintenance debts from other countries.

   http://www.irishstatutebook.ie/1994/en/act/pub/0028

23. Family Law Act 1995: raised the minimum age for marriage to 18 and required three months' written notice to local registrar, abolished petitions for jactitation of marriage (falsely claiming to be married to someone), provided for declarations of marital status, and ancillary orders after judicial separation or foreign divorce.

   http://www.irishstatutebook.ie/1995/en/act/pub/0026

24. Domestic Violence Act 1996: extended safety, barring and protection orders to non-spouses, gave health boards powers to apply for orders, allowed arrest without warrant for breach.

   http://www.irishstatutebook.ie/1996/en/act/pub/0001

25. Family Law (Divorce) Act 1996: allowed divorce and remarriage, with all ancillary orders.

   http://www.irishstatutebook.ie/1996/en/act/pub/0033

26. Children Act 1997: recognised natural fathers as guardians, allowed children's views to be considered in guardianship, access and custody matters, permitted parents to have joint custody.

   http://www.irishstatutebook.ie/1997/en/act/pub/0040

27. Family Law (Miscellaneous Provisions) Act 1997: amended the law in relation to notification of intention to marry, barring orders, powers of attorney and distribution of disclaimed estates.

   http://www.irishstatutebook.ie/1997/en/act/pub/0018

28. European Council Regulation 1347/2000: allowed—subject to certain conditions—the mutual recognition in all EU member states (except Denmark) of court orders relating to divorce, legal separation, nullity or child custody.

   http://europa.eu/legislation_summaries/other/l33082_en.htm

   Replaced by:

29. Children Act 2001: authorised courts to order health boards to convene a family welfare conference where a child requires special care or protection. The health board can apply for a care order or supervision order if necessary.

   http://www.irishstatutebook.ie/2001/en/act/pub/0024

30. Domestic Violence (Amendment) Act 2002: amended the Domestic Violence Act 1996 to provide eight-day limit for *ex parte* interim barring orders, changed grounds on which *ex parte* orders could be granted.

   http://www.irishstatutebook.ie/2002/en/act/pub/0030

31. European Council Regulation 2201/2003: concerned jurisdiction and the recognition and enforcement of judgments in matrimonial matters and matters of parental responsibility.

32. Civil Registration Act 2004: reorganised and modernised the system of registration of marriages, divorces and nullity.

    http://www.irishstatutebook.ie/2004/en/act/pub/0003

33. Civil Liability and Courts Act 2004: allowed the publication of decisions in certain family law proceedings, subject to not identifying the parties.

    http://www.irishstatutebook.ie/2004/en/act/pub/0031

34. Enforcement of Court Orders (Amendment) Act 2009: introduced warning systems "in ordinary language" for maintenance debtors, plus a right to legal aid and limitations on imprisonment for those unable to pay a maintenance debt.

    http://www.irishstatutebook.ie/2009/en/act/pub/0021

35. Adoption Act 2010: mandated consultation with fathers of children to be adopted.

    http://www.irishstatutebook.ie/2010/en/act/pub/0021

36. Civil Partnership and Certain Rights and Obligations of Cohabitants Act 2010: provided for the registration of civil partners and the rights and obligations of cohabitants.

    http://www.irishstatutebook.ie/2010/en/act/pub/0024

37. Child Care (Amendment) Act 2011: gave the High Court statutory powers to hear HSE applications for special care orders where children's welfare might require that they be held in a special care unit.

    http://www.irishstatutebook.ie/2011/en/act/pub/0019/

38. Civil Law (Miscellaneous Provisions) Act 2011: amended the 1996 and 2002 Domestic Violence Acts, transferred the mediation functions of the Family Support Agency to the Legal Aid Board, amended the 2010 Civil Partnership and Certain Rights and Obligations of Cohabitants Act and gave District Judges greater powers to jail for contempt for refusal to pay maintenance.

    http://www.irishstatutebook.ie/2011/en/act/pub/0023

39. Jurisdiction of Courts and Enforcement of Judgments (Amendment) Act 2012: amended the 1994 Maintenance Act to give effect to the 2007 Lugano Convention.

    http://www.irishstatutebook.ie/2012/en/act/pub/0007

40. Courts and Civil Law (Miscellaneous Provisions) Act 2013: amended *in camera* rules for family courts, strengthened provisions for the enforcement of maintenance orders, increased civil jurisdiction of District and Circuit courts.

    http://www.oireachtas.ie/documents/bills28/bills/2013/3013/b30c13d.pdf.

RULES AND REGULATIONS

1. District Court (Maintenance) Rules, SI No 614/2003

    http://www.irishstatutebook.ie/2003/en/si/0614.html

2. European Communities (Judgments in Matrimonial Matters and Matters of Parental Responsibility) Regulations, SI No 112/2005

    http://www.irishstatutebook.ie/2005/en/si/0112.html

3. Rules of the Superior Courts (s 40, Civil Liability and Courts Act 2004) SI No 247/2005

    http://www.irishstatutebook.ie/2005/en/si/0247.html

4. Civil Liability and Courts Act 2004 (s 40(3)) Regulations SI No 337/2005

    http://www.irishstatutebook.ie/2005/en/si/0337.html

5. Civil Liability and Courts Act 2004 (s 40(4)) Order SI No 338/2005

    http://www.irishstatutebook.ie/2005/en/si/0338.html

6. Civil Registration Act 2004 (Commencement) Order 2007 SI No 736/2007

    http://www.irishstatutebook.ie/2007/en/si/0736.html

7. Circuit Court Rules (Case Progression in Family Law Proceedings) 2008 SI No 358/2008

    http://www.irishstatutebook.ie/pdf/2008/en.si.2008.0358.pdf

8. Circuit Court Rules (Hague Convention 1996) 2011 SI No 121/2011

    http://www.irishstatutebook.ie/2011/en/si/0121.html

9. European Communities (Mediation) Regulations 2011 SI No 209/2011

    http://www.irishstatutebook.ie/2011/en/si/0209.html

10. European Communities (Maintenance) Regulations 2011 SI No 274/2011

    http://www.irishstatutebook.ie/2011/en/si/0274.html

11. Rules of the Superior Courts (Civil Partnership and Cohabitation) 2011 SI No 348/2011

    http://www.irishstatutebook.ie/2011/en/si/0348.html

12. Circuit Court Rules (Civil Partnership and Cohabitation) 2011 SI No 385/2011

    http://www.irishstatutebook.ie/2011/en/si/0385.html

13. District Court (Civil Partnership and Cohabitation) Rules 2011 SI No 414/2011

    http://www.irishstatutebook.ie/2011/en/si/0414.html

14. Social Welfare (Consolidated Claims, Payments and Control) (Amendment) (No 6) (Civil Partnership) Regulations 2011 SI No 604/2011

    http://www.irishstatutebook.ie/2011/en/si/0604.html

15. District Court (Fees) Order 2012 SI No 108/2012

    http://www.irishstatutebook.ie/pdf/2012/en.si.2012.0108.pdf

16. Circuit Court (Fees) Order 2012 SI No 109/2012

    http://www.irishstatutebook.ie/2012/en/si/0109.html

17. Supreme Court and High Court (Fees) Order 2012 SI No 110/2012

    http://www.irishstatutebook.ie/2012/en/si/0110.html

18. Pension Schemes (Family Law) (Amendment) Regulations 2012 SI No 254/2012

    http://www.irishstatutebook.ie/2012/en/si/0254.html

Other Reports and Useful Sources

Rights and Duties of Cohabitants (82-2006) Report [2006] IELRC 82 (December 2006)
Aspects of Intercountry Adoption Law (89-2008) Report [2006] IELRC 89 (February 2008)
Alternative Dispute Resolution Consultation Paper (LRC CP50-2008) [2008] IELRC CP50 (July 2008)
Legal Aspects of Family Relationships Consultation Paper (LRC CP55-2009) [2009] IELRC CP55 (September 2009)

www.citizensinformation.ie/en/birth_family_relationships/eu_and_family_law.html
http://www.dcya.gov.ie/documents/publications/Post_Separation_Parenting.pdf
http://ceflonline.net/wp-content/uploads/Ireland-Parental-Responsibilities.pdf
http://ceflonline.net/wp-content/uploads/Ireland-Divorce.pdf
http://www.jsijournal.ie/html/volume%202%20no.%202/2%5B2%5D_sheehan_cohabitees%20and%20the%20law.pdf
http://courts.ie/judgments.nsf/6681dee4565ecf2c80256e7e0052005b/6c2a6b8ed70110f880256cc300452db4?OpenDocument&Highlight=0,mk
http://www.solo.ie/news/14097.htm
http://www.hcch.net/incadat/fullcase/0289.htm
http://www.lawreform.ie/_fileupload/consultation%20papers/cpFamilyCourts.htm
http://www.jdsupra.com/legalnews/family-law-property-law-litigation-41527/
http://static.rasset.ie/documents/news/domestic-violence-2012.pdf
http://www.inis.gov.ie/en/JELR/PrenupRpt.pdf/Files/PrenupRpt.pdf

http://www.fsa.ie/fileadmin/user_upload/Files/Contact_Centre_Full_
Report_31_M_201045.pdf
http://www.hkreform.gov.hk/en/docs/rwills_e.doc
http://irishlaw.livejournal.com/1003.html
http://ec.europa.eu/justice/civil/family-matters/index_en.htm
http://www.coe.int/t/dghl/standardsetting/equality/03themes/access_to_
justice/CDEG_2011_8_EN_Case_Law_ECHR%20(2).pdf
http://www.intratext.com/x/eng0017.htm.

Useful free websites:
Courts Service: http://www.courts.ie.
Supreme Court website: http://www.supremecourt.ie.
Dept of Justice on family law: http://www.justice.ie/en/JELR/Pages/Family_
law.
British and Irish Legal Information Institute: http://www.bailii.org British,
Irish case-law and legislation, and European Union case-law.
Kieron Wood's website: downloadable forms and more family law information
http://irishbarrister.com.

Useful Contacts

Legal Aid Board
47 Upper Mount Street, Dublin 2.
www.legalaidboard.ie
info@legalaidboard.ie
Tel: 01-644 1900

Free Legal Advice Centres
13 Lower Dorset Street, Dublin 1.
www.flac.ie
Referral line: 1890 350 250
Tel: 01-874 5690

Law Society of Ireland (solicitors)
Blackhall Place, Dublin 7
www.lawsociety.ie
general@lawsociety.ie
Tel: 01-672 4801

Law Library (barristers)
Four Courts, Inns Quay, Dublin 7
www.lawlibrary.ie
barcouncil@lawlibrary.ie
Tel: 01-817 5000

Accord (Catholic marriage
counselling)
Columba Centre, Maynooth,
Co Kildare
www.accord.ie
admin@accord.ie
Tel: 01-505 3112

Mediators' Institute of Ireland,
Pavilion House,
31/32 Fitzwilliam Square South,
Dublin 2.
www.themii.ie
info@mediatorsinstituteireland.ie
Tel: 01-609 9190

Association of Collaborative
Practitioners (nationwide)
http://www.acp.ie/
http://www.acp.ie/form/form.php

Relationships Ireland,
38 Upper Fitzwilliam Street,
Dublin 2.
http://www.relationshipsireland.
com/
info@relationshipsireland.com
Tel: 1890 380380

Aim Family Services,
64 Dame Street,
Dublin 2.
http://www.aimfamilyservices.ie/
aimfamilyservices@eircom.net
Tel: 01-670 8363

Clanwilliam Institute,
18 Clanwilliam Terrace,
Grand Canal Quay,
Dublin 2.
http://www.clanwilliam.ie/
office@clanwilliam.ie
Tel: 01-676 1363

Elmwood Centre,
22 Upper Baggot Street,
Dublin 2.
http://elmwoodcentre.com/
info@elmwoodcentre.com
Tel: 01-667 6928

Turning Point,
23 Crofton Road,
Dun Laoghaire,

Co Dublin.
http://www.turningpoint.ie/
admin@turningpoint.ie
Tel: 01-280 7888

Al-Anon,
5 Capel Street,
Dublin 1.
http://www.al-anonuk.org.uk/
Tel: 01-873 2699

Samaritans,
112 Marlborough Street,
Dublin 1.
http://www.samaritans.org/your-
community/samaritans-work-ireland
jo@samaritans.org
Tel: 1850 60 90 90

Bereavement Counselling Service,
St Ann's Church,
Dawson Street,
Dublin 2.
http://www.dynamicintent.com/bcs/
dubcentres.cfm
Tel: 01-676 8882

One Family (single parents),
2 Lower Pembroke Street,
Dublin 2.
http://www.onefamily.ie/
info@onefamily.ie
Tel: 01-662 9212

ISPCC,
20 Lower Baggot Street,
Dublin 2.
http://www.ispcc.ie/landing
ispcc@ispcc.ie
Tel: 01-676 7960

Deserted Husbands' Association,
54 Foster Terrace,
Ballybough,
Dublin 3.
Tel: 01-855 2334

Separated Persons' Association,
23 Ashington Close,
Navan,
Co Meath.
Tel: 01-838 0600

Amen,
St Anne's Resource Centre,
Railway Street,
Navan,
Co Meath
www.amen.ie
info@amen.ie
Tel: 046-9023718

Minus One,
68 Lower Leeson Street,
Dublin 2.
Tel:01-676 5596

Parentline (parents under stress),
Carmichael House,
North Brunswick Street,
Dublin 7.
http://www.parentline.ie/
info@parentline.ie
Tel: 01-873 3500

Cura (unwanted pregnancy),
Columba Centre,
Maynooth,
Co Kildare.
http://www.cura.ie/
curacares@cura.ie
Tel: 01-1850 622626

Adoption Authority of Ireland,
Shelbourne House,
Shelbourne Road,
Dublin 4.
http://www.aai.gov.ie/
adoptioninfo@aai.gov.ie
Tel: 01-230 9300

Society of St Vincent de Paul,
SVP House,

91-92 Sean MacDermott Street,
Dublin 1.
http://www.svp.ie/Home.aspx
info@svp.ie
Tel: 01-838 6990

Treoir (unmarried parents and
children),
14 Gandon House,
Lower Mayor Street,
IFSC,
Dublin 1.
http://www.treoir.ie/
info@treoir.ie
Tel: 01-670 0120

Dublin Catholic Marriage
Tribunal,
Archbishop's House,
Drumcondra,
Dublin 9.

http://www.dublindiocese.ie/
content/diocesan-offices
dublinrmt@eircom.net
Tel: 01-837 9253

Registrar General,
General Register Office,
Government Offices,
Convent Road,
Roscommon.
http://www.groireland.ie/
Tel: 090 6632900

UK Divorce Registry
First Avenue House, 42-49 High
Holborn, London, WC1V 6NP
www.justice.gov.uk/guidance/
courts-and-tribunals/courts/principal-
registry/contacts.htm
PRFD.divorcea@hmcts.gsi.gov.uk
Tel: 0044-207 947 600

Questions and Answers

These are just a few of the questions emailed to Kieron Wood by the 1,000,000-plus visitors to his website at http://irishbarrister.com. Some details have been altered to protect the privacy of inquirers.

Q. Congratulations on your excellent website. You say: "You can't get an Irish divorce unless at least one spouse is domiciled in the Republic of Ireland or has lived in the country for a year before bringing proceedings". Does this mean you must live in Ireland for a year immediately before bringing proceedings or at any time during your life?

A. A person must have lived in Ireland for at least one year on the date of institution of divorce proceedings.

Q. I have come to Ireland and found the love of my life and we want to get married. The lady in question had a Catholic Church annulment of her marriage. Does that mean we can marry or does she have to get a divorce also?

A. A Church (or ecclesiastical) nullity has no effect on the status of a civil marriage. It relates only to the religious element of the marriage and simply means that the Catholic Church will permit that person to marry in church. Your girlfriend will need to get a divorce to marry you.

Q. Could you please give me guidelines for an Irish person living in America seeking a divorce? My spouse still lives in Ireland with our three children.

A. The Irish courts may grant a divorce where either spouse was domiciled in the state on the date of institution of proceedings or where either spouse had been ordinarily resident in the state for one year, ending on the date of the institution of proceedings. You also must have been separated for four out of the past five years.

Q. Wondering if you can direct me to information regarding marriage of Irish citizens abroad who are marrying citizens of another country. I am not Irish and I am divorced and we are having a hard time with getting a certificat de coûtume. Any help would be appreciated.

A. A marriage abroad is subject to local law. Whether or not you are a foreigner or divorced is a matter for local law, not for Irish law. If you were divorced in Ireland, you can obtain a copy of the decree from the family court office. You can obtain further information from the Registrar of Marriages.

Q. What proof do we need to provide to the court that we have been separated for four years? During that period, we moved out and back more than once. Do both parties have to agree on the length of the separation?

A. *As long as you were separated for four of the five years before applying for a divorce, that will satisfy the statute. It has nothing to do with the agreement of the parties; it is a matter of fact. If you both agree on the dates, the court is likely accept them, unless other evidence is produced to the contrary. Proof of separate addresses (such as utility bills) would be helpful. Living apart does not necessarily require living in separate houses, but it does mean that there was no marital relationship.*

Q. Can you please tell me how long it takes to obtain a divorce under Irish law? I am resident in Holland, as is my wife.

A. *You can't seek an Irish divorce unless at least one of you is domiciled in the Republic of Ireland or has lived in the country for a year before bringing proceedings.*

Q. I was married in England but my four children and I have been resident in Ireland for two years. My husband is seeking a divorce as we have been separated for over four years. He lives and works in England. Can I be represented by a solicitor in Ireland or do I have to use a solicitor based in England?

A. *If your husband has already initiated divorce proceedings in England, it would be usual to use a solicitor practising in England, although, under EU law, any practising lawyer in one state can practise in all other EU states, subject to certain limitations. If he has not yet initiated proceedings, you should consider issuing proceedings in Ireland.*

Q. Is there a way to go about getting a legal separation without going through the courts? Are there any forms for this?

A. *You and your husband can draw up a separation agreement and this can be ruled by the court, giving it the force of law. Alternatively you can apply to the courts for a judicial separation if you fulfil the criteria set down in the 1989 act.*

Q. Can you tell me how much maintenance is and whether a child's father should contribute towards the costs of child care? I received €200 per week from my daughter's father but, since she has started big school, he has deducted €30. I still have the cost of after-school care.

A. *There is no set scale for maintenance. It depends on the parents' means and requirements, and the needs of the children. If your husband was paying maintenance under a court order, he is not entitled to vary the order without returning to court. If he was paying maintenance voluntarily, you should discuss the matter with him. If you are in need and you believe he can afford to pay more but he refuses to do so, you can apply to court for a maintenance order.*

Q. If a divorce is not contested—that is we have reached an agreement suitable to both of us—do we both still have to be represented by a lawyer? Should all papers be drafted, agreed and signed before the court case?

A. No. Yes.

Q. We have been married for only 11 weeks, but almost from the start knew it was not meant to be. Stupid I know, but is there any way out for such a short-lived marriage?

A. Just because you have decided after a short period that you should not have got married does not mean that you are entitled to a decree of nullity. However, if you believe there was a defect in the consent for the marriage, you should apply for a decree of nullity now. If your marriage is ruled valid, you can apply for a decree of judicial separation after a year, unless there are exceptional circumstances which permit an earlier application. A divorce requires separation for four of the previous five years.

Q. I'm a US citizen. My ex-husband lives in Ireland and obtained a divorce there without informing me. He stated that we had been separated for four years, though we had only been apart for three years. I never received anything official from the court, only a copy of the decree from his attorney.

A. Separation does not necessarily mean living in separate houses; it can also mean living apart but under the same roof. If you think you can prove that you and your husband were having a marital relationship within the four years before his divorce application, you should contact the court and inform the registrar. By the way, if your ex-husband knew your address, he should have served the divorce application papers on you. You should contact an Irish solicitor to confirm the validity of the divorce decree.

Q. My brother's wife is seeking a legal separation. If that should occur, would I have any rights to see his children who are my nephews and nieces?

A. Any relative of a child may apply to the court for permission to seek access to that child. The court will take into account the applicant's connection with the child, the risk of disruption to the child's life and the views of the child's guardian(s).

Q. My partner and I are not married to each other but we have a five-year-old son. My partner now wishes to assign all his assets to our son but, as he is in mid-divorce from his wife, this is very difficult. What are our son's inheritance rights at present?

A. If a husband disposes of his assets in order to deprive his wife of what the court may consider to be her share, that disposition may be set aside. The court would look with suspicion on any attempt by a party to a divorce application to divest themselves of all their assets. The needs of all your partner's children will be taken into account by the court when dividing the marital assets. Marital and non-marital children have identical rights to their parents' estates. If your partner died without making a will and before the divorce, his wife and all his children – marital or non-marital – would have a right to share his estate. You may have a right to a share under the Civil Partnership and Certain Rights and Obligations of Cohabitants Act 2010. The situation would be more complicated if your partner had made a will. You should also be aware that remarriage normally invalidates all previous wills.

Q. My partner has recently obtained a judicial separation. Next April, it will be four years since he moved out of the family home. Will he then be entitled to a divorce or does he have to wait four years from the date of the judicial separation? Now that he has a judicial separation, will he automatically get a divorce without having to file papers again?

A. He can apply for a divorce if he has been separated from his wife for four of the past five years. He will have to file a separate application for the divorce, but the judicial separation arrangements will be taken into account by the court.

Q. I live in the US and have three questions. If a person is legally separated and all issues are settled, how long does it take to obtain a divorce once it has been filed with the courts? Would either or both parties need to be present? Does Ireland recognise a foreign divorce obtained in Mexico or Haiti?

A. Waiting times vary, but there is currently a waiting list for uncontested divorce cases in Dublin. Normally both parties are required to be in court but in certain circumstances where both parties are agreed on all matters, it may be possible for just one spouse to be present. A foreign divorce will be recognised in Ireland if one or both parties were domiciled in the country where the divorce was granted, and the divorce was recognised as valid in that country.

Q. If a wife leaves the family home due to unacceptable behaviour, such as her husband's alcohol dependence, are her legal rights to the family home adversely affected?

A. Desertion might adversely affect a spouse's right to the family home, but leaving the home for good and sufficient reason would not be considered desertion.

Q. Have you come across any instances where a father was granted custody of a small child, instead of the mother?

A. Men do obtain custody, but it is fairly rare in practice. The Irish courts have ruled that, where a child is very young (all things being equal), a mother should have custody.

Q. What is the legal definition of a minor? Does a child have to abide by a separation agreement to see one of his parents at the weekend, even if the child is not willing to?

A. The legal definition of a minor is a person under 18 years old, but if a child of, say, 16 or 17 refuses to see a parent, there is very little anyone can do. However, in many separation cases, one parent will claim that a young child of, say, 8 or 9 does not wish to see the other parent. Sometimes that can just be the custodial parent applying pressure on the child. The courts are required to do what is best for the child and will take a dim view of a parent applying pressure on a child to defeat the other parent's right to access or the child's right to see the other parent.

Q. I am going through a divorce. We have four sons, three of them over 18 and working. Do I have to pay maintenance for them? My wife also says she wants half my pension which is my only income. How much is she allowed of that pension?

A. The court may order maintenance for dependent children up to the age of 18, or 23 if in full-time education. There is no specific rule about the division of a pension. All your assets and income—and all your wife's assets and income—are taken into account by the court in deciding what constitutes "proper provision" in relation to maintenance or pension adjustment. If your circumstances later change, you can apply to the court for a variation.

Q. I had a little boy six years ago but his father and I weren't married and didn't stay together. My ex now wants to take our son on a two-week holiday. I said that was too long but my ex said he was taking him, no matter what. Can he take our son on holiday without my permission?

A. The situation depends on a number of matters. Is he a joint guardian of the child? If not, you are entitled to make all the decisions about the child's upbringing unless a court decides otherwise. However, if your ex-partner has been given access rights by a court, you have no right to change those unilaterally. If you are unhappy about the situation, you can apply to the court for a variation of the access arrangements.

Q. I was granted a judicial separation in 2007, and was awarded maintenance and the family home. I was divorced in 2010. My ex-husband has now threatened to stop paying maintenance because his daughter has no desire to see him. Is he within his rights to do this? Will I have to go back to the courts? Also, I'm earning more money now than I was in 2007. Can this be taken into account?

A. Your husband is not entitled to vary a maintenance order without your agreement or a court order. If there is an access order for the children, you are not entitled to vary it without agreement or a court order. Your current income and outgoings will be taken into account if your ex-husband applies for a variation of the maintenance order, as will his.

Q. I lost contact with my husband years ago and don't know where he lives. Can I still get a divorce?

A. Your solicitor should ask the court for directions as to the steps you should take to trace him (such as advertising in newspapers in the area where he might live) in order to serve him with the divorce application. If the court believes it is impossible to trace him, it may allow you to proceed with your application anyway.

Q. If a couple got married abroad, and later got married in Ireland, would the Irish marriage be void, on the basis that there was an existing valid marriage (albeit to each other)? The foreign marriage was a civil ceremony, and the Irish wedding was a Catholic marriage, with the civil register signed. They have two marriage certificates.

A. If the couple were already validly married when they went through the ceremony in Ireland, the civil element of the Irish ceremony would be of no effect. However, they would still be validly married under the law of the foreign country and therefore not entitled to a decree of nullity (unless there were other reasons for such a decree).

Q. My husband and I married five years ago in Ireland and have been living in the USA for the past two years. We're separated for almost one year now and wish to file for divorce here in the US. Will this be recognised in Ireland? Could we apply for a divorce in Ireland instead?

A. If you are domiciled in the USA and obtain a divorce there, it will be recognised in Ireland. Domicile essentially implies a decision to remain in a place permanently; that is decided by a number of factors. You may only obtain a divorce in Ireland if one of you is domiciled in Ireland on the date of institution of proceedings or if either of you has been ordinarily resident in Ireland for one year ending on that date.

Q. I live in England and my marriage has irretrievably broken down. My wife is still a resident of Ireland, with our children. What is the difference between applying for a divorce in Ireland and England?

A. I can't advise you on English family law, but there are several websites which deal with it. Among the main differences are the waiting time for a divorce (four years' separation in Ireland) and the absence of any "clean break" provision in Irish law.

Q. I am interested in obtaining specific information on divorce in Ireland and would like to contact you to discuss this. I would appreciate if you would let me know your fee structure.

A. You would need to consult a solicitor, as the Bar Council forbids barristers to deal directly with members of the public in these matters, or to advertise their fees. A solicitor is required to give you guidance about the likely level of legal fees, which will depend on the complexity of the case.

Q. My mother died seven years ago and my father has now sold the family home in Kerry where I used to live. The house was in my father's name. Does the Family Home Protection Act provide for this kind of situation?

A. No. The Family Home Protection Act only protects spouses' rights. Your father is entitled to sell his home if he wishes. If your father dies and leaves you nothing in his will, you may consider making an application for proper provision from his estate, but this application must be brought within six months of probate being taken out.

Q. Our house is registered in joint names. My husband has always paid the mortgage from his own account and somebody mentioned to me recently that, if anything ever went wrong between us, I would not have any claim on the house as I am not contributing towards the mortgage.

A. A spouse may contribute towards the family home in cash or "money's worth" (such as staying at home and looking after children or paying other bills). Both are among the many factors taken into account when dividing property in the case of marriage breakdown.

Q. My partner left the family home three years ago. Just recently we heard that his wife had been saying that he would have to wait a long, long time for a divorce. Can she prevent the divorce in any way? I also read that divorce is not recognised by the Catholic Church. Does that mean that if he divorces, he cannot legally remarry?

A. Your partner can apply for a divorce when he has been separated from his wife for four of the previous five years. His wife cannot prevent the divorce as long as he fulfils the criteria set down in the Divorce Act. A divorced person may remarry in a civil ceremony, but a Catholic who was validly married may not remarry in the Catholic Church until his or her partner dies. A person who obtains an ecclesiastical nullity decree may marry in church.

Q. I got a judicial separation three years ago and accepted €50,000 to transfer the ownership of the family home into my husband's sole name. He also took over payment of the mortgage. I assumed the house was worth about €150,000 at the time, but homes in that area now sell for more than €250,000. Can I ask the court to change the agreement?

A. It appears that you agreed to the division at the time without a property valuation and are now unhappy because the house is worth more than it was. The court is unlikely to vary the original order unless there was some impediment preventing you receiving proper advice at the time.

Q. My stepfather has applied for a divorce from my mother. The family home and business were originally bought with my mother's money but my stepfather says he's entitled to half of everything. They are planning to sign an agreement splitting everything down the middle. In the meantime, he has refused to leave the family home, and is being abusive and threatening to my mum and brother. What can we do?

A. A court will not necessarily give "half of everything" to each spouse in a divorce. It depends on a number of factors, including the amount each spouse has contributed towards the property in money or "money's worth". Pending the hearing of the divorce, your mother can consider obtaining a protection, safety or barring order against your stepfather. She should not sign any agreement until she has been properly advised by a good family law solicitor.

Q. I'm anxious to know approximately how much I'll be entitled to when my divorce comes before the courts in the next few months. I do have my own lawyer, but he says he is not happy about the Circuit Court judge in my area.

A. It would be unethical for me to advise a person who has a lawyer on record. If you are unhappy with the outcome of your divorce, you can always consider an appeal to the High Court.

Q. I got married to a Nigerian national last year. I was just 18 and we had known each other only five months. He forced me to arrange the notification, and even while I was taking the vows, I just wanted to run away. The other day he punched me in the face. He claimed to be 18 when we married, but he has admitted to me that his birth cert and passport are fake. I don't even know who I am married to! Do you think I'd be able to get an annulment?

A. I presume you are no longer living with this man. If you are, you can apply for a barring order on the grounds of his violence. You should report your suspicions to the gardaí immediately. If he gave false information to the registrar, this could be grounds for nullity. Duress would also be grounds for an annulment.

Q. I am separated from my husband for just over four months and have applied for a decree of a judicial separation. If I get a judicial separation, will this affect my right to apply for a divorce in later years? Also I am considering moving to the North of Ireland with my two young children. Could my husband bring charges of child abduction against me?

A. A decree of judicial separation will not affect your right to apply for a decree of divorce after four years' separation. If you have joint custody of the children, you must obtain your husband's consent before taking them out of the state to live. If he will not give consent, you can apply to the court for permission to go. The judge's decision will be based on the best interests of the children.

Q. My husband and I are Irish citizens who married in the Republic of Ireland. We have now moved to Canada to live permanently. Can we file for divorce here or would we have to return to Ireland?

A. You cannot apply for a divorce in Ireland unless one of you has been ordinarily resident here for 12 months. If you wish to apply for a divorce in Canada, you should consult a Canadian lawyer.

Q. My wife and I were both 19 at the time of our marriage in 1994 and had only been together for about eight weeks as a couple. She was pregnant when we got married. After a few months, I came home from work one evening and found that my wife had left, taking my daughter with her. She is now living with another man and they have two more children. Would I be entitled to a nullity?

A. *The shortness of your relationship with your wife, your respective ages and her pregnancy would certainly be relevant factors in any nullity application. You should consider applying for a nullity with a fallback position of seeking a divorce if the nullity is not granted.*

Q. I am separated nine years from my husband. He now lives in Spain. (I have his address). Can I serve the divorce documents on him in Spain?

A. *You would need to apply for permission to serve the papers on your husband outside the jurisdiction. Your solicitor will advise you of the procedure.*

Q. I am in the process of separating. My daughter, who lives with me, is profoundly mentally and physically handicapped. Someone told me that, if you have a handicapped child, you are entitled to get the house in your sole name. Is this so?

A. *No. If you have custody of the handicapped child, the likelihood is that you will be allowed to remain in the family home until your daughter no longer needs special care, at which stage the property may be sold and the proceeds divided between you and your husband. That would depend on the circumstances at that time.*

Q. I know of two people who were married in a Catholic church in Ireland just 22 days after they met. The girl was 23 and on holiday and the man was 29. They married before the new law requiring three months' notice. Are they validly married?

A. *If the couple were free to marry one another, complied with the legal requirements at the time and gave their full consent to the marriage, they are validly married.*

Q. Is it true that a woman who leaves the family home before a separation has been finalised, loses any rights to a share of the family home if it is sold? I have been told that this is classed as deserting the family home.

A. *Desertion may be taken into account by a court when dividing assets, but it does not necessarily mean a woman loses her rights to any share in the family home. Leaving the family home for good reason does not count as desertion.*

Q. I am an Irish citizen currently living in the US. My wife is seeking a judicial separation in Ireland. It has now come to my attention that she has got engaged to marry someone else without having a separation or divorce. Can she do that?

A. Your wife is quite entitled to tell someone that she will marry him in the future. However, she cannot marry anyone else after a judicial separation, as she would still be validly married. She would either need a decree of divorce or nullity—or for you to die.

Q. My husband has been barred from the family home, which is in joint names. Can I sell our home without a court order or his agreement, as I am now the only occupant of the house?

A. No.

INDEX